Promise You'll Take Care of My Daughter

For
Leyone

RN JPI '93
OIL 1 '93

Also by Ben Wicks

NO TIME TO WAVE GOODBYE

THE DAY THEY TOOK THE CHILDREN

NELL'S WAR

WHEN THE BOYS CAME MARCHING HOME

Promise You'll Take Care of My Daughter

THE REMARKABLE WAR BRIDES OF WORLD WAR II

BenWicks

Foreword by Pierre Berton

Copyright © 1992 by Ben Wicks

Published in 1993 by
Stoddart Publishing Co. Limited
34 Lesmill Road
Toronto, Canada
M3B 2T6
(416) 445-3333

First published in hardcover in 1992 by
Stoddart Publishing Co. Limited

Canadian Cataloguing in Publication Data

Wicks, Ben, 1926-
Promise you'll take care of my daughter

ISBN 0-7737-2570-9 (bound)   0-7737-5565-9 (pbk.)

1. World War, 1939-1945 — Women.   2. Wives —
Canada — History — 20th century.   3. Canada —
Emigration and immigration — History — 20th century.
I. Title.

D810.W7W5 1992   306.84'5'0971   C92-093269-X

Jacket Design: Brant Cowie/ArtPlus
Cover Photograph: National Archives
Author Photograph: Toronto Star Syndicate

Printed and bound in Canada

To new Canadians
across this great country

Contents

Foreword

One of the great and unheralded mass movements in recent history has been that of the English war brides who arrived in Canada following World War II. This timely book about a new and unexpected kind of immigrant tells the story in their own words and is long overdue.

Canadian servicemen spent more time away from home than any other nationals. Some were absent from their native land for as long as six years. This explains why so many young men, cut off from parents and families, found new families in the Old Country. The Canadians certainly spent more time in England than anybody else, including many English servicemen. In the early years of the war they were all that stood between Blighty and Hitler. Except for a brief diversion at Dieppe, no Canadian soldiers got into action until the summer of 1943.

By then they had adopted the English or were adopted by them, learning the ritual of the British pub, exploring the English countryside on leave, relishing everything from afternoon tea to the girls at the Windmill in Piccadilly.

As Ben Wicks points out, Canada made a trade with Great Britain — our young men for yours. While British Tommies were fighting in the desert, the Canadians replaced them at home. Some, of course, boasted of owning a ranch at the corner of Granville and Hastings, or a gold mine on the prairies. Some alliances didn't last. But the remarkable postscript to the story of the war brides is the indisputable evidence of marriages that worked. They were a remarkable group, these war brides, making what has always been a radical decision — to say goodbye to families and friends and follow a stranger to a new world. The country is the better for them.

PIERRE BERTON

Preface

Once I had finished three oral history books on World War II —
No Time to Wave Goodbye, The Day They Took the Children,
and Nell's War — I decided to end the series with the final days of
the war and their effects on those waiting and those returning.
Thus was born the book When the Boys Came Marching Home.
However, among the more than two thousand replies I received
from wives, husbands, and those who had been children at the time
were a number of letters from war brides. I must confess that this
was a group that I had totally ignored in my previous books, and
on reading their letters I was amazed at the stories these remarkable
women had to tell and felt they deserved a book of their very own.
The present volume, Promise You'll Take Care of My Daughter, is
the result.

Almost 48,000 women — the flowers of Britain and Europe —
travelled to a strange land thousands of miles from their loved ones
to begin new lives with their Canadian husbands. They travelled
into the unknown, without the comfort of their husbands' presence,
and many brought young children with them. Their letters tell of
courage and endurance—crossing the Atlantic by ship, then setting
off on a train journey across a huge country, and then perhaps
being driven by horse and buggy to a remote farmhouse on the
prairies, where it was so cold that washing the floor created an
indoor ice rink. This is the story of thousands of women who did
that and much more, women who made good on a romance that
flared brightly in the few weeks and months before their men made
a crossing of their own from training fields in England to the killing
fields of World War II.

In many respects, this book is the history of our country, the
story of a group of people who pulled up stakes and headed for
Canada to begin a new life. But unlike most immigrants, the war
brides were not motivated by fear of persecution or the need for a
better way of life. They came because of the love of a man — a

stranger who one day walked into their lives and led them from the old into the new.

Once smitten with the idea of writing Promise You'll Take Care of My Daughter, *it was important to get in touch with as many of the war brides as I could. Fortunately, one of my first contacts was war bride Gloria Brock, who introduced me to the many war bride organizations that exist across Canada. In April last year (1990), an international reunion took place in Regina. More than four hundred and fifty war brides, many with their husbands, attended the three-day get-together, and the large ballroom was packed with the jolliest of people. The years rolled away as once again these women were in the company of those with whom, so many years ago, they had boarded the ships that took them away from home and family.*

The partying in Regina continued on the following night, and I went to bed exhausted at eleven o'clock, as once again they decided it was time to "Knees up Mother Brown." On Sunday morning the war brides said tearful goodbyes, but they will meet again next year and the year after and the year after that. They are a sturdy group of women who will never grow old. They were young when they left the land of their birth, and they will remain so; for like old soldiers who never die, the war brides of the two world wars have overcome obstacles that few of us could envisage.

Like my other books in this series, this book deals with separation. It was not easy for those we contacted to write about their experience, for it had affected them deeply. Many had left homes in wartime Europe, and they could still feel the comforting arms of their loved ones as the ship sailed away. These same loved ones would soon be thousands of miles away.

Because it was so emotional, the chapter that covers the farewells of the war brides was the most difficult to do. I could so easily identify with their parents. I myself am now a grandfather, and I found particularly moving the poignant stories of those who left for Canada with babies and young children. This sense of identity with those who were kind enough to contact me has played a major role in the success of the books I have already mentioned. Each of us can feel the pain and recognize the courage of those who are telling us their story. For them it was a happening that changed their lives forever.

Fortunately for us, most of these remarkable Canadian women are still alive and thus are able to relate how they personally played a part in Canadian history. Through their eyes we are able to revisit the period and, in so doing, feel the debt of gratitude that we owe to those we know simply as "the war brides." That most of their marriages survived is a tribute to these remarkable women.

BEN WICKS

Acknowledgements

In acknowledging those whose assistance was indispensable in the preparation of this manuscript, I must begin with the remarkable war brides and their husbands. As well as those whose letters and interviews are included in these pages, there were hundreds of others who took the time to write and phone. My only regret is that there was not the space to include everyone's story.

Gloria and John Brock, Peggy Gliddon, and Kay Garside, of the Saskatchewan War Brides Association, went out of their way to help me gather information. Today's Seniors, the Toronto Star, and other Canadian newspapers provided a means of contacting the war brides. Sheri Mulkewich and Mercia Harrison of the Canadian Red Cross and Victor and Irene Manning also provided assistance.

I thank my remarkable assistant Sandra Tooze, who researched and shaped the manuscript. My dear friend and agent of twenty years, Matie Molinaro, was always there to give encouragement and to take care of aspects of business that continue to mystify me. And I thank Doreen, my wife, who despite her own incredible work in the developing world, never ceases to find time to give me support.

1

Hey, Cowboy, Where's Your Horse?

*I*T WAS WARTIME *and the first of Canada's servicemen were heading for Europe and war. Most of them had enlisted to escape a mundane civilian life and to see the glamorous cities of London and Paris, far from the restrictive glare of parents. True, they had a country, freedom, and a way of life to defend, but few placed that ahead of their chance to run from the constant search for work and, "if lucky," the stifling boredom of the eight-to-five shift. So an army of young Canadians boarded ships in Halifax, looking towards the high adventure that awaited them overseas.*

On arriving in England, they looked in surprise at the undersized fields, lanes, and houses that slipped past the windows of their troop trains. They found it hard to believe that this was a country at war. The first year of the war had seen little action. For Britain, the preparations centred on a defensive role, as most of the country looked towards the skies for the expected invasion. By the end of 1939, British men who were fit and of the right age had already been conscripted and were either serving overseas or training at the various camps scattered throughout the countryside.

As the Canadian servicemen settled in, they soon became aware that there were many local inhabitants whose friendliness more than compensated for the damp weather. Most Britons welcomed them with warmth and kindness, trying to alleviate the homesickness that many of the men suffered. The Canadian troops had arrived in a land that was largely deprived of British sons and husbands. Many of the single young women were therefore eager to fill the void of male companionship as soon as possible. They found the Canadians more than perfect substitutes for the absent

British soldiers. Being better paid than their British counterparts, the Canadian servicemen proved to be generous, and they displayed a warmth and personality that soon endeared them to the British population.

Wartime Britain held surprises for the Canadians. Rationing and the blackout were new experiences, and as the trains scattered the new arrivals throughout the countryside, many of them found themselves in isolated areas with only the constant training drills to occupy their time.

Although no one wanted to fight, most felt that since that was what they had come to do, the sooner it was over the better. But the early arrivals had a long wait. Most of the men of the five Canadian Army divisions stationed in Britain did not see action until the summer of 1943. In some areas the Canadian servicemen had to prove themselves to a wary population, whereas other districts welcomed them immediately. George Edward Zwicker experienced a bit of both:

The Aldershot residents did not exactly take kindly to the Canadian soldiers. I was transferred to a reconnaissance squadron and we moved to the Oxford area, and it was with this unit that I served for the duration of the war. It was not until after the departure from the Aldershot Command that my true and fond relationship with the British people, which includes the Scots, Welsh, and Irish, was fully established.

Although many service personnel from around the world could be seen in Britain during the early part of the war, the Canadians commanded a special respect. The American troops had yet to arrive, and word quickly spread that the visiting servicemen with North American accents not only enjoyed a good time but were able to pay for it. After arriving in Scotland aboard the Queen Elizabeth, *Signalman Rufus Chudleigh immediately found himself mistaken for an American:*

Coming off the boat the first Scotsman to speak to me said, "Hey, cowboy, where's your horse?"

The weather was a surprise for some, for they fully expected that the worst Britain would have to offer would be rain. Stu Brooks, who arrived in Aldershot in January 1940 and found the ground covered with snow, remembers that the English jokingly blamed the Canadians for bringing such weather.

As the Canadians settled in and grew accustomed to their new surroundings, many of them headed for the cities when they were on leave. There, service clubs and dance halls were readily available to ease the loneliness that the British felt existed among the troops stationed in their country. And romance began to bloom, intensified by the passions of war.

It was certainly a comedy of errors when Jean Imrie Deshane met her future husband at a dance at the Overseas Club canteen in Glasgow:

In order to break the ice, they had a number of Paul Jones and musical chairs. Every time the music stopped I was grabbed by this same soldier, and we managed to stay in the game right down to the last three couples. After we eventually lost our chair and were walking off the floor, he turned to me and said, "You know, you don't feel as heavy as you look." Great start!

Anyway we sat at a table with his buddy and my girlfriend, and they got us each a Coke. The soldier waved his arm at one time in the conversation and over went the Coke, right onto my brand-new dress. I had scrimped on my coupons in order to get this new dress. It was made of crêpe and started to shrink right up. I was a sight to behold!

So we left for home. The guys offered to escort us and we got on the tram. My escort said in a loud voice, "Here, I'll pay," put his hand in his pocket and, with the whole tram watching, said, "Just take what I owe." Well, you know there were some "ladies" making extra money off the overseas troops and, with the state of my dress and the Canadian flash on his shoulder, my reputation immediately took a nosedive.

Six months after the war began, Canadian soldiers started to arrive in Sussex. For Joan Dumaine, in Lewes, it was a story of very young love:

It was a Saturday evening, and Mother was in the garden when the back gate opened and this young French Canadian came in and asked if he could leave his new bicycle in our yard while he went to the movies. Of course, she said yes. I came into the garden and we met. In broken English and hand signs, he asked if he could take me to the movies. Mother said I could go and to bring him back for supper afterwards. I was fourteen and a half years old and Paul was eighteen. We fell in love, and on my fifteenth birthday he asked me to marry him.

Those living in villages close to the camps made a special effort to arrange dances and other functions to show the troops that they were welcome and to ensure that they felt at home. It was a natural response, since some had sons, daughters, and husbands also serving their country far from home, and they hoped that their loved ones were being given similar treatment wherever they were stationed.

When Vera Davison received an invitation from the local camp to attend the weekly dances there, she readily agreed:

Transportation was provided. So once a week, for quite a while, a group of us climbed into an army truck and were whisked off to the dance. Not quite Cinderella style, but more fun. And fun we had, dancing in a cloud of reddish dust off the cement floor to the big-band sound of the camp's band.

It was music that brought Mary Hayward Pedersen together with her future husband Andy. He was stationed in her village of Copthorne, Surrey, when his major decided to start a dance band to improve morale:

They didn't have a pianist, so Andy was delegated to invite me to join the band. We had lots of happy times playing for dances in the surrounding areas while trying to ignore the frequent air raids.

One special evening comes to mind. I was asked to play the piano at an officers' Christmas party in 1942 at Balcombe House — a stately old country mansion in the centre of Balcombe Forest. It was a gala evening, in spite of wartime austerity, complete with a Christmas tree and a visit from Father Christmas. At the end of the evening the major sat beside me on the piano bench. He thanked me for providing the music and said, "I would do anything for you."

Taking him at his word, I replied, "Well, there is something you can do. Andy is on guard duty over Christmas and you can give him time off."

"Certainly," he answered. "How long does he want?"

"Oh, five days would be fine."

Then he said, "I'll do it if you kiss me under the mistletoe." This duty accomplished, he said, "Do any of the other boys want Christmass leave?" Needless to say, I wasn't very popular when I said no.

Upon arriving home with Andy, my father was waiting up for me (as all good fathers did in those days). I was greeted with, "What's he doing here?"

"Oh," I said, "Andy's spending Christmas with us."

"But he's on guard duty over Christmas, isn't he?" Dad asked.

"No, he's not," I answered. "I got him off."

"*You* got him off? How could you possibly do that?"

"Oh, I kissed the major under the mistletoe."

After all these years I can still see my dear father, an ex-Grenadier Guardsman who had stood sentry duty outside St. James's Palace, turn red, then white, then red again, and exploded with, "What a bloody army!"

The British soon grew to enjoy the company of the newly arrived Canadians. Young women, in particular, were impressed by these young servicemen who spoke with an accent that was new and fresh. Olive Warner readily agrees. During the war she and her sister used to bicycle to the nearby town of Colchester, Essex, to go to dances and to enjoy cheese-stuffed potatoes and cups of Ovaltine in the potato bar:

One particular evening a tall, good-looking Canadian soldier passed by and commented on the fur-backed gloves that I was wearing. It was the first time I had heard a Canadian speak so, of course, it had a very romantic sound.

When we arrived at the potato bar, the place was packed and there was nowhere to sit. We looked about for an empty table and someone said, "Why don't you take my seat?" It was the Canadian who had passed by on the street. We began talking and before we left had arranged to meet the following week. The friend he was with that night told me that after I had left the potato bar he said, "That's the girl I'm going to marry." A year later we did.

Yet those Canadians had more attributes than just their accents. Years later, a war bride explained to Maclean's *magazine:*

The great majority of Canadian men, no matter what their background, are instinctively gentlemen. . . . He flatters you and makes you feel good in a dozen different ways. Frankly, British men could learn much from the Canadians in their subtle way of appealing to a woman's vanity and keeping her happy. Their attentions certainly swept us off our feet, and we soon found ourselves completely in love with them.

She was not alone in her praise. As more and more women were left to fend for themselves on the home front, they began to enjoy the company of Canadian servicemen, and many were impressed. Because the future was so uncertain, there was a sense of urgency in the air. The wartime attitude of living for the day led what might have been casual romances in peacetime into quickly made commitments to marriage. Kit (Locke) Hardcastle's story is a case in point:

We were on the tube going from Hammersmith to Piccadilly when my future husband boarded our train . . . and within twenty-four hours he had proposed to me!

As more and more men left the factories and farms to be called into the armed services, women stepped in to fill their jobs. The Women's Land Army was formed to replace men who had been working on the land. Helena Hammer joined it and was eventually stationed in her home town of Dundee, Scotland:

I was fond of skating, and it was at the Dundee Ice Rink that I met my future husband. Our versions of how we met differ. I still say that he stuck out his foot and tripped me up! We were married a year later.

We formed a Canadian Wives' Club in Dundee, and some of my best friends are girls that I met at the club in 1944. We had speakers at our meetings from the Canadian Wives' Bureau in London. They did their best to describe Canada to us, but nothing quite prepared us for life in this vast country.

A mutual friend introduced Doris Rhindress to her future husband Bob as they walked down the High Street in Epsom, Surrey. "Bobby Dazzler," as Doris's mother called him, was a hit with her family from the start, and the couple were married in November 1941. But a frightening incident occurred shortly before Doris left for Canada:

When I moved to East Grinstead, I worked as an usherette at the Whitehall Theatre. One early evening, on 9 July 1943, while the first film was being shown, a German bomber dropped a 500 lb. bomb, which landed directly on the theatre. There were many casualties. I was injured, although not seriously. Bob spent hours helping to carry bodies from the wrecked theatre, fearing all the time that one of them would be me. Someone finally told him that I had been taken to the hospital. He didn't know which hospital, so he went from one to another looking for me.

The raid occurred at 5:20 PM and he didn't locate me until 8:30 PM. I can tell you, he looked far worse than I did. His face was as white as a sheet. We were so young and scared. I wasn't quite twenty and Bob was twenty-one. We had just found out that we were going to have a baby and were both terrified that the injuries I sustained might have affected the baby in some way.

Soon after the raid, Bob's unit was sent to Sicily. That same month, November 1943, I set sail on the *Mauretania* for Canada and a whole new life.

Although the Canadians were welcomed in Britain as allies in the fight against Hitler, people with teenaged daughters harboured a particular mistrust of anyone in uniform. Most parents recognized that these servicemen were far from home and might therefore be none too worried about their own behaviour. Some fathers had served in World War I and remembered that they had most certainly not been innocent travellers when abroad, so it was natural that they should want to protect their daughters.

Evelyn Nicholson received some parental advice which she has been very glad she never followed:

"Don't talk to any of those Canadians," my mother warned me as I set off for a week's holiday, staying with relatives at Aldwick, near Bognor Regis, Sussex. It was September 1942 and thousands of Canadians were stationed in southern England.

One evening during my holiday, I was invited to go to the pictures with my cousin and her friend, a Canadian soldier. Returning home on the dimly lit upper deck of a bus, there was an empty seat beside me. The bus soon filled up with noisy, happy Canadian soldiers. It was payday and most of them had been to the pub. There was a clatter of army boots as two made a dash for the empty seat. The "winner" talked to me, but I only answered in monosyllables and looked out the window. He followed me off the bus, and although he was surprised to find that I was with another couple, he said he would walk me home. My aunt asked him into the house, and for the first time I could see this handsome soldier, Nick.

We met during that week and I gave him my parents' address in Balham. Once home, things became more difficult. The first time Nick called at the house, my father was polite but my mother kept a frosty silence. She remembered that during the First World War, girls married Canadian soldiers who turned out to be married already in Canada. Some were left with children to raise. On this point she need not have worried, as this time the Canadian government was very careful, and it took three months of investigation before anyone could marry.

Of course, the main reason was that they did not want their daughter to marry and go to live in Canada. It was the other end of the world to them; even I had no desire to leave England. But we were "only friends," I insisted, and that was true. I had other friends closer to my age. Nick was a mature twenty-four. Eventually, my parents thawed, and we shared many Sunday dinners with Nick. He always praised my mother's apple pie, which was a good move on his part.

A year later, my feelings had changed towards Nick and we talked of engagement. Once again, the fight was on with my parents, and he was not welcome in the house, so I had to sneak out. Then Nick suggested that we would live in England after the war. It took a lot of talking to convince my parents, but they finally agreed to our engagement, as long as I waited until I was twenty-one before I married.

I was happy to be engaged, but with the second front ahead of us and life in London's air raids, I wondered if we would ever marry. Nick went to France just after D-Day and was wounded near Caen. I will always remember that Red Cross postcard, with ticks in the appropriate places, telling me he had been wounded in the leg. Then there was a long silence, waiting to hear more. Finally, a letter came from him and he was back in an English hospital.

Early in 1945, I begged my parents to give their permission for us to be married in June, as I would be twenty-one in October. They relented and we were married. My grandma gave me clothing coupons so that I could have a plain white dress made by a dressmaker, and I borrowed a veil and shoes. The wedding ring came from Canada in a parcel, secure in the pocket of a khaki shirt. A reception was held in a room over my father's shop. It was quite a feast for those days, with lots of salad decorated with hard-boiled eggs, some very thinly sliced ham, trifles, and even a wedding cake made by my mother. Nick and I spent a week at Torquay and we were very happy.

When it came time to be demobbed, my husband's parents wrote asking him to consider returning to Canada, for, after all, they had not seen their son for nearly six years. They also thought that I would be missing the opportunity of a lifetime if I did not come out. Much to my parents' consternation, we agreed to do this and Nick sailed home in June 1946; I followed in July.

In any budding romance, one of the first problems facing an overseas serviceman was to get accepted by the woman's family. Despite warnings from her father, Marjorie Landry became involved with one of the Canadian soldiers stationed in London:

I worked on the King George Dock in a canteen. I served a group of four Canadian soldiers, and it didn't take long to establish the interest of one of them, for we made a date. I guess — you will laugh—it was love at first sight. Incidentally, my father was helping to train the Canadians and he warned me that he did not want to see me with any soldiers, especially Canadians. So we dated in secret, until my sister blurted out that she had seen me downtown with a Canadian. Anyway, by this time my father had befriended the men, so we were able to come out in the open, and all the boys became regular callers at my home for meals and outings, etc.

In June 1944 we became engaged, and wedding plans were to follow at some future date. I had joined the NAAFI by this time, and I was stationed at an air base in Lincolnshire. So we met when we could. All of a sudden I received a telegram: "Go home, buy ring, arrange church, etc., getting married 24 Aug." I rushed home and said, "I'm getting married on Tuesday." I will not tell you what my father said.

We were married on 24 August and the next morning we went to Littlehampton to join the rest of my husband's unit. At 6:00 AM the following day they all marched under my window on their way to Europe.

Not all parents disapproved. Rita Williams's whirlwind courtship began with a little help from her mother:

My mother was a dance pianist in Liverpool, and my sister, brother, and I used to go to meet her at the end of the dance and take her home in the blackout. One night we were waiting for the tram when a young Canadian soldier approached us, asking if this was his "streetcar." My mother assured him that it was, and we all climbed aboard.

Mum was a gregarious type and we were laughing and talking about making chips for supper. The young man said, "Gee, that sounds great." Mum said, "Well, Canada, you're welcome to come along."

Unknown to me, my sister had given the soldier my address and in three weeks I received a letter from him. Six months later we were married!

Another young woman who met her future husband in the company of her mother was "Lady" Solomon. She met Tony while out window shopping in Glasgow one Saturday evening in August 1945:

Hearing music nearby, we investigated and found a group of neighbours celebrating the return of our boys from POW camps in Europe. Bright lights were strung across the street and food and beer was available for all, so we joined the merry making. Soon a tall, dark, handsome fellow asked me to dance. While dancing under the circle of lights, I saw by his shoulder flashes that he was a Canadian soldier with the Royal Winnipeg Rifles (little black devils). He was on leave from Holland. At the end of the evening, when we stepped apart after the last waltz, the brooch on my jacket lapel got caught in his tunic. His clever remark was, "I guess we're hooked."

Most Canadian camps were situated in the country in the hope that they would be far enough away from city life to keep the men out of trouble. A stroll to a local inn or to the village dance would seemingly give them little opportunity to find true romance. Yet it happened. Vera Davison was doing farm work for the Women's Land Army when she and her friends became acquainted with some Canadian soldiers stationed nearby:

I did not meet Earl, my future husband, right away, but one night he dropped in to the dance and my fate was sealed, as they say. Not that it was a whirlwind romance by any means. In fact, we left our final decision to marry too late to be married in England. Earl was afraid it would be too drastic a change for me — a Londoner, used to a big city — travelling so far from home to a small Canadian village in Nova Scotia. The decision was made, though, and I secured a berth on the *Ile de France* a year after Earl left. If we had married before Earl went home, I would have travelled courtesy of the Canadian government.

My parents were not at all happy with the engagement. Not because they did not like Earl, but because of their worry for me and the distance there would be between us. They feared they would never see me again. My mother and I were very close, and Dad told me that she cried for a week. In fact, he said that if I had been under twenty-one, they would not have given their consent. I felt unhappy to be hurting them, but young love can be very selfish.

Betty Hleucka's husband-to-be was stationed in the south of England but was on a trip north in search of a storybook hero when she met him in September 1940:

I was in the ATS stationed at Chilwell barracks and was attached to the artillery regiment. Some friends and I decided to go into Nottingham, as it was payday, and go to a picture show. But on the way we saw a Canadian soldier standing on the corner. He wore a very large beret which hid his face from the side view. We decided to toss a coin to see who should walk by and find out what he looked like. I was lucky enough, as I was later to find out, as he was to be my husband for fifty wonderful years.

I strolled by him and looked into his face. I received a wonderful smile and I, in turn, winked my eye and hurried back to my friends. He immediately came over; we all introduced ourselves and went for a drink. He explained that he and his friends had chosen to come to Nottingham to go to Sherwood Forest to see where Robin Hood had supposedly lived. But instead he found me.

Life can be strange. What appears to be a setback one day may turn out to be all for the good. Elizabeth Smythe did not want to leave school in Ireland when she was fourteen, but her family could not afford any more education for her so she had to go into domestic service in England. Yet Betty would never have met her future husband if she had stayed in the land of her birth:

12

We used to go to Irish dances where we met other Irish people. There were a few Canadian soldiers, mostly of Irish origin, who also went to these dances. The Irish guys were pretty jealous because all the girls were crazy about the Canadian soldiers and also because they had money.

I remember meeting my husband Patrick in 1941 at one of these dances. He was with the Royal Montreal Regiment of the Canadian Army. He was from Tanderagee, County Armagh, and had gone to Canada when he was seventeen. I remember that he was lots of fun and a crazy dancer. We started going to the dances steadily, and I kept his dancing shoes for him. His were black patent and mine were silver, and we'd carry them to the dances in a black bag.

The dances were in Wimbledon, and we had to take the underground to Wimbledon. There were all these people sleeping on the underground platforms, and we crazy nuts used to step over them to get on and off the trains going to our dances. These poor people used to look at us like we had lost our minds.

As even more Canadians arrived, most young women were quite happy to be seen in their company, especially those, like Ann Gurdon, who had been restricted in their everyday life:

I met my husband at Paddock Wood, Kent. I and several other nurses had been in quarantine for more weeks than I like to remember. The children in the nursery where I worked kept coming down with jaundice, etc. That weekend the matron said we could go to the dance if we all had a bath in carbolic soap. Needless to say, we did not smell like roses; however, it did not stop my future husband dancing with us and taking me back to the nursery where I worked. He promised to come the following week if. . . . Two weeks later I received a letter saying he was in hospital with — what else? — jaundice. I often wondered who was the carrier.

Pamela Woollam remembers that her peaceful village of Horseley was quiet until the "invasion":

Not of Germans, but of thousands of young Canadians in khaki and heavy boots, which struck sparks as they walked. The village was like a military camp, much to the excitement of the local girls and apprehension of their parents. All the young Englishmen had gone, to be replaced by the Canadians who were billeted on the local families. After first being looked upon as wild, licentious soldiery, suddenly the people of the little villages realized they were boys taken from their homes and families and dumped in a strange, damp, cold land with nothing to do but prepare for a war that only now began to seem real.

The Canadians of the 1st Medium Artillery Regiment were adopted, and they made a lasting impression on the Horseleyites. For years after, they would return on leave to their British "families." Indeed, when the Horseley boys came back after the war, almost all the local girls had married Canadians, including me.

With the carefree attitude that is common to those who are far from home, the Canadians soon began to enjoy their stay. A population battered and scarred by constant bad news suddenly became aware of these young men with happy smiles and realized that they were just the tonic that was needed. For eighteen-year-old Audrey Roberts, the happy-go-lucky, charming Canadian serviceman she was later to marry was certainly just what she needed in those troubled times:

By the end of 1943 I was saving clothing coupons for a trousseau and wedding dress, and we were hoarding what unperishable rations we could lay our hands on. Orange juice allocated to my baby brother was mixed with gelatine to make rubbery jellies for the wedding breakfast, and hoarded tins of salmon (sent from Canada) and tins of Spam were used to make finger rolls and sandwiches. The fruit and sugar for the wedding cake was sent by my husband's family in Canada, as were gifts of flowers for the tables.

Although the initial attraction for many young women may have been the Canadian accent, these marriages were based on much more. When asked what had attracted her to her new Canadian husband, a British woman responded to Maclean's, *"We wanted to marry Canadians because we were in love with them—perhaps in some cases there was the added attraction of going to a new country." She went on to describe how they "represented romance": "Why did the Canadians marry us? They tell us it's because they could sit down and talk to us seriously, plan for the future with us." No doubt, this was rather unfair to the Canadian women at home.*

Another British woman commented, "I think the British parents as a whole do not spoil their children, particularly daughters, in the same way that Canadian women were spoilt." The validity of this comment is questionable, however, since it was made by someone whose closest link with Canada had probably been watching a Mountie in a Nelson Eddy movie. Whatever the reasons for the "bug," it finally bit Nellie Arbuckle in 1942 when she answered the phone at the War Office in Whitehall and heard a North American accent coming through from the other end:

I started talking to a Canadian soldier who was in the North Nova Scotia Highlanders. We talked for a while, and I thought he was quite cheeky when he asked me for a date. I don't know why I consented to meet him, but I did. We kept on seeing each other until he was sent to Italy. In June 1945, when he returned to England on leave, we were married.

In February 1946 I was rushed to King's College Hospital and had emergency surgery for TB in the womb. This meant I would never be able to have children. But we adopted a little girl, born to an unwed mother that month in the same hospital. Eventually, after a lot of trouble trying to get permission to take her to Canada, a sympathetic judge at the Old Bailey gave me a certificate to allow me to take her with me.

Maisie King's favourite form of recreation was ice skating at a rink in Purley, Surrey. But soon the locals had to share their facility with the Canadian troops stationed nearby:

One Sunday afternoon in the autumn of 1941, a fault developed in the rink's freezing plant and there was an inch of water over the entire ice surface. The going was sluggish. I fell several times and my skirt became so heavy with water that I went to the side barrier to wring it out. Suddenly I was aware of a Canadian soldier, a corporal, looking at me with a lopsided smile. He was handsome, with curly hair and a romantic wave falling over his face.

"Why don't you come round with me," he said in a pleasant Canadian voice, "and I'll teach you how to skate properly."

I retorted, "Skate properly! I've been skating since I was eleven years old!"

The smile widened. "Well, you'd never know it," he said, indicating my sodden skirt.

That was the beginning.

As the war progressed, civilians found themselves becoming part of the front line. More and more, people found a need to escape the dreary life of wartime Britain. A favourite pastime was a trip to the movie house, which provided a means of travelling to the vastly more glamorous world of Hollywood. Two young women in Bournemouth, Barbara Stanley and her older sister, decided to go to the Odeon Theatre on their day off:

This particular Saturday we went to see a Veronica Lake movie. The ticket queue was long and boring. Ahead of us were two soldiers who kept fooling around trying to attract our attention. Our response was cool, as I was already engaged to a Canadian soldier, and I thought nothing more about them.

The usher seated us in the darkened theatre, and I soon realized the same two soldiers were seated on my left. I took a quick glance and read CANADA on his shoulder flash. During the movie, this soldier offered me a cigarette and asked if my mother would like one too. Laughter nearly overtook me at the thought of his mistake. I passed the cigarette to my sister and said, "Canada wants to know if my mother would like one too!" Between the two of us we were almost helpless with silent laughter.

During the intermission, he asked me if I always laughed a lot and I said yes. They invited us for coffee and offered to walk us home. We accepted the coffee but, as we had to catch a bus home, we declined their escort. As I was about to board the bus, this cheeky Canadian soldier grabbed me and kissed me. I got on the bus and waved goodbye, never thinking I would see him again.

The next Saturday, my sister and I again went to the movies. There were the same two Canadian soldiers! Six months later, I agreed to marry this crazy Canuck, who had pursued me on every legal, and sometimes illegal, absence from camp.

When the Canadians first came to Iris Peachman's home town of Basingstoke, Hampshire, she and her friends swore they would have nothing to do with them. But things changed when, as a nurse, she was asked to take a patient to the Canadian plastic-surgery section of the hospital:

Upon entering the hospital, standing just inside the door was a tall Canadian soldier, a dispatch rider. At his feet was his dispatch case and, not seeing it, I tripped over it. The soldier said he had never had a lady fall at his feet before! After helping me to my feet, he asked me for a date, which I accepted. It wasn't too long before we were both in love and planned to be married.

Patricia Lorange also met her future husband through her work. Seldom has a wrong number led to so much. In the autumn of 1940, when she was working as a civilian telephone operator at Wallington, near Croydon, a misplaced call changed her life:

It was a busy night and, due to an air raid somewhere in the vicinity, I was having difficulty getting a call for a local subscriber through to somewhere else in Surrey. Every time I dialled I got a very faint male voice saying, "Canadian Corps Headquarters." Every time I cut the connection and redialled the same voice answered. Fate!

I asked the voice if he was manning a switchboard. "Yes," he answered. I asked if he could connect me to a number in his area as I was having trouble and my subscriber was getting a bit irate. "Sure," he said, he'd be happy to oblige. The roundabout connection was made, much to my caller's relief.

When my subscriber hung up, I could see from the light on my switchboard that the distant voice at the Canadian Corps HQ was still on the line. To make a long story short, we spoke with each other between doing our jobs as operators. As our hours of work coincided, we got into the habit of talking each evening. This was strictly against all rules, of course. I was paid to work a proper shift, not chat with some soldier while on duty—and a Canadian, too! Nor was chatting with English girls the business of the Signal Corps.

After two or three weeks I met Alex, the young man with whom I'd been having these nightly conversations. He'd arranged to come up to Wallington to meet me. It was my twentieth birthday. Celebrations were interrupted by an air-raid warning. My parents, my sister, Alex, and I took to the air-raid shelter in the garden just before a 500 lb. bomb lifted our house off its foundations and dropped it back down again, filling it with soot, ashes, pieces of metal, and shards of glass. We were safe, although we had to wait for debris to be cleaned off the shelter entrance before we could get out.

That was the beginning of a year-long courtship that included near-daily trips from his billet in Ashstead to Wallington on the Green Line bus. His stop was at a church near my house aptly named St. Mary the Virgin. (In those days, daughters were repeatedly warned by their fathers that this prized condition was not to be changed by any Canadian soldier who might be "just passing through" or, worse still, have a wife back home in Canada.)

After being told by the bus driver that he might as well marry me as he'd "just about bought the ruddy bus," we did just that. We were married in Wallington on 27 September 1941. The bus driver and conductress were among those who threw rice as we left the church.

The natural meeting place for young people in the 1940s was, of course, the dance hall. With the sound of a big band in the city or a small group in the village hall, it was possible to hold each other without the glaring eyes of disapproving parents.

In a crowded dance hall in Leeds, Gloria Brock almost broke her neck as she fell over a pair of feet blocking the aisle. That was how she met her future husband, John. For Cecilia Knight, the fateful meeting occurred at a dance in Bournemouth. For Mary Thompson, it was at a dance in Dundee. Mary and her good-looking Canadian continued their romance by mail:

We really got to know each other through letters. There was a letter every day. Then he came up on leave with a friend, and my sister married his friend!

For Joan Buan, the meeting place was the Palais in Edinburgh:

Everyone met their husbands there. We got married after the war was over. I wasn't going to marry him but we went to a pub and he said, "Why don't we?" "No, I don't want to go to another country." But we had a few drinks and I said, "Well, what the hell." We got married the next morning and my mother nearly had a fit!

Many were those who met at dances: Maureen and George McDonald, Stella and Rufus Chudleigh, Eileen Bruguiere-Taylor and Bill Taylor, and Harry and Ivy L. Cline. Ivy's meeting was dramatic:

During an "excuse-me" dance, Harry touched my partner's shoulder to excuse, only to discover that the man was a childhood friend from Waterloo, Ontario. I was locked into a huge hug between the two, and our romance went on from there.

Joan S. Oakes was another who met her husband-to-be at a dance. She had found that being tall made it difficult to find an ideal dancing partner — that is, until the Canadians arrived:

My girlfriend and I went to the Dome dance hall in Brighton and we were both very tall and we never could find partners taller than us. We stood watching all the people coming in and my friend said, "The first tall fellow I see, I'm going to tag him." I said, "Okay, if you get around the floor a couple of times and I haven't got a partner yet I'm going to tag you," because I was a little shy. So she did her couple of turns around the floor and I hadn't got a partner yet so I tagged her — and it was my future husband.

We started putting in for our permission to marry, which was a lot of palaver to go through, about two or three months after we met. They were checking on whether the servicemen were already married back in their own country and also checking that the women didn't have husbands that were away in the war.

My husband's family lived in Athabasca in northern Alberta. He told me that he was sixteen years old when he joined up, he had nothing when he joined up, and nothing to come back to, so we would be starting right from rock bottom. He was much more honest than a lot of fellows were from what I hear. When he talked to my mother the night before we were married, he said he was scared of taking me from my own home, my own family, my own country and he had nothing.

Joan makes a good point when she speaks of the difficulties of marrying a Canadian serviceman. The red tape could be daunting. Part of the screening process for the women could include being interviewed by the commanding officer or chaplain at the base. This was so that the Canadian authorities could assess the serious-ness of the couple's commitment and whether the woman was willing to accept a totally different life in Canada. She was often asked if she "had" to get married.

As for the men, they were required to fill out Form 1000/110 to determine whether they could support a family after their dis-charge from the armed forces. To back this up, they were asked to state what their work and earnings had been before enlistment. If these answers were satisfactory, both parties were then required to have a blood test and medical examination.

When all the documents and certificates had been received, approved, and signed, the wedding date could at last be set. The commanding officer was then informed and permission was granted. This was posted on the daily orders, telling the parties concerned that the serviceman could marry on or before a given date. At least two months had to pass from the time of consent to the actual date.

A Maclean's *interview at that time quotes a British war bride: "It isn't an easy matter to marry a Canadian—particularly if he is in the army and below officer rank. He must first of all show his good intentions by saving about $200. He must get his command-ing officer's permission to marry and must wait some weeks before the marriage can take place. In the Air Force it is not quite so* *difficult, but the commanding officer's permission must still be granted." As if all this was not enough, "the bride to be must produce proof in the form of letters from clergymen, employers or others that she is a girl of good character and likely to be a success at homemaking in Canada."*

Ruth Delmage was one of those who came up against the regulations. She and her future husband had had a whirlwind romance after meeting near Sandringham in late September 1943, and they hoped to get married that November. But that was not to be:

When he presented this date to his padre he figured we hadn't known each other long enough. They did let him come on leave to my home for ten days in December to see if we still felt the same way about each other. Then our permission to get married was granted for 1 January 1944.

Even worse was the experience of seventeen-year-old Molly Houle and her French-Canadian fiancé Roland, whom she had first met by chance when walking to a tea shop:

My mother said that as I was her first daughter to get married, I was to have a very nice wedding. She started saving some of our rations, and the neighbours also gave us their ration coupons to help out. My mother sewed the bridesmaids' dresses and I borrowed a lovely white wedding dress from a friend. We ordered a wedding cake, which had to have chocolate icing as white icing was not to be had. Everything was going well.

The wedding day morning came and Roland arrived at the house all upset. His captain had informed him that his permission to marry had not come through. So Roland went all the way back to his base to see someone higher up. Finally, he returned, but very upset. They had told him that all the papers had gotten lost. We could not get married then and we would have to repeat the paperwork process and try again in another six months!

My mother said that we would have to go to the church and tell everyone to come back to the house. We would have to go ahead with the reception. All of the carefully rationed food could not be lost. We managed to cancel the cars, but not all the flowers. It was such a big disappointment for everyone. The neighbours started whispering that Roland was probably married back in Canada and that was why the army never gave him permission to marry me. But we knew that it couldn't be so with the many letters that I had received from his parents and sisters in Canada. We went ahead that day and had a great party anyway. My Mum said that when we did get married, we wouldn't be able to have another reception.

Another six months passed by and the papers finally came through. During that time, Mum had started to save ration coupons again, and my future mother-in-law sent over food and fruit to make another wedding cake, along with white icing sugar so that we could have a white wedding cake this time. On 1 August 1942, we had a wonderful wedding and another great party!

Since a large number of British women had been called into the services before the bulk of the Canadians arrived, they often met Canadian servicemen through their jobs. Sheila Johnson was in the WAAF and worked as a radio/telephone operator in the control tower of an airfield in Waddington, Lincolnshire. She met her husband-to-be when he was training bomber crews and waiting for D-Day:

Frank and I are still deciding who picked up whom at a mess dance on Good Friday, 1944. The band was playing Vera Lynn's "Yours," and it's been our song ever since. We became an instant duo and in two weeks we were engaged.

Such happiness was not for long, as two short months later D-Day arrived and Frank left for the European war zone as a Typhoon pilot — a day I knew was coming with fear and trembling in my heart. We met on emotionally charged short leaves until the next Good Friday, when the dreaded telegram arrived: "missing in action." Only one who has experienced receiving this type of telegram can understand the feeling of utter anguish and despair.

Within weeks VE Day arrived, and amidst the joy there was still no news of Frank, alive or dead. My heart was filled with dread, but on 14 May a telegram arrived from my mother in London: "Phone home at once — good news." Frank was back in England! After six weeks of being reported missing, he had crash-landed his aircraft, suffered a broken back, been captured by the enemy and marched behind their lines, been helped by his comrades when he often passed out from pain, stoned by the residents of cities bombed by the Allies, and eventually ended up in Stalag LUFT I on the Baltic coast. Finally, he was released by the Russian army. He returned to Canada in a walking body cast on a hospital ship in July 1945, but not before we were married in June. As the love story says — we both lived happily ever after!

Patricia Enright-Howlett was serving in the WRNS, performing top-secret work decoding German messages using the Enigma machine. When she and her friend got forty-eight-hours' leave, they decided to splurge on a hotel in London, as they were fed up with staying in hostels:

We stayed at the Cumberland Hotel. It was divine, pure luxury to us after living in WRNS quarters with so many girls. To have our very own bathroom, twin beds with thick, fluffy eiderdowns and cosy, bedside lamps.

We went down to the lounge to have a drink (gin and lime — how sophisticated!). A pianist was playing soft music and at the next table there were three or four Canadian airmen. One eventually drifted over and asked if he could buy us a drink. Soon we were all at the same table, and there I saw the tall, dark, and very handsome navigator who would become my husband.

In order to avoid interference with wartime production, many of Britain's factories had moved away from the potential bombing targets of the cities and set up shop in rural areas. When the war began, seventeen-year-old Jean Margaret McArthur was evacuated to the country with the company she worked for. Her story begins with a blind date with a Canadian soldier:

I was very dubious about the whole thing because it was said that they would either rape or murder you. I guess we got that impression from the *News of the World*. On the second date he proposed to me and I told him he was crazy, as he didn't know me and I didn't know him. He was adamant, however, and replied, "As soon as I looked at you I said to myself, 'Here is the girl I am going to marry.' " Well, the disease must have been catching because before long I was also crazy, and so we were married.

We got married on a forty-eight-hour pass and my husband couldn't tear himself away and stayed an extra twenty-four. When he got back to camp his officer said, "You must be tired after your honeymoon, so I will give you a chance to rest up — twenty-one days CB, twenty-one days KP, and twenty-one days loss of pay." The cost of love was very high during wartime, but it was worth it.

Although Elsie (Styles) Turgeon's girlfriend dreamed of moving to Montreal, Elsie said that she would never leave England. But all that changed when she met Tony walking along the banks of the River Ouse in Lewes:

Tony, who spoke very little English, asked me to go to the movies the next night. I agreed, but said I would meet him at the theatre, as I was only seventeen and my father was very strict. Also, the Canadians were not totally accepted by the people in our small town.

With the help of my aunt, we continued to meet secretly for a few months. I eventually became more courageous and introduced Tony to my father. They immediately hit it off. After that, our home was always open to the soldiers as long as they behaved like gentlemen. After all, my father had to protect the virtue of his five daughters. We slept upstairs, my dad on the landing and the Canadians on the floor in the living room!

With Doris Nelly Adams, it was a case of mistaken identity that provided her introduction to her future husband. She had met a soldier, Andrew, during a blackout, and when she went to meet him for a date, she was not too sure what he looked like:

When I saw a couple of soldiers coming down High Street in Guildford, I ran up to one and said, "Oh, here you are. I've been waiting on the corner for fifteen minutes." So we got acquainted and went for a walk. Three weeks went by, and one night my friend pushed me in a doorway and said, "My name is not Andrew — it's John. I never saw you before we met that day you ran up to me!"

The happy-go-lucky attitude of the Canadians soon made an impression on the war-weary women of Britain. Most of them enjoyed the attention they were getting from these troops. As the numbers of Canadians serving in Britain increased, so did the chances of meeting them. Joy Stanfield was not yet sixteen when she met the man of her dreams:

This should start "Once upon a time . . ." because it is like a fairy story. Behind our house was a large garden, a big farmer's field, a main railway line to London, and a large Canadian Army camp. From my bedroom window one March afternoon in 1942, I watched a small group of soldiers playing ball. One happened to look over and wave. I waved back, and so began a love story that has lasted forty-nine years. Between us, we wigwagged signals to meet and did so at a small pedestrian tunnel under the railway line. I pedalled my bike down the road to the rendezvous, and he lugged an army bike over fences from the camp. The moment we met, I knew this was the man I wanted to marry.

Many Canadian regiments were stationed near Shoreham by Sea, Sussex, during the war. Phyllis Clements met her husband, Joe, when he was on guard at a place called Buckingham Park, which was just a few minutes from her home. Her mother had taken their dog, Flash, for a walk and returned with the news that there was a very nice, shy young soldier she had been speaking to at the park gates:

I immediately decided Flash needed another walk. I met Joe and started seeing him often. I was fifteen years old and, like many girls, just loved the uniform and accent. We became engaged in 1944. Joe had borrowed money from my mother until his payday to buy the ring in Brighton. I borrowed two bridesmaids' dresses from a girl I met in the hospital where I had my tonsils out. My poor mother had been very busy saving rations and scrimping to manage a lovely luncheon for our reception, which was held in our back garden.

Canadian servicemen sometimes found themselves stationed in the same military camp as the woman of their dreams. Ronnie Fleming was in the ATS *and was enjoying her first leave in Reading along with three friends. They had bought some apples in a greengrocer's and were strolling along biting into the juicy fruit when they passed a group of Canadian soldiers:*

They spoke to us, and we stopped and chatted with them. There was this one soldier — tall, blond, blue-eyed — standing very quietly on the edge of the group. Our eyes met and that was that; the chemistry had started to work. Jack and I sat and looked at each other for a while, then we became talkative. My heart was pounding so fast I was scared he would hear it. He drove me back to camp that night. He told me that he had fallen in love with me and that one day I would be Mrs. Fleming!

Now that Jack has passed away, Ronnie looks back fondly on the way they first met:

Jack often used to tease me about tempting him with an apple. A tear often falls when I eat one now.

Henriette Reid's story is different from most — it began in Canada. She had been at the World's Fair in 1939 and was due to take the Queen Mary *back to England on 5 September. When war broke out on the third, her trip was cancelled. Henriette was alone and stranded in New York. She travelled to Montreal, where she landed a secretarial job, since she could get no funds from England and her money was running out:*

One day in 1941, coming in from lunch, I was given an urgent message to call Cooks' Travel and found my parents in London had managed to get me a passage back to England. They were so worried about their daughter in the colonies among the Indians! I had only a few hours to pack, pay some bills, and catch a train to

Halifax that night. It was wild. En route to Halifax there was a train wreck ahead of us at Mont Joli, and our train was held up for thirty-six hours. There were many Canadian servicemen also going to Halifax. One air force officer told me he was en route to London to be assistant director of public relations at air force HQ and asked if he could phone me when he got there.

When we finally met in London, I was working at Reuters on Fleet Street. He used to meet me on my late shifts and walk me home in the blackouts. Six months later we got married at Caxton Hall, Westminster. A pub we frequented was the meeting place of the Irish Guards from the Palace. They insisted they would be an honour guard at our wedding. Neither of us wanted that, so we got married quietly a couple of days earlier and then celebrated with them all at the pub.

Our house was the smallest in Westminster, owned by the publisher of the magazine *Punch*. Our home was open house to many airmen, including Buzz Beurling and others.

The war brides of World War II were not exclusively British. Canadian servicemen on the Continent also married women whom they brought back to Canada. Joukje Will was living in Eelde Drenthe, Holland, at the end of World War II, and it was there that she met her future husband, Robert:

My father dug a trench at the back of our place for me to hide in if the Germans happened to return. I spent the last six months of the war inside the house, never daring to look out and often taking refuge in the trench. By the time the armistice was signed, I was filled with such fear I couldn't bring myself to come out of hiding. My family finally convinced me it was safe to go outside.

After six years of extreme hardship, lack of food, and fearing for our lives during the Second World War, my family and I heralded the coming of our liberators, the Canadian soldiers. This period of time was also my teenage years. This was May 1945 and a short time later, when I was on my way to see my grandparents, I met a young soldier, Trooper Robert Thedford Will, standing on guard at the airfield. We became good friends and were engaged in August of that year. On 20 October 1945 we were married by the Burgermeester in an extravagant ceremony. I was the first girl in the village to marry a Canadian soldier, and a crowd of about two thousand well-wishers gathered outside the city hall.

Ann Byle, who was to become one of the almost nineteen hundred Dutch war brides, remembers how she met Art:

The Dutch people were, of course, delighted that the Canadian troops liberated us in April 1945. In the town of Assen it was 13 April. My mom and dad opened their home for Canadian soldiers — to keep them off the streets and away from the girls who just threw themselves at the boys!

One day Dad brought this fine-looking Canadian over. I had never had a boyfriend and found him very handsome. He also could speak Dutch quite well, with an interesting accent. Well, it didn't take long before we fell in love. Even though I was only sixteen, I was quite mature for my age. The war years made us grow up fast.

Mina Jones met her husband-to-be on a bridge just outside Rotterdam:

My future husband, who was a dispatch rider, was on his motor cycle and I was on my faithful bicycle. Instead of air tires, I had parts of a garden hose wrapped around the wheels! I had been wondering, after watching the first Canadian troops entering The Hague, how to get hold of some Canadian cigarettes, when my future husband pulled up beside me, asking if I could speak English. It must have been love at first sight, because we got married soon after!

Simone Marie Poupinel was a seventeen-year-old Parisian who had spent most of her teenage years under the terror of German occupation. Her courtship was anything but whirlwind — she did not marry Mickey until 1950:

I spent the war years mostly in Paris and lived through all the privations. I have been hungry and terribly cold in winter; I never saw a candy in the house, not even an orange or a banana. I was not allowed to go to movies because my father did not want me to see the German propaganda. I cried over the deaths of older cousins killed in the Resistance, and I heard of family friends or even schoolmates being sent to German concentration camps. In the middle of the night, sometimes, the air-raid sirens woke us up. I could hear the planes flying over Paris and the noise of the anti-aircraft guns. But we knew that someday the Allies would come to deliver us from the oppression.

When we learned that the Free French under General Leclerc had made their entry into Paris, the population was euphoric. I watched with my family the arrival of the American soldiers on the route to Paris. We had homemade flags that we waved and we screamed our joy to the troops. As I spoke some English, I made friends and kept in touch with some of these Americans. I soon learned to sing "God Bless America," "You Are My Sunshine," "Roll Out the Barrel," and many more songs.

I joined the Canadian Club in Paris. On Saturdays, with other girls, I would guide some Canadian soldiers through the city. We would visit the Eiffel Tower, the Louvre, Notre-Dame, etc., and come back to the club for tea and sandwiches. Boy, what a treat! I had not had goodies like these for years. Sometimes I invited a Canadian to my home for a party. My father was very hospitable with my guests, as he kept a fond memory of the Canadians who had been allies of France in the 1914–18 war.

It was at the Canadian Club that I met a sergeant-major, Mickey, a blue-eyed, dark-haired Nova Scotian of Irish descent. I was impressed by his quick mind and his knowledge . . . and he was good looking. The first day I met him he told me I was the kind of girl he would like to marry. He was a determined man and he had decided he would see me again. He was posted in Holland and arranged to have some leave to meet me in Brussels when I visited relatives there. We kissed once, in my aunt's living room, and he promised to write me from Canada, where he invited me to come. He wanted to have his university degree before I came to Canada to marry him. We wrote for five years!

A young Scottish woman, Katherine Biggs, served as a quarter-master with the Red Cross in Europe. She transported the wounded to or from the hospital trains and hospital ships. When she went on leave with several Canadian girlfriends it was to — where else? — Paris, of course:

We had done a couple of days of sightseeing, and the second or third evening we went to the Canadian officers' club. During the course of the evening, one young officer came over and asked me to dance. He danced in a way I wasn't used to at all—like a hopping hen — and I was trying to follow that! He was a country boy and had never had an opportunity to have dancing lessons, so I thought I could take this person in hand. I suggested, "Perhaps I could help you to learn to dance." He escorted us around Paris for the rest of the week and then, when we went back up to Belgium, he hitch-hiked in the car we were going in. Then he would come down on the weekends from Germany and see me.

Joyce Hassard's story has a different twist. Her mother had been a war bride of World War I, and Joyce was born in Saskatchewan and lived there until her mother's death in 1932. The family survived with several different housekeepers, one of whom, coincidentally, was her future husband's sister. Then her father moved them back to Peterborough, England:

I was washing the lunch dishes at the sink in the scullery when a soldier walked by the window. We'd only said our goodbyes to one Canadian soldier the week before and from the build and the stature it looked like he was back again. I flung open the back door, saying, "Hi, Bud, what are you doing back again?" — and my mouth fell open at this stranger who said, "No, it's not Bud. It's Lorne." That's how I came to meet my future husband. He was very smartly dressed, nice pressed trousers and a nice clean smell (which I later found out was Noxema), curly black hair and warm brown eyes . . . and he played cribbage. My dad, a crib fanatic, took to him like a duck to water. Every leave thereafter, we had him for a visit.

On his leave before he sailed for North Africa, Sicily, and the Italian campaign, we became engaged. He had his sister send me the ring from Canada. He was gone for over a year and then we were married. He signed on for the army of occupation and came back on leave every three months or so until his final leave in April 1946, before he returned to Canada. I remember it so well. I had cooked his breakfast — my week's ration of bacon, my month's ration of eggs, my week's ration of butter for his toast—and it sat on the kitchen table congealing and getting cold while we said our tearful goodbyes. Neither one of us could eat.

Naturally, many of the women whom the Canadians met already had boyfriends. Gertrude Savage had planned her future with her English fiancé, that is, until she was pressured to go on a blind date in Aldershot:

I had a cousin staying with us in London, and she had a date with a Canadian soldier one night. My mother felt she was responsible for this teenager and she said, "Oh, you can't go to Aldershot by yourself. Gertie will have to go with you." I was already engaged to an English fellow in the British army and I said, "I'm not going to Aldershot. I don't want to get involved in all this." My cousin was desperate and had already told this fellow she was coming and bringing me, so he said he would bring a friend.

So when we got to Aldershot, they took off and I was stuck with the friend. I wasn't very impressed. Then, when it was time to go home, they wanted to come with us and take the milk train back down to the coast. During the night there was an air raid, and my mother got up and saw these army boots under the kitchen table! She wanted an explanation.

My parents really fell in love with this fellow, and they didn't like the man I was engaged to at all, so they did everything to encourage us. They liked him before I did. The day that he asked me to marry him, we were crossing the main street in Kingston and there were buses and cars going by, and he stopped in the middle of the street and said, "Gertie, will you marry me?" So I said, "I guess so and I'll call the other thing off."

Those who found their friendship developing into more than a casual acquaintance had many obstacles to overcome long before the wedding day. First, there were the concerns of the British parents. They would truly be losing their daughter, for the young couple would be setting up house thousands of miles away. The parents were bound to ask themselves whether their little girl had merely fallen for a uniform. Or had she perhaps been swept off her feet by glamorous tales of what lay ahead for her in a faraway country? What type of life was in store for her in a remote land with a man they hardly knew? What of the in-laws their daughter was about to meet for the first time? Betty Taylor did not need to wonder about this last point. She knew she would have mother-in-law problems before she even met her husband's mother:

The telegram on the day of our marriage to our best man was: "Stop these children. They don't know what they're doing."

Constance McKenzie came from a struggling family and she had had to grow up fast. She was only fifteen when her head was turned by a stranger from another land:

Art used to come to see me every weekend. We did most of our courting in the air-raid shelter. It was romantic in its way. Don't forget, he was the first to make a fuss over me — it was nice.

Art asked Mum if we could become engaged and bought a beautiful ring with five lovely stones in it. Mum, looking on the bright side and hoping she would now not have to keep me forever, was only too pleased to say yes. He soon broke down my defences and we were making love as if we were married already. Very quickly I was in the family way and on the way to the registry office for the wedding. I became the second Canadian war bride on 3 June 1941.

There I was, just sixteen, dreading the thought that now I was a Canadian war bride and would have to face life in a strange country. The only comfort was Art; he was my husband and I was his wife. When I asked Mum what she thought of it all, it was very plain to see that owing to the hard life we were having at that time, she chose the easy option and said we had done the right thing. Then, of course, there was the scandal of being unmarried and having a baby. People at that time were very narrow-minded. It was okay to have sex, but if you got caught and had a child without marrying the father, not only you suffered but the child as well.

The wheels had been set in motion for Joan Smale to meet her future husband when, as a child, she had begun a correspondence with a pen pal in Canada:

Little did I think that the pen friend I acquired when I attended grammar school would be instrumental in introducing me to my future husband. Through countless letters over the years, I learned so much about Canada from the perspective of a girl my own age who lived in what is now Thunder Bay. Her parents had what seemed to be a perpetual open-house policy for many of the soldiers of the Algonquin Regiment, stationed nearby during the war years. Several were given my address when they were posted overseas, but only one contacted me—the man I was to marry.

Eventually, the Canadians were packing their bags and were once again on their way. Other areas of the world demanded their attention, so they had to leave those in Britain they had come to know and, in some cases, love. Not all were able to put the experience behind them. Love had a way of digging its claws in deep, and only the promise of unending devotion from both parties could ensure that the relationship would continue.

After dating for about a week, Betty Benn's life with Ken had been getting "better and better," but the embarrassment of their leave taking almost ended their relationship:

I was the only person seeing the train off at Uxbridge station. As an afterthought, he handed me money, to get his civilian shoes repaired and clothing cleaned, in clear view of all the troops hanging out of the window. Did I get a rousing appraisal! So, with head held high and a red face, I walked proudly down the platform. This naive Canadian almost ended the beginning of a lovely courtship.

After serving a term in Europe he was due for some leave and we had decided to get married. Ken said I did the proposing, but you know women don't do those sort of things. Most people today would say we were ridiculous, getting married without knowing each other for long. I even had to take his cousin along to meet Ken at the boat train, for I wasn't sure if I would recognize him!

Those who found themselves walking down the aisle with a Canadian serviceman knew that they would soon have to part. But their separation would not only be while their husbands were in the war zones of Europe. Later, these men would be going home to Canada either before or after their wives. Waiting for transport across the Atlantic could be agonizing, as these young women pondered an unknown future in a land 5000 miles away.

While Connie Robitaille was waiting for word to join her husband Roger in Canada, she and her friend puzzled over a Canadian custom that seemed very strange:

In one letter which Roger had written after he returned home he mentioned his brother was getting married. There was to be a bridal shower, and he said everything had to be clean because there would be so many women there. I told this to my girlfriend, and we decided it must be the custom for the bride-to-be to take a shower in front of all the other women. My friend said, "Aren't you glad you were married over here?" and I did agree with her!

This was wartime and the unexpected often happened. Tom Pascoe found he was being shipped home to Canada so soon that he would miss his own wedding. He and Marian had to move quickly:

We were married that afternoon, had a small family reception, and left for York for our one-night honeymoon. Wouldn't you know, we were unable to find accommodation anywhere. Later that night we found a boarding house, and we were invited to wait in case someone with a reservation did not appear. Upon entering, we found several other couples also waiting. During the course of the conversation, the fact that Tom and I were just married was discussed. Sometime later a room did become available, and the kindness of the other couples who were waiting will always be remembered. They insisted that we take the available room.

The next day Tom returned to his RCAF station at Eastmore, and it was almost one year before I saw him again.

The Canadian Department of National Defence not only provided the means for the war brides to travel to Canada, but it offered other necessary services too. Many of the wives needed to be released from wartime jobs, and all required exit permits. As well, the transfer of reasonable amounts of bank deposits was made possible through the Bank of England, the movement of endowment insurance was facilitated, arrangements for baggage were made, and details were provided about the journey onward after arrival in Canada.

For the wife of a Canadian serviceman, the euphoria of new-found love was balanced by her realization that she would be leaving behind many friends and, above all, the people who were closest and dearest to her. The decision to pay this price was not easy, and many war brides gave it long and serious thought. Kay Garside, who had won the heart of a Canadian private and would be living in Saskatchewan, described the situation:

I was introduced to my husband by his sergeant. The sergeant and I had been dancing together at a local hop and he invited me over to the pub during the interval for a drink. My husband-to-be was there on his own, so my partner called him over and introduced us. We all returned to the dance and during the evening, after several dances together, Fred asked if I would meet him for a date. The sergeant and I were only friends, so I agreed to meet Fred. It later became a joke with us that that was the only time a private ever beat out a sergeant!

After losing touch with one another and then becoming reunited, we discovered our feelings for each other were more than friendly. We saw each other as often as his duties would permit and he wrote often. Finally, Fred asked me if I would like to go to Canada with him to live after the war ended. It has been a family joke that he never actually asked me to marry him. My reply to the question— so he said—was, "I thought you'd never ask."

I was an only child and it was understandable that my parents were less than thrilled when we broke the news to them. They liked Fred, but the idea of their only daughter leaving home to live in a strange country thousands of miles away, knowing nobody, didn't make them happy. I was twenty-two and didn't need their consent, but I hoped they would give me their blessing. Realizing I was determined, they reluctantly agreed.

Many forms had to be signed, both from the army and my church. I was Catholic and Fred was United. At that time, church rules were strict about mixed marriages. I had to obtain a special dispensation from the church in order for the marriage to take place. This took time. Also, Canadian servicemen were required to have a certain amount of savings before marriage. How Fred managed to accumulate this, I'll never know.

Finally, on 29 January 1944, we tied the knot. It was a small wedding, family and a few friends. A one-layer wedding cake, small barrel of beer, and two bottles of liquor. I needed a winter coat more than a white wedding dress. One had to be practical, especially when clothing needed coupons. The reception, if you could call it that, was held in the small front room of my parents' tiny flat. My aunt played her accordion. To top off the evening, we all stood at the back door watching an air raid in progress! Next day, Fred and I left for a two-week honeymoon in Manchester, staying with his cousin. All we could afford. Then Fred's unit moved to Italy and remained there for thirteen months. We wrote often, but sometimes I felt as if our marriage was a dream, except for the wedding ring on my finger.

In March 1945, Fred returned to England. He was able to spend most weekends with me. Not much time to get to know each other again. The war was winding down and it looked as if peace was finally coming. The knowledge that I would be leaving England, home, and friends became very real. For a while, Canada had looked like the promised land. After almost six years of bombing, rationing, and doing without, it seemed exciting to talk to my friends about my new life. Suddenly, it wasn't so romantic. This was the real thing. By this time I was pregnant with our first child, and when the letter came in June advising me to report to a location in London in readiness for sailing to Canada, I just wanted to be with my mum.

Trying not to think about the future, we went shopping for a trunk. Dad packed this so well only one glass was broken on that long sea voyage. We weren't allowed to bring much money with us. Further amounts would be sent on to us at intervals—if we had any. I had seen pictures of Fred's parents and written to them, and they had sent me parcels. They seemed kind. I knew they were not in good health and older than my parents. They had emigrated to Canada from England after World War I, so at least they should understand how I might feel on arriving in a strange country. I was scared — no doubt about that. But the die was cast and I can honestly say I never entertained any thoughts that I would not go. Marriage was for life as far as I was concerned, wherever it might lead.

Kay Bleakney, who had no intention of getting married when she started dating Ken, had a frosty reception from her family when she married a Canadian:

The Christmas before Ken went overseas, he dropped a bombshell — he had asked permission to get married! Of course, I refused. But after much pleading and pressure from a couple of friends, we did get married. My mother never spoke to me on that day and my sister said, "You'll go to Canada and we'll never see you again!"

Many organizations were willing to assist the war brides with their transition to a new way of life. The Salvation Army Red Shield Services sponsored war bride clubs in Britain. Canadian personnel gave lectures on Canadian culture, taught Canadian cooking, helped with travel problems, set up Canadian libraries in the clubs, and taught the war brides Canadian expressions. Some clubs organized tours, which gave members the opportunity to meet others who were about to set out on the same adventure, as well as giving them the chance to see parts of Britain they had never visited. When the Brighton war brides' club went to London, it was the first time many of the women had been there.

In August 1944, when the armed services took over the transportation, comfort, and welfare of the war brides leaving for Canada, the Canadian Wives' Bureau was set up in London as a branch of Canadian Military Headquarters. Its main administration office was in Sackville House, just west of Piccadilly Circus. Previously, arrangements for bringing the women to Canada had been conducted on a very small scale. Now, young war brides were encouraged to organize clubs in their own parts of the country so that they could get together to familiarize themselves with Canadian conditions. All four auxilliary services — the Salvation Army, Knights of Columbus, YWCA, and the Legion — assisted the war brides by providing information and study courses. Religious education about the activities of the various religious denominations in Canada was given by padres.

Several other Canadian organizations also got into the act and did wonderful work for these new wives. One of the best sources of information was a small brochure, "From Kith to Kin," prepared by the national chapter of the Imperial Order Daughters of the Empire (IODE). It was written in a chatty, newsy, and welcoming manner for the women who were soon to become fellow citizens. "You will find our accents hard clipped in some parts of our country," it warned, and it provided a range of useful information on trains and other matters: "At first sight, perhaps our 'sleepers' upset more people, unaccustomed as they are to them. They are perfectly safe, usually very quiet; the porter is on duty all night. If you would go directly from Halifax to Vancouver it would be a journey equal to four round trips from London to Edinburgh" . . . "Two out of three farm houses have radios, one out of two has cars and about one out of three has a telephone." The brochure also stressed the importance of mail-order catalogues to the rural shopper, as well as describing Canadian history, racial strains, the system of government, courts, legislation, health and welfare, the schools, the Canadian climate, clothing, and sports. Probably of most interest to the brides, the brochure explained what hard water was and how they could best protect their famous English complexions.

When a Canadian serviceman married and claimed for a dependant allowance, the information was fed through the office at Sackville House, and in due course an application form was sent to the wife to fill out for her transportation to Canada. On its acceptance, she was told to report to Dr. Jupp, on the second floor of Sackville House, for a medical examination. Any wife who was more than five months pregnant was not allowed to travel. Similar offices to the one in Sackville House were set up in other large cities in Britain.

The rules, regulations, and preparations no doubt paid off, for as Maclean's *of January 1944 declared, "Under this rigorous sys-*

tem of checking, the unhappy marriages are not so likely to occur as they would be if there was no interval during which the parties could stop and think things through." Maclean's *was probably right*. But although the wedding was the first item on the agenda, the hardest part was yet to come.

2

One Last Hug

*U*NLESS YOU *have had the experience of leaving your loved ones and moving to a foreign land, it is difficult to understand the pain. With a country at war, such separation was even more difficult. Most of the departing war brides had been part of a tight-knit family that had suffered hardship and had consequently been very close. Many had lived through bombings and had shared small spaces. Parents who had protected their daughters during the war suddenly found that these same children were grown and were packing their bags to go and live in a country far from their reach. Furthermore, many war brides had young children. So parents were saying goodbye not only to daughters but also to grandchildren.*

Some war brides were leaving families who had lost brothers, daughters, or fathers to the war. They felt an added sense of guilt in leaving a home that was already torn apart. And in a day and age when travel was a luxury, families were not sure that they would ever see their loved ones again.

This was the first time in history that the Canadian government had provided home-to-home transportation for the dependants of its servicemen. The Department of National Defence had worked overtime through its Canadian Wives' Bureau to deal with the transportation and welfare services it provided for the young women. War brides from all over Britain and the Continent were transported to London, where they were lodged in hostels while waiting for a ship. One such hostel in Mayfair had been the home of an Italian count.

Once the Admiralty had word that space was available on a Canada-bound ship, the wives with the highest priority were told to report to one of the London railway stations, where still more documentation was carried out, along with the necessary ticketing for the ship. Canadian authorities at the station gave each woman a travel certificate and a Canadian train ticket to her final destination.

Canadian regulations made it clear that each dependant was entitled to one journey only and that the war brides would not be given Canadian exit permits to return to Britain while the war was on. If they returned to Britain anyway, they would not become eligible for free transportation a second time. For fiancées of servicemen who wanted to go to Canada to marry, arrangements could also be made through the Wives' Bureau with one proviso — they had to pay their own way.

Once a wife's application to travel was completed, her registration and travel documents were placed in a long brown envelope. These were numbered and given a certain type of priority, such as pregnancy, number of children, or a husband already in Canada. Each wife also had to send a photo, which was placed on her Canadian travel certificate. The same applied to children over a certain age; otherwise, they travelled on their mother's certificate.

Wives who did the journey during the war often had little opportunity for last-minute goodbyes, for there was a need for secrecy about the sailing of ships. People were reminded that passing on the slightest piece of information could result in a U-boat attack.

Laura Lillian Burris had married in 1942, having met her husband at a dance in Birmingham. He was anxious that she should go to Canada, since there was a lot of bombing in her neighbourhood. But there was danger on the sea as well:

I received a letter from London dated 21 May 1943, telling me to be prepared to leave on short notice. Needless to say, preparations for the trip were hurried and very secretive, the motto of the day being "Loose lips sink ships." I was sorry not to be able to say goodbye to friends and fellow workers, but it was wartime 1943, a bad time to be travelling.

My husband was allowed to go to Liverpool with me. The next day we went to a large bus depot where a bus waited, encircled by sailors with guns. The war brides leaving that day were a small test group, approximately ten of us. The few relatives seeing us off had to remain at a distance as we boarded the bus and, with the sailors still on guard, proceeded to the dock area. No last minute hugs and kisses for us.

Misconceptions about Canada made some partings even more stressful, such as that of Betty Spencer, who was heading for Penzance, Saskatchewan:

My dad knew of Canada as having Indians which scalped people. He made sure I had return-fare money if the place was full of savages. But I had the nicest in-laws, which made my life easier. I later went back to London for a visit and to show my dad that my scalp was safe.

Madge Kiel, who was married three days before VJ Day, remembers the amount of work involved before she could finally set sail for Saskatchewan:

I was getting papers by the score to fill in from the Canadian government. Dad and Mom came to London, then they travelled to Southampton to wish me bon voyage. I remember it as if it were yesterday because they were having a victory parade in London, headed by King George VI and Queen Elizabeth. The next day we travelled to Southampton. My folks were on the pier. It was sad for them, but I was happy. An army band was there, playing "Rule Britannia" and "Auld Lang Syne."

Another woman facing a mountain of paperwork was Jean Margaret McArthur who, like other war brides, soon learned that getting to Canada would not be easy. She had moved to London after her marriage so that she could be near her family before leaving them forever, or so she thought. After a near miss with an incendiary bomb, her husband begged her to go to Canada:

So, I set things in motion and, after filling in the most immense forms five times over, I got word to leave on 31 March 1945. My parents travelled with me to the other side of London. It was the worst thing of all to have to leave them on a street corner and say goodbye for ever. I cried all the way to the meeting place, and they told me my parents had followed me on the other side of the street and stood outside crying. I was twenty-two years old and my babies were two and ten months old. What had I done? I couldn't believe I had done it, but I had burned my bridges and must make the most of it.

Margaret Lindsay headed for Saskatoon full of a sense of adventure, "scared, but determined to like my new country" — yet she was sad to leave her family:

Saying goodbye to my mom was maybe the hardest. Mom said, "I'll never see you again, Margaret," and she never did.

Monica Lewis Hale had married her Canadian in March 1945 and had become president of the Canadian Wives' Club in Dorking, Surrey. She set out for London, Ontario, a year later:

Early in June 1946 a large envelope arrived from the Canadian Wives' Bureau in London, containing instructions and address labels for our luggage. The "Not Wanted on Voyage" label went on my big black trunk, packed with clothes, family treasures, and baby bedding. The "Wanted on Voyage" label was stuck onto my one suitcase, which contained Cow and Gate powdered milk baby formula, baby bottles, gowns, booties, some slacks, and a couple of sweaters and a few underclothes. My son's carry cot was loaded with diapers—terry cloth and gauze liners—leaving room for him on top.

I made a round of family visits, but can honestly say that I never had any apprehension or deep feelings about leaving. Ours was not a demonstrative family, and displays of deep emotion were not encouraged. I was convinced that our future lay in Canada and felt deep down that I was doing the right thing.

I had splurged five guineas—a lot of money then—on a model hat to wear on arrival in Canada. It was a forward-tilted, navy pillbox, with pale blue feathers arranged to look like flowers over each ear. With a navy spring coat, blue dress, and navy shoes it made quite a presentable outfit, I thought, and hoped my mother-in-law would agree.

On the appointed day we caught the train up to Waterloo, joined a group of other wives and children, and were taken by bus to an old London hotel, which the Canadian government was using as a hostel for us. Conditions were not good, and we had to stay an extra day because the Victory Parade was taking place through London and we couldn't leave.

The time soon passed, and it was so nice to be with other girls having the same experiences. Some of them had grave doubts about leaving and there was a queue for the phone as they made tearful last-minute farewells. Then it was time to get on the bus again, to return to Waterloo, and onto the train for Southampton. Canadian soldiers were at dockside to help carry our luggage and help with the children.

Joyce Hassard's husband had already left for Canada, and she patiently waited for word that would allow her to follow:

Another war bride and I regularly travelled to London to Canada House to shake them up and keep our names to the forefront. Eventually, I was advised I would sail from Southampton on 14 September 1946 on the beautiful ship, the *Queen Mary*.

It was the end of my life in England. I was leaving a wartorn country of rations and hardships, bombings and death—a country I had come to love, a life I had come to love, everything familiar and loved ones who were so dear to me. What would lie ahead? I was filled with apprehension, but overriding all was the fact that I was going to be reunited with my darling husband and I was returning to the land of my birth. I was coming home.

Mary Jane Brooks and her son left Tunbridge, Kent, one morning in March 1945, bound for Kingston, Ontario:

My father said goodbye, telling me to do my best to get along and leave my English ways behind. My mother was ill but came from her bedroom to wave goodbye. I went back three times. Then my sister wouldn't allow us anymore time. I never saw my parents again.

Ellen Tinney had not seen her husband for a year, so she was anxious to join him in Belleville, Ontario. Nevertheless, parting from her family was a very difficult step:

My mother was ill in bed. My father was sitting reading his morning paper up at his face. I thought, Why is he doing this at a time of parting? When he dropped his paper to say his goodbyes, I knew why. It was to hide the tears streaming down his face. This shook me most of all, as the dad I knew never seemed too emotional. His advice to me was, "You meet your new friends more than halfway and you will do just fine."

Then I was off to the railway station, my trunks gone ahead of me. When I was looking out of the train window, I saw many people waving towels in the wind.

As Beryl Haines Ward's home was in Southampton, she did not have far to go to board the ship. But her family was not pleased that she was off to the "colonies." There was no farewell party, only a visit to the cinema with a friend the night before. The film was Brief Encounter, *and they "cried buckets":*

The day of my departure, my mother went out; she didn't wish me well. I threw the rest of my meagre belongings in a bag and, before calling a taxi, I phoned my friend Hazel and asked her if she would like to come along for the ride. I remember that we chatted, in typical English fashion, as if I left for another country to start a new life every day of the week! Then I said "Cheerio" to Hazel at the gate and headed for the *Ile de France.*

We left dockside in the evening, before last light. I stayed up top to watch the coastline for as long as there was light. I didn't feel a thing! I remember working hard trying to feel sad, excited, nervous —I just couldn't dredge up an emotion. Many of my companions hadn't left home before and they felt everything! I spent much of my time playing mother hen, big sister, and nurse.

Isabella Low, a policewoman in Glasgow, was heartbroken because she did not get to say goodbye to her father, who had returned home to retrieve her forgotten coat. She describes her emotions as she left Central Station, Glasgow, that day:

One can only imagine how I felt. Words cannot explain the lonely feeling. I was leaving my parents, my brothers and sisters and friends. As a family we were very close and had come through so much together: the happy times before the war, the holidays we spent at the seaside, and the feeling we all had when war was declared. We shared our air-raid shelter as the sirens sounded in the middle of the night, waiting for the all clear to sound. My brothers were both in the services, one a prisoner of war. We had gone through the rationing of food, lining up for extra treats that might have come into the stores, and being allowed one egg a week. As the train swiftly passed by the beautiful countryside, my thoughts were of walking in the blackout, being designated a runner during the air raids and as a fire watcher, working in a munitions factory, and then being transferred to the Glasgow Police.

Interrupting my thoughts, a young lady opposite me in the compartment asked if I was as lonely and frightened as she. We both smiled, and after getting to know each other, we decided we should look to our new adventure and enjoy the trip and stop worrying. The train was filled mainly with war brides, some with children, and those without helped those with their little ones.

Kay Garside's parents accompanied her to the departure point in London:

I remember Dad telling me that if things didn't work out I was to come back. He didn't say what I should use for money. It would be nineteen years before I returned, and I never saw my dad again. He died two years after I left. That was one of the many things we didn't think about when we married Canadians — what it would be like when family members passed away and we couldn't go back to see them. At least, many of us couldn't; there was just no money to do it.

Mum didn't say much, except to warn me to try to get along with my in-laws, as I would be living with them for a while until we got a place of our own, if we did. The plan was for Fred's parents to retire and he would run the farm. I can't believe I didn't ask questions about living conditions and other important things.

When we boarded the coaches to take us to the station for our journey to Liverpool, I looked out the window at my parents and suddenly realized this was it. The finality of it hit me and I burst into tears. Too late now—I was on my way.

Although it had been exciting to look forward to a new life in a strange land, the moment of parting was often excruciating. Mothers hugged their daughters and fathers attempted to hide their tears. For this was not a temporary journey. It was the end of one life and the beginning of another.

One of the wives had been only fifteen when she met her future husband near her home in Rochester, Kent, and she was still very young when she set off to join her fiancé:

I will never forget that journey to a new life. Just one week after notice from London to be prepared to travel, I was at Waterloo Station, loaded onto a bus, as were hundreds of other girls, and we sat there watching our mothers, sisters, and aunts—those who had come to see us off—waving and crying. It was the very worst part of leaving. We spent the night in London. I can't remember where, except that there were eight of us bunked in one room. One girl wrote letters for hours, some were crying, and the rest of us tried to put on brave faces.

Teatime—no, we must call it supper now—army cooks at long tables dishing up sausages and mashed potatoes. But who could eat when emotions were running so high? There was sadness at leaving all that was familiar, excitement over the journey ahead of us, and happiness at finally having the wonder of being together always with the one we loved, instead of existing on letters, forty-eight-hour passes, and all-too-infrequent leaves. We were a motley lot, most with small children, and a few, like me, just alone in the crowd.

Breakfast next morning was a repeat of the evening before — lining up for more sausages and mash—then onto the buses again. Next stop Southampton.

Sixteen-year-old Pauline Elizabeth Ament received her call to leave for Canada in May 1946. She had told Lloyd that she was a year older when she first met him in Beckenham, Kent, never dreaming that they would be married and that she would be travelling so far from home:

Now I wondered, how can I leave my family? Dad was away at sea and my dear little mum, who had done so much for me, was the best in the world. Anyway, we were sent to a hostel in London. There were so many of us. They said there were two thousand brides and five hundred children. What a night! Between tears and cigarettes we somehow got through it and were off to Southampton to board the *Queen Mary*. We were six to a cabin, and all we could hear was the song "I'll Be Seeing You," which didn't help us one bit.

Like many other war brides, Marjorie J. Crawford went through a gamut of emotions when leaving home for the unknown:

How will I ever manage? I can hear my father saying, "Have an orange every morning and a walk around the deck. Keep your mind off the ship going up and down." Joy, it worked! And the journey across the ocean aboard the *Aquitania* wasn't that bad for me. How sorry I felt for some of the girls!

A young Scottish woman, Joan Fletcher, described how agonizing it was to leave behind a special person she loved dearly:

It was such a wrench to leave, as I knew there was very little chance I'd see my granny again. I remember kneeling by the chair where she sat as we said our goodbyes. She lived on the second floor of a tenement, and I remember coming out of the close sobbing all the way as I crossed the road. I walked backwards and she was at the window watching me until I got to the corner, where I had to turn out of her sight. I stood there and threw her kisses as tears streamed down my face, and I'm sure she was the same. Then I had to turn the corner and go — that was the last time I saw my granny.

Although their hearts might say that the man they had married was one in a million and the one they wanted to be with for the rest of their lives, it did little to lessen the pain of leaving. Margaret C. Haggerty thought she had gained the very best Canada had to offer when she married Ernie in 1946. Still, Scotland was the land of her birth, and leaving it proved to be a heart-rending experience:

The news had finally arrived — I would be leaving for Canada. I was told to be at the Caledonian Station in Edinburgh on 1 September 1946, leaving for Liverpool. There were a lot of war brides gathered there, saying their goodbyes to their families. As we were being escorted onto the train, a pipe band was playing many old tunes, bringing many a tear to our eyes.

This was a very low day for my family. It was to be the last time my parents would see their daughter. To this day, I will always remember my mother running alongside the train, hoping not to let go. Yes, it was heartbreaking for us all.

It was a long time before we could compose ourselves, but once we started to talk to each other, our eyes were no longer full of tears. I knew I was leaving the most wonderful woman behind — my mother. But I always felt I would see her again, and this made parting easier. That day never came.

For some parents, the pain was one they preferred to suffer in the private of their homes. Freda Muriel Donaghy's mother was one:

My father came to see me off. My mother wouldn't come — she cried — and I cried all the way to London. We were in the hostel overnight. I was too upset, I don't recall too much about that, but I had my little eleven-month-old boy to look after.

Gloria Brock, a woman who has worked tirelessly to organize and promote war brides' groups, reflects on her own trauma at leaving her loved ones behind:

I don't think it really hit me that I would be leaving all my family behind until my brother was taking me to the depot. The last memory I had of my parents was of my dad with his arm around my mother's shoulders, and they turned and walked into the house and shut the door. My brother said, "Don't look back, just keep going."

After Gertie Abelson married Austin in 1943, they lived in Ealing, where Gertie joined the Waiting Wives' Club, which had been formed in an attempt to prepare the war brides for life in Canada. Although it helped with information, it did little to lessen the tug for home and family when the ship set sail:

There was a band playing "There'll Always Be an England," and women were crying as they boarded the *Queen Mary*. I had fears and tears—fears for the unknown, what we might face, and tears to leave all we had known and loved. It was sad to leave our homeland. Since having just been through years of war, we had been through a lot together: lost loved ones, blitzes, worries of rationing, etc. Some girls were seen leaving the ship before we sailed. It would seem the emotional ties to home were too strong. But I was eager to join my husband, to start our life together, and to learn about my new country.

No sooner had Freda Muriel Donaghy begun to settle on board the Queen Mary *than a member of the crew made an unfortunate remark:*

He said, "Well, girls, you'd better go up on deck and take your last look at England." There wasn't a dry eye on the deck. It was very touching. A band played and we all cried.

Margaret Bannon left Glasgow on the Queen Mary *in July 1946 to join her husband in Seaforth, Ontario. She still found it hard to believe that she had left her home in Glasgow:*

We all realized this was it, that tuppence ha'penny wouldn't take us back. Tears were streaming down our cheeks, wondering what was ahead for us. As we were heading for the pier, we could hear the band playing "Here Comes the Bride."

Like most other war brides, Ruth Delmage had great regrets about leaving her family behind. Her family's circumstances probably made it even more difficult:

It was quite a decision; you had mixed feelings. You hate to leave your family. I think it was very hard on my mother because I had two brothers that were in the war, one was a prisoner of war in Germany and the other was captured in Singapore — and about a month before I left, we got word that that brother had died two years before in Thailand. Of course this was very devastating to my mother, for the three oldest children to leave home. She said, "Oh, I'll never see you again." It was very hard for her, but for myself I knew I was going to make a new life.

Naturally, there was a limited amount that a war bride could take with her. Family photographs were a priority and were gently laid for safe keeping between the few clothes that could be packed. Pat Moon Heath, who had met her future husband when he was recovering from an appendectomy in a Surrey convalescent home, remembers the problem she faced as she prepared to travel to Ottawa with a four-month-old baby:

We were allowed 500 lb. of luggage. I had just purchased a lovely maroon carriage, the first to arrive in our town after the war. My older sister packed it full of tea-towel diapers and tins of baby formula. My mother tore up old sheets into diaper size and packed an old case full of them for my journey. What a godsend, as we were given 6 × 9 in. squares of cotton batting for diapers.

We went to London by train and lodged in a large house overnight, sleeping in metal bunk beds. All the girls and babies cried all night. The next morning we took a train to Southampton, where we boarded the *Aquitania* for Halifax. The two upper decks were for war brides; the lower decks were for returning soldiers. As the boat sailed out of the harbour, the crying started again. But the authorities were smart — they put us through boat drill until the shores of England had disappeared.

Not all war brides cried. Some were in a dreamlike trance that left them in a state of delayed shock. For many, the train was the final sign that there was no turning back. As they waited for the guard's whistle to sound a new beginning, their minds began to etch a deep notch that would be with them for the rest of their lives. Doris Paterson has the scar to this day, and, at the slightest jog, that moment in time returns:

Will I ever see my parents again? It's time to go. My brother will see that I am on the train. At our gate, my mother and father cry and wave goodbye. Tears don't come into my eyes. I can't speak. I seem to enter a trancelike state. I do this when I know that I have to go through something unbearable. Walking, getting on the train, getting a taxi in London — all done like a robot. It will soon be over and I won't be able to turn back.

I arrive at the designated house. A group of about thirty women and children are gathered together so that we can be escorted to the boat the next day. I am shown to a large, sparse room, bunk beds in four tiers against the walls. It's strange to sleep with so many people. Not like my dear home in the country with only the sound of the birds. A child is fretful. God, it must be hard to explain this to a little one! A lady in the bunk above me is crying.

Then, at last, it's morning and we are shepherded onto a train for Southampton. I talk to the other ladies in the railway carriage. We show each other pictures of our loved ones and tell about where we came from. By the end of the journey we seem to have developed a bond. I guess you do that when you are involved in the same process, cut off from your usual support group.

Veronica J. Moore was living in Devon in March 1946 when she was notified that she would be leaving for Saskatchewan shortly. She was told her itinerary and issued tickets to catch a certain train to London, where she would be met by a member of the Canadian Armed Forces:

On finding out that I had been born and raised in London, my chaperone had me guide her all around. We were finally billeted at a large mansion-type house just behind Marble Arch. This was to be our home for the next few days, until everyone was gathered together. We finally travelled south to Southampton, after having escorted quite a few girls around London to show them the sights, before we all left forever, as we all thought.

It was a particularly anxious time for those with small children or those who were about to have a child. Pat Janzen desperately wanted her child to be born in Canada, but in May 1946 she was already four months pregnant. Since the authorities would not let war brides travel after they were six months pregnant, waiting for the news was particularly stressful for Pat:

Finally I received notice that I was to sail around the middle of June. At the time, I didn't realize how heart-wrenching this parting must have been for my mother. She and my young sister travelled on the train with me from Hailsham, Sussex, to London, to be together for as long as possible. But I was hurried away with crowds of other girls almost immediately. My mother's trip was in vain. It was twenty-two years before we saw each other again.

We spent the night in London in a huge depot with wooden bunk beds to sleep in. Some girls took off and never came back!

Elsie Nadeau had had plenty to occupy her mind after marrying her Canadian soldier, Norman, in Redhill, Surrey, in 1941, for she had given birth to her son on a Saturday morning in July 1942 with dozens of strangers looking on:

The birth took place in a public air-raid shelter in South Merstham, because I could no longer get down in our Anderson garden shelter or under our Morrison table shelter.

I had forgotten about going to Canada until September 1944, when I received a letter from London asking me to be in London on 24 September. I went to Canada House for a medical (boy, that was something!), had my picture taken for a passport, and had a lecture on Canadian currency, weather, shopping, etc. We were told to stay at one address, have our trunks ready, that prams and pushchairs must be wheelable, and that we could manage our own hand luggage.

Mom and Dad came to Victoria with me. A Canadian nurse met me and took my baby, and a soldier loaded my pram and trunk into a truck. I said goodbye to Mom and Dad, and the nurse took me out of the station and put me on a bus. It was almost full of war brides and babies. We got off at a large building and were given a meal and another talk about the different customs in Canada. We went back to the bus, were put on a train, and off we went to Greenock on the Clyde.

Winifred M. Pope had met her Canadian soldier at an army dance and married him only after he delivered an ultimatum. She says that waiting for her notice to travel to Canada was absolutely nerve-racking, and she suffered from black moods and depressions:

Finally, I got word to leave on 8 June, my birthday, and report to a hostel in London, where we were billeted overnight — our last chance to change our minds! One girl did walk out in the middle of the night.

Most of the parents, including mine, came to see us off on the train to Southampton. What a scene — everybody crying, everybody! I did not use much makeup in those days, but that morning I put on mascara because I was determined not to cry. But, of course, I did and mascara was running all down my face. Charming!

Who was it who said, "To say goodbye is to die a little"? I'm sure we all died a little that day. The sense of loss and fear of the unknown were practically unbearable . . . and yet there was also a highly charged sense of adventure. As I said, we were young.

Before leaving England in 1943, Doris Rhindress had been injured in a bombing raid on the theatre in which she worked. Although she was anxious to begin a new life in Amherst, Nova Scotia, she was haunted by the fear that her unborn child might have been affected by the trauma. There was also the trauma of parting from her family:

I left many good friends in England, but the hardest one to part with was my darling mother. Thinking about meeting all new people was the hardest, but it must have been just as hard on them, having a pregnant stranger who looked like a beached whale thrust into their midst. I was so nervous that for my last meal in England I went by myself to a "greasy spoon" hole-in-the-wall on a dark street in London and ordered rabbit stew. But I *hate* rabbit stew and always have!

Myra Mirka was a war bride from Glasgow who had met her husband John when he was in Scotland on leave. They were married on Boxing Day, 1945, and John still teases that "we've been boxing ever since!"

Along with many other war brides, I left Glasgow by train from St. Enoch Station on the first stage of our journey to Canada. It was hard saying goodbye to family members and friends who had come to see us off and wish us luck. As the train pulled out of the station, I remember wiping tears from my eyes, and on glancing around I discovered all the other girls in the carriage were doing the same. I guess we felt a bit foolish as we had a "wee greet." Then suddenly a tall, well-built girl jumped up from a seat by the window and did a sort of heavy-footed tap dance as she sang "Dum-di-di-dum, dum, dum, dum!" This broke the ice and our tears changed to laughter. We were soon talking and exchanging stories, and the rest of the trip to London wasn't too bad.

As Jean M. Chartrand said goodbye to her husband Wilfred in January 1946, her only worry was that she would not be with him when he returned to Oak Point, Manitoba. It was to be almost a year before they could be together once more:

How I longed for word that I would soon be able to join him! But time passed and no notification. Then I discovered I was pregnant, so that put me further down the list.

In the meantime, I still kept on teaching and once a week I worked with war brides in the Rose and Maple Leaf Club in Nottingham. I felt very sorry for many of the girls. Some expected to see a handsome man in uniform; instead, they received a photograph of a working man in union-striped overalls fixing a fence. "Not the man I married!" Others bragged of the "gopher ranches" that their husbands owned! One even boasted that her husband owned a restaurant on Fifth Avenue in New York. It turned out to be a hot dog stand. What a rude awakening many of these girls received!

Time passed and our son Garry was born, but still no word of sailing to Canada. As it got closer to Christmas, I fully expected to be spending the festive season with my parents and my sister. Lo and behold, on 4 December 1946 there was the official notification that I would be sailing for Canada on the ninth and that I would have to leave home on 8 December and take the train to London. For months I had been putting odds and ends into the trunks, but when the crunch came, what a rush! What do I take? What do I leave behind? Finally all was ready: trunks were packed (128 lb. overweight), all forms were completed, and we were ready to leave for London. My family accompanied me on the trip south. After a hurried goodbye, we were taken to a YWCA hostel, where we spent the night. The next morning we boarded the train for Liverpool. What a waste of time for me, as I could have gone across the country in less than half the time!

Pamela Parsons had first met her Canadian soldier in Brighton. Then fate stepped in and they ran into one another again at a dance at the Wintergarden at Eastbourne. Although the tears were falling all around her, Pamela felt the sense of adventure so keenly that she could think of little else but the new life that awaited her in Smiths Falls, Ontario, far across the sea:

I remember that it was just pouring rain and there was a little trio of musicians who had braved the rain, playing "Auld Lang Syne" until the ship was out two miles from the dock. Then they packed up their stools and left. I looked around me and there was a girl crying her eyes out. I couldn't understand her because I was so excited at this new adventure. The thoughts of this twenty-one-year-old girl were only of being with her husband.

Gladys Ludwig had married a Canadian soldier she met while working in the cafeteria of a training school in Lewisham:

Leaving my parents and brothers and sisters was not easy for me. We were a very close and happy family. The war brides had forty-eight hours' notice and had to be packed and ready to go. I had to leave a lot of personal things behind, as we had limited space for luggage. My family came as far as Waterloo Station to see me off, and after that I was on my own. We spent the night in a hostel in London with many other brides and babies. That was the start of an unpleasant experience for me.

We boarded the train at Euston Station and had a very long and terribly slow ride to the Liverpool docks. The children and adults were hungry and tired. After we had been on the train for hours, we were given cold baked beans and Spam, and that was it until we got to Liverpool. It was very late at night when we arrived, and the children were crying. Gosh, it was awful! We all wondered what we had let ourselves in for. Finally, we were assigned to our cabins and it was very crowded.

Many war brides would have envied Jean McGoey; she got to fly to Canada to marry her fiancé. On 26 March 1947 she set off on her great adventure, following her heart. Her mother went with her to Prestwick the night before her departure:

I spent the rest of the night cuddled with Ma in the room while she gave me all kinds of tearful advice. We got up bright and early and in a dither whether the flight would leave on time or not.

In those days you walked out to the tarmac and climbed a set of stairs and into the plane. Ma strolled right along with me at the tag end of the line, still in two minds whether to let me go or not. A few steps up the stairs the steward told Ma she wasn't allowed to come that far. Ma was having none of that and proceeded to tell him I was her only daughter, heading off to a wild country, and he should at least let her see me to my seat. He must have made some sort of signal to security, as Ma was grabbed from the waist and pulled down the stairs!

The last glimpse of Scotland for me as we taxied down the runway was Ma standing there looking forlorn in her smart brown hat, orange feather waving in the breeze . . . and a puddle of blue silk around her ankles! Ma had a perfect horror of being in an accident and being shamed by well-worn underwear. But I guess wartime elastic couldn't stand the strain when she was firmly pulled down the stairs, more or less by the seat of her skirt.

Elsie (Styles) Turgeon was moving from her home town of Lewes, Sussex, to Verdun, Quebec:

The day I left home it poured rain. My father travelled up to London with me and my daughter and all our possessions in an old steamer trunk. We were loaded into an old army truck with other war brides and babies, to be taken to Liverpool. I could see my father waving goodbye while we looked out of little holes in the side of the truck. I don't think I'll ever forget that day my father and I said goodbye.

The next day we boarded the SS *Arigunai*, but we couldn't sail right away as there were mines in the harbour. As we finally left shore, some of the dock workers sang "Wish Me Luck as You Wave Me Goodbye."

Joan Bryant Butler had met her future husband Bill when she was crossing Trafalgar Square. He had stopped her to ask the way to Canada House. Like other war brides, she found it heart-rending to leave family and home behind when she set off for Toronto:

How can I describe the feelings of my parents and myself? Their only daughter and grandchild were leaving for another country so far away and, as we truly thought at the time, it was for good. I felt heartsick. I loved my parents dearly and also loved my homeland. It was with mixed feelings — loathing to leave, yet looking forward to Bill and our babies starting a new life in Canada—that I packed all my wordly goods.

As instructed, I set off early in the morning with Michael. Mum came along to help carry the hand luggage, etc. Somehow my dear dad had managed to slip away from his job and was there waiting.

Michael was seventeen months old and quite a handful, plus I was five months pregnant. So I was really grateful to have Mum and Dad there with their help.

We were climbing the stairs inside the school, after being told the war brides and children were on the top floor. Partway, we were confronted by a military policeman coming down the stairs. He looked at my parents and in an authoritative bark told them they had no business being in the school and they must leave immediately. I asked if they could accompany me to the door on the top floor, but it was to no avail. The man watched while we stood for a moment on the school landing saying a tearful goodbye. I've never forgotten that heartless man.

It was a long, dragged-out morning at the school. More war brides and children arriving, everyone upset, children crying. Finally, after lunch, it was time to gather our children and luggage to board a coach which would take us to the station and our evening destination, Liverpool. From my window seat on the bus I could see a small knot of people standing at the school gates. I told myself that Mum and Dad couldn't possibly have stood there waiting all those hours. But as the bus slowly drew past the gate, Mum and Dad craned their necks, saw me and Michael, and gave one last wave. It took all my courage not to stop the bus and go back home.

The whole country was on holiday that August day in celebration of the victory over Japan. So we had to sit in port one more day until the tugs came the following day to pull us out to sea. As our ship left the dock, everyone was on deck beside the rail. It was a touching moment—ship horns blowing, dock workers and cleaners standing waving brooms and handkerchiefs. There was hardly a dry eye.

3

On Board Ship

*T*RAVELLING BY TRAIN *to their port of depar-
ture, the war brides and their children stared out of the windows, wondering what the future held. And as the rich green fields
gave way to the sooty tenement houses of the dockyard areas with
their bomb sites and damaged houses, these young women were
reminded yet again of the perils they had endured with their families, whom they were now leaving. Perhaps their thoughts also
went back to the time they had met the men whose love had urged
them into this fateful journey.*

*It had been commonplace to move troops in wartime, but trans-
porting thousands of civilian women and their children was an
entirely different problem. Available ships were refitted to accommodate these novel passengers. Regulations established the amount
of luggage with which each person could travel: 500 lb. for up to
three dependants, with 150 lb. permitted for each additional
dependant. Breakfast and lunch were provided for the equivalent
of 75 cents, and dinner cost a dollar. Special aid was available for
those with unforeseen problems.*

*This was the first time most of the women had ever travelled by
sea. Lonely and apprehensive, they stared at the giant hulk that
waited at the dockside to gather them into its innards. Once on
board ship, the period before sailing was devoted to interviews —
as well as giving those with second thoughts their last chance to
turn back. Maps and books were available to give the war brides
information about their future home.*

*The departing war brides were big news locally, especially those
like Sheila Johnson on board the* Mauretania *who were part of the*

first large group to leave for Canada. As they pulled away from the dock, everyone, including the mayor of Liverpool, was there to see them off:

Newspapers and band all came out to wish us well. It was a very jolly atmosphere. Off we went, only to return to harbour due to fog. Twelve hours later, at the next tide, a second attempt was made to leave. There was no mayor and no band, but the newspapers, cameramen, and dock workers wished us well (again). This time the jolly group of wives and children were not quite as jolly, the strain of leaving one's homeland painfully visible.

We were *still* destined to return to the dock a third time, as fog again prevented our departure — another twelve-hour wait for the final, successful attempt. This time no mayor, no band, no newspapers—no one except one person, who shouted, "You'll be sorry!" Although I didn't see it personally, I heard that one bride and steamer trunk went back down the gangplank. I managed to keep smiling . . . thinking of my happy landing at Frank's ranch at Queen and Yonge.

Bridie Ames, who was travelling with her one- and two-year-old children, had a terrible start to the journey:

A Red Cross nurse offered to carry my baby to the ship, the *Letitia*. After getting through customs, I headed for the ship, only to find there was no sign of my baby or the nurse. Well, as you can imagine, I was most upset, and the ship was due to sail within the hour. They scanned the ship from stem to stern—no baby. Another hour or so had gone by when they found my baby and the nurse three docks away . . . on a ship headed for Australia!

Olive (Briggs) Ripley, who had met her future husband when skating at Purley, recalls the anguish of many war brides as they sailed away from the dock in Southampton:

I remember some of the girls realized, after we were well out to sea, the reality of it all. Would we ever see England again? How did our parents feel? As a matter of fact, one girl did try to commit suicide. I often wonder what happened to her. Did she stay or go back to England? I will never know.

Joan Elsie Zwicker had met her future husband George at her sister's wedding to another Canadian soldier. She has similar memories:

Most of the war brides, including myself, were quite apprehensive, not only about the trip itself but also about what lay ahead in our new country, Canada.

We were aboard the ocean liner *Scythia* and were one day out when the ship developed engine trouble, so we had to turn back and anchored off Belfast, Ireland, for repairs. Had we been docked, I feel sure at least half the brides would have disembarked!

Joyce Harrison also travelled to Canada on the Scythia, *and the ship ran into trouble on her voyage too:*

It was an old ship which had been used in the Boer War. After two days at sea we were attacked by the Germans and had to return to Liverpool to join a convoy. One girl got off the ship then, and later a baby died and was buried at sea.

Gladys Ludwig was another who travelled while the war was still going on:

The food was good, but most of the passengers were seasick. On deck we had nothing to sit on, so we used our life jackets for a cushion, but the captain said that was a no no. Every day we had life-boat drill; it was the same routine for seven days.

Vera McDonald had been engaged to marry her childhood sweetheart when she was swept off her feet by an RCAF navigator. After their marriage they had a baby girl, and they seemed destined for a happy future. But while Vera was still in the hospital, she received the dreaded telegram telling her that her husband had been killed in action. Although his family had practically made him promise not to marry "one of those English girls," they were now anxious

*to meet Vera and their new granddaughter. Frightened and grief-
striken, Vera set out for Canada in the spring of 1944 on board
the* Mauretania:

I will never forget the tears, laughter, and misgivings that were felt
as we set sail and gradually headed out into the Atlantic Ocean.
Most of the girls had a baby or two, and all seemed to be telling
them, "We are going to Canada and soon you will be seeing Daddy."
My emotions were of a different kind. My little girl had no daddy
to see and I had no loving husband. Nevertheless, I didn't talk
about this to the others and tried to join in and have fun with them,
laughing about how we had met our spouses, where we were going
to live in Canada, etc.

I well remember all the boat drills and learning to put on our
life jackets. We had to practise every day. At that time, the Atlantic
wasn't the safest place to be and we were all a little afraid, even
after living through years of sirens and air raids.

Above all the anticipation about meeting a new family and living
in a new country, I was astounded to find myself surrounded on
board by reporters and photographers. Because my husband had
lived in Nova Scotia, this was a news item: "Local Boy's Widow
and Daughter Arrives." There were photos of Diane and me in the
local papers—not exactly the sort of publicity I enjoyed.

*Sylvia E. Richardson had tried to prepare for life in Canada by
attending lectures at war brides' meetings, but almost all they did,
she recalls, was to stress the importance of a clean coffee pot.
Nearly a year after her husband returned home, Sylvia finally had
word that she would be sailing aboard the* Queen Mary:

Only then did I begin to have second thoughts about leaving England. But my husband had a new home waiting for us, so how
could I have second thoughts? So I said my sad farewells to Mum
and Dad, family friends, and neighbours, who waved me goodbye
with the Union Jack.

The first two days we stayed at a mansion in Park Lane. All
those stairs to climb with two babies, up to what was the servants'
quarters, I suppose. That was when I almost had the urge to run

back home. However, we were soon on our way to Southampton and aboard the *Queen Mary*. Prime Minister Mackenzie King was on board, and during the voyage he welcomed us and our children to Canada. England's loss, but Canada's gain.

The morning we sailed into Halifax, the air force flew out to meet us, for the prime minister's benefit, I believe. On the PA system they played "There'll Always Be an England," and the tears started up again. A band was playing as we docked. Our turn to get off came at midnight.

Only the bravery she had gained during wartime — and the fact that she was in love—gave Doreen M. Christoffersen the fortitude to go through not one but two farewells to Britain:

I and other war brides sailed on the ship *Empire Brent*, which at that time was called the *Letitia*. We left Liverpool early in the morning. We were not far from the docks when a bump was felt. Not knowing what had happened, we found the ship sailing back to the dock. A cattle boat had collided with the *Empire Brent*, damaging her, and she had to be repaired. Back to London we were sent.

The wireless had a newscast saying that the *Empire Brent* had collided and that war brides leaving for Canada were being returned to London to the hostel. It was not known if any of the war brides had been injured. My mother heard the newscast. She phoned my father at work. They both rushed to the hostel in a panic.

We had to wait for two weeks before the *Empire Brent* was repaired. Did we want to set sail once again? I believe most of us had second thoughts.

Joyce Young and her two young sons left her parents in Fulham just before the war's end and set sail on the Nea Hellas, *which had been a troop ship:*

When we left Greenock, the navy dropped depth charges just outside the harbour. It was a little terrifying. On the whole it was a good trip, but it was hard with two children. There were no doors on the toilets, just curtains. You had to wash diapers in salt water; that was quite a chore. When we arrived in Halifax and saw all the lights, some of us cried, as we had been living in the blackout for nearly six years.

Gloria Brock recalls leaning on the rail of the ship as it left the dock, and taking a last look at England:

As soon as we were moving away from the shoreline on the boat, then I started to look at the distances. It's getting wider, it's getting wider. Then I thought, You know, this could be permanent. You might never get back.

But then the hustle and bustle started again, searching around the ship, so your mind is taken up again for a few days. Then you've got a lull again when you've settled down, and you sit on the deck and you think and you review your life. I remember sitting there one morning and there was a cloud formation and I could see my father, mother, and brother in it. It kind of shook me. But then I got violently seasick, and I was expecting our first child anyway, so I didn't think about much else until I got to John's home.

I had no pictures of my family, but in the Christmas parcel from my folks that year they sent a photo—it was the very picture I had seen in the cloud formation from the ship. It was nerve-racking, because they were in the same position and had the same clothes on. That really shook me and I started to think, Will I ever see my folks again?

With her new family in Saskatchewan getting closer by the day, Kay Garside began to feel that her journey would soon be over. But she was in for a rough time:

Our ship, the SS *Samaria*, was waiting for its passengers in Liverpool: war brides, children, and troops returning to Canada. She wasn't the *Queen Mary* by any means, but looked pretty big to most of us. Six of us were in a cabin meant for two. Portholes were closed and blacked out because the war with Japan was still on. One container of water to each cabin was all that was allowed.

Four of us were pregnant. Once the ship moved out to sea and reached the Irish Channel, one of the roughest stretches of water in the world, I became very sick — a mixture of pregnancy and seasickness. I stayed that way for the entire seven days of the trip. If only I could have stayed in my bunk! That wasn't allowed—"Up and at 'em" came over the PA system every morning. Mum had heard that lemons helped seasickness and managed to obtain two of these precious fruits for me. I sucked those darn things till there was nothing left, to no avail. I would get to the dining room, smell the food, and I was gone. The other girls brought me oranges.

Our life jackets were our pillows, and we had to carry them at all times. No chairs on deck, so we sat on the life jackets. Lifeboat drill occurred often. We were allowed in the officers' lounge for an hour every afternoon. We were all excited now that the farewells had been said to families. Youth bounces back quickly, fortunately, and we chatted away, telling each other where we were going to live—not that we had a clue where it was.

Most of the wives visited the ship's orderly room, which was the heart of the operation. Here, information was dispensed to troops and wives, and standing orders were posted each day and were typed out in a "thou shalt" or "thou shalt not" format. Lost children were often brought here, where staff were on hand to care for them. On one ship, the men working in the orderly room were nicknamed the Diaper Brigade.

For Isabella Low, who boarded the Aquitania *in Southampton, a missing child was not the problem:*

One of the brides was missing. After a delay, we learned that she had changed her mind and could not leave her family. The ship pulled out, and we were soon on our way to our new lives.

The formulas for the babies were prepared in the ship's galley by a Red Cross worker. She had to have all the formulas ready and the galley cleaned up before the cook began making meals for the adults. And what meals they were! After the strict wartime rations, most war brides, including Pat Miller on board the Britannic, *found the amounts and quality a special treat:*

I was one of 1300 war brides on board, many with children. We were escorted by a navy convoy. The trip was wonderful, for food was in great abundance and, compared to our war-starved diet, the meals were regular banquets, served by white-coated stewards who seemed to enjoy our enthusiastic cramming. This quickly resulted in the most miserable bunch of seasick brides ever encountered, yours truly being thus indisposed for two or three days and wishing that she could die before ever reaching the "Land of the Maple Leaf."

Some found the amount of food overwhelming. Veronica J. Moore recalls:

We all had so much food on the *Aquitania* we wanted to save it all and send it home. We had more meat on our plates for one meal than we had seen as rations for a week per family.

Dot Ford, who sailed on the Letitia, *has similar memories:*

We were eating such good meals with white bread, and it was almost more than some of us could stand. I actually saw girls put morsels of bread into their letters home, just to let folks see what white bread looked like!

The white bread delighted many of the wives. Madge Kiel, who was on the Queen Mary, *remembers that "everyone was eating it as if there was no tomorrow." Again, it was the food that war bride Jean M. Chartrand remembers. On board the RMS Samaria, she was one of the lucky ones who escaped seasickness, and she revelled in the wonderful meals:*

All this after wartime rationing! I found myself in a cabin with five other girls and their babies, all under a year old. I was the only one breast-feeding my baby but, being the only one not getting seasick, I became the "gopher," picking up feeding bottles for the others.

Apparently we had seven hundred troops, five hundred brides, and three hundred children aboard. Sad to say, some of the girls were caught fraternizing with the officers on the boat deck. This meant instant return to the UK without seeing her husband. The husband of one of these girls had come up from New Brunswick. He was on the dock and she was up on "A" deck. If she wanted to come back to Canada, she would have had to pay her own passage and hope that her husband still wanted her.

Another sorry story about the trip across the "herring pond" was about the girl who had a penchant for Kayser-Bond lingerie from the laundry area. It never came to anything.

Not all war brides travelled on the large ships that made regular crossings of the Atlantic. Betty Hawkins, who had met her husband while she was a volunteer making beds at the Maple Leaf Club in London, left for New Brunswick aboard the Lady Nelson:

Travelling on a small ship, I now realize, was in lots of ways luxurious compared to the numbers using the facilities on the large liners. Troops were on board and teased us unmercifully on what we would find in Canada. One of our group was a hairdresser, and somehow she found an unlimited supply of eggs and lemons, and we all had fantastic shampoos — disgraceful after our rations for years!

Although the company of other war brides going through a similar trauma helped somewhat, once the novelty of shipboard life wore off, new feelings of homesickness developed. Pat Janzen found that despite the wonderful food, it was not a happy voyage:

The sleeping conditions below decks in crowded dormitories — with the muffled tears of already homesick and seasick girls and the crying of tired, bewildered children — meant that few of us got much rest. I spent most of the time up on deck, as my father, a marine engineer, said that was the best place.

As the ships made their way across the Atlantic, the Embarkation Transit Unit Movement Control (ETU) was busy in Halifax. Days before a ship arrived, ETU received a cable that it was on its way, and meetings were then held to plan the next stages of the opera-

tion. *The landing program, immigration schedule, and train depar-
tures across Canada were finalized and information sheets prepared
for each war bride.*

*For the first few voyages, medical staff with three or four nursing
sisters were overworked attending to the wives and their children.
Seasickness proved to be a major problem, along with the smell of
full diapers and prepared formula. A call was eventually sent to
Red Cross nurses, who arranged for crates of disposable diapers
to be loaded on board the ships.*

*Anyone who has travelled the North Atlantic by sea knows how
unpleasant it can be. When I worked as a crew member aboard the*
Queen Elizabeth, *I frequently watched wealthy passengers turn a
dark shade of green before heading for their cabins. To travel as a
war bride, without the benefit of modern pills and comforts, must
have been rough indeed.*

Motion sickness plagued both Ann Gurdon and her infant son:

My son, like many other babies on board ship, slept in a hammock
fixed on my bunk bed. I was on the top bunk and every time I
passed under the hammock my son vomited over me. I was not
smelling like a rose when I finally met my husband.

*For those travelling during wartime, the journey was that much
more harrowing, as Joan S. Oakes discovered. She had left her
home in Huddersfield, Yorkshire, in early 1945 and was heading
for Edmonton:*

Our dreams and excitement turned into nightmares while crossing
the Atlantic Ocean. A journey which normally would have taken
six or seven days turned out to be twenty-one days! I got so sick I
didn't care whether we landed in Canada or not. We were informed
later that our convoy was travelling a zig-zag pattern, north and
south, to avoid contact with the German U-boats and that we had
lost two ships in the convoy.

Laura Lillian Burris sailed during wartime aboard the Empress of
Canada, *without a convoy:*

A submarine warning in the middle of the night made us realize how necessary were the rules regarding drills and sleeping fully dressed with our lifebelts on at all times. Like our departure, arriving in Halifax was also quiet and uneventful, even a little depressing.

Although it was also a wartime trip for Jean Margaret McArthur, she found that travelling on the troop ship Franconia *was both good and bad:*

Good because everyone was nice to us and the food was out of this world compared to what we were used to. But there was only fresh water for a short period each day and so we had to go down to the hold of the ship to wash. It was hot and noisy down there and so hard to drag two babies down with you. As a result, we arrived in Halifax looking definitely grubby around the edges, and that upset me.

Kay Bleakney's departure had been very rushed. In January 1946 she had been told to report to Canada House and, once there, was informed she was leaving for Canada the next morning:

It was night when we boarded the ship, and the next morning we took off to the tune of "Auld Lang Syne" and coins being tossed into the water. As it happened, we put back twice due to fog and it was almost two days before we actually sailed.

We came by France and the journey took ten days. My companions were all seasick, but I ate everything put before me. I helped with the children in the nursery, saw films, and read. They claimed it was a dreadful journey; there were very strong winds and days we were not allowed on deck. Tablecloths were soaked to prevent dishes from sliding. But the film shows still went on, which was a distraction.

There were a thousand troops aboard, but we were instructed not to communicate with them. Nevertheless, I heard that two girls were being sent back to England.

Pat Janzen, who was four months pregnant, travelled on the Letitia:

It was a wartime hospital ship which had no radar. Because of this and also because it was iceberg time, the ship slowed almost to a stop each night. Consequently, it took ten days to reach Halifax.

Few of the war brides had experienced life outside Britain, and fewer still had ever sailed on a luxury liner such as the Queen Mary. *Built in the thirties, she was the pride of British shipbuilding. Famous personalities had waved from her decks on both sides of the Atlantic. Now she had been pressed into postwar service, and thousands of war brides arrived on the docks to find themselves staring up at this magnificent ship. Joyce Horne was one:*

She was our bridge to a new life, and what splendour we found on her! Growing up in utility England, we were not prepared for rose-coloured carpets in the huge dining room, white tablecloths on round tables set for four, and beautifully upholstered chairs on which to sit. We sailed at 5:00 PM that night on the tide. I remember hearing the BBC overseas news broadcast at that time. My old life ended there, and a new and exciting one was beginning.

My first meal on board was in the second sitting at 7:00 PM, after the mothers and children had eaten. Turkey, fresh vegetables, and *white* bread—food such as I had forgotten existed. Unfortunately, I was not able to retain much of these goodies; so much excitement and a floor that did not stay level did not help me enjoy the sea trip for the first day or so.

I was lucky to share a good-sized cabin with just one girl and her two small boys. Heavy curtains were at the doorway in lieu of a door and no sheets on the beds, just beautiful, thick white blankets. Upon opening my eyes the next morning, I spied a big fat red bug about two inches from my nose—he, too, was immigrating.

The *Mary* broke the transatlantic crossing record that trip, and four days later to the hour we arrived in Halifax harbour. The docks were crowded with people to welcome us: Red Cross, Salvation Army, and even a big brass band. A lady at least fifteen years my senior was standing beside me at the rail keeping a watchful eye on her five children. The band struck up "Here Comes the Bride," and she rolled her eyes heavenward and then towards her children and muttered something like, "Some bloody bride!"

Those brides destined for the Atlantic provinces disembarked that night, and luggage from the hold was unloaded by crane to the dockside. One huge netful of trunks broke open and the contents sank into the water.

Evelyn Buzzell also arrived at Southampton to find she would be travelling on the Queen Mary. *She was more than seven months pregnant:*

And looked it! About halfway over I was called on the PA system to report to the purser's office. He was very nice but told me I was really too far advanced in my pregnancy to travel. "However," he said, "seeing that I can't turn the *Queen Mary* around in the middle of the Atlantic, I guess we're stuck with you." Thank goodness!

Ten women shared the cabin that Monica Lewis Hale had been assigned to on the Queen Mary, *but they did have their own bathroom, which used sea water for baths and flushes:*

Even now I am filled with admiration for those who organized our exodus. It must have been a horrendous task, but arrangements were splendid. The five days passed in a blur of making up baby formula, sterilizing bottles, washing diapers, going down to meals — which were absolutely marvellous after our wartime rations — walking round the decks, and visiting with new friends. And at night we had movies. Imagine sitting up on deck on a lovely summer night, the throb of the ship's engines in the background, while we watched Betty Grable from both sides of the screen — if we were on the wrong side, all the wording of the credits was backwards. Prime Minister Mackenzie King was on board and took the opportunity to drum up some votes.

We arrived at Ocean Terminal, Halifax, and a regimental band was on the dock to greet us with "O Canada" and "Here Comes the Bride." I remember seeing the little red and white lighthouses, so different from those on the English coast.

Other well-known ships were also doing their bit to transport troops and war brides to Halifax. But times had changed since the idle rich had travelled the seas in peacetime. Elsie Nadeau, who sailed on the famous Ile de France, *was very disappointed:*

Everything was sopping wet, as the crew had hosed down the ship after the Canadian troops coming over had disembarked. We were told that everything possible would be done to make us comfortable. Mothers with babies were to take the lower bunks. Life jackets must be worn at all times. Brides without babies had to help at mealtimes. Doctors would make rounds every morning.

One morning I went to get some fresh air. The ship was almost still so I asked a seaman about it. He said, "The bloody sod is hiding out there somewhere and we are zig-zagging." He meant a U-boat.

We arrived in Halifax eight days after leaving Scotland. Halifax was fog-bound, so we lay out in the harbour overnight. A customs officer came aboard, stamped our passports, and gave us train tickets. That night four of us helped each other to pack. We washed and laughed at how bruised our legs, backs, shoulders, and bottoms were — they were black and blue. Oh, those steel bunks!

When Jean Stevens travelled on the Ile de France, *there were six hundred brides aboard, no babies, and three thousand troops:*

We were on the top deck and weren't allowed to go anywhere else. I can remember us looking over the top deck and there'd be the troops on the deck below, and some of them putting a blanket over themselves and talking in high-pitched women's voices, pretending they had a girl down there under the blanket — just for laughs.

Because there were so many of us on the boat, they couldn't serve us lunch. So at breakfast the bread and cold meat were put out for us to make ourselves a sandwich and take it away to eat for lunch. We slept in three-tiered bunks and washed in canvas sinks. I was very seasick, as were a lot of the girls. They handed out capsules to relieve our nausea, but we had never seen anything like them before. We very carefully took them apart and swallowed the insides, because we didn't know you could swallow the whole thing.

We landed in Halifax on 13 May, 1946. The pier was crowded with people because of the three thousand troops coming home. Coming from austere and rationed Britain, I couldn't get over all the girls on the pier with flowers tucked in their hair. All the soldiers were waiting to be demobbed, but some of them had to wet-nurse us. We would step forward and a soldier would carry our luggage to the train that was waiting to take us further into Canada. The soldier I was with wasn't too happy about doing this; he really just wanted to go home.

Doris Paterson was one of the few war brides who knew what it was like to travel on a luxury cruise ship, but she soon discovered that things were now different — except for the food:

When I go on board the *Aquitania* it is obvious we are not on a cruise ship. Partitions have been put up and bunks squeezed in everywhere to accommodate as many people as they can. But the dining room is as I remember on cruise ships. Everything there is elegant and — can you believe your eyes? — *white bread*! We haven't seen white bread since the onset of the war. It tastes like cake. We are reminded that we are going to a land of plenty compared to England, poor dear country.

The end of the first day, and it hasn't been so bad. I did feel a lump in my throat as we passed Land's End—the last sight we will see of England. And if only the girls would stop telling all the horror stories: a mother-in-law in a wigwam smoking a pipe, a husband regretting marrying and who now has a Canadian girl-friend, or the pictures he showed you of the lovely mansion he lived in was just a photo he took of a wealthy person's home. The real truth could be pretty awful. But I know my Ted. He would never lie to me. He's as straight as an arrow.

This is the second day. The night was terrible. It seems there is something wrong with the milk on board. The babies are all upset, vomiting and crying. But the sun the next day is wonderful. Without being aware of it, the sea air, the sun, and the wind combined have tanned my skin. I am starting to get excited to see my new homeland and to be with Ted again. It has now been three and a half months since I have seen him. What reception will I get from his family?

The third day and we're more than halfway there. The babies are losing weight and the mothers are fretting. The ship's doctor is concerned and has prescribed a milk substitute. My newfound friends and I feel as though we have always known each other. One comes from Holland. She is beautiful and I adore her accent. So charming. She told me that she hates it. Her husband thought it was cute to begin with, but by the time he left he was yelling at her, "Get it straight, for Pete's sake!" and complaining that the accent got on his nerves. I guess there will be a lot of that. Wartime does that to you, brings you horror and dread but also romance and adventure. It's only when you've had the romance for a long period that you face the realities.

Day four and finally the babies are a little better, if thinner. We are getting used to being on board and the sounds that go with it. Tomorrow we dock in Halifax. Tomorrow, tomorrow—the stomach churns. Nervous and excited. What can I expect of this Canada? Open spaces, grandeur. (The posters of the Banff Hotel linger in one's mind.) Fresh-faced people. Men who don't expect much from their wives. Lots of hopefulness for the future without the depression of having to rebuild the ruins of the war. Lots of ration-free food. Ah, well, we will see.

Charlotte Farrow was classified on her embarkation papers as being two months pregnant, though she was not pregnant at all. But it was too late for her to rectify the error:

My first trip to the dining room was one of surprise and disbelief. My surprise was that all pregnant brides were escorted and seated safely by Canadian soldiers. I felt so guilty having all this attention showered on me. There was nothing I could do or say that would change things, so I just relaxed and enjoyed every minute of it. After a simply delicious meal, with white crusty rolls, fresh fruit, and milk—things we had not seen for years—I was escorted back to my cabin. What bliss! I could hardly believe my good fortune.

Florence Reid really was pregnant when she set out to join her husband Clayton in Montreal. She remembers the "most appalling wartime sausages" and dry biscuits that were fed to the war brides on the train to Southampton. But things were very different on the ship:

On board the *Queen Mary* at last! We couldn't believe our eyes when we sat down at tables laden with bowls of apples and oranges and baskets of snow-white bread rolls. We were served the kind of meal we had only dreamed of in the last years of the war. We had been eating brown National bread for so long that some women at my table sent out a warning: "Don't eat the bread. Flour isn't that white. It's got chemicals in it!" As we left the table, the fruit bowls were hastily cleared by those with children, and I greedily stuffed an orange into my handbag for a bedtime snack.

Because clothes had been rationed for so long, we hadn't much in the way of a wardrobe. My mother had given me her coupons to buy a summer maternity outfit to arrive in, but the things I wore on the ship were getting shabby. As we approached Halifax, tattered bras, panties, and underslips went flying out of portholes into the sea, as we put on our one good set of everything.

There had also been some war brides in World War I. One of them was Daisy Horn, who sailed in September 1919 on board the SS Canada. *After all these years, she still remembers one night very vividly:*

I was asleep when someone in the next cabin came in and woke me up, and there were rats running across right by my face! I just screamed murder. A purser came in and shut my mouth quick. I was waking everyone up. He said, "Don't worry about the rats. We like them on the ship because as long as they stay on the ship it'll never sink. We've got Fluffy, Ginger, and Patsy. If they leave, we drown because rats don't leave until a boat is going to be wrecked." I tried, but I couldn't believe it.

One lady left her pyjamas on top of her bunk and the rats had a bunch of babies in there! The rest of our girls didn't like her, so we were pleased. She was over forty when she got married and told us we got married too young.

Although Cecilia Knight crossed the Atlantic after the war was over, the voyage was not without danger:

I wasn't sick at all, but my baby was quite sick. The conditions were really rather dreadful. It was a hospital ship and we were very crowded. Nowhere to adequately bath the babies or do the laundry (and, of course, there was no such things as Pampers in those days). It was very difficult.

We ran into fog and icebergs, and the boat had to shut down its engines and just float all night. In the daytime they would cruise along a little bit, but at night we had to stop because the radar was picking up these icebergs and we were in a thick fog. I'll tell you, there is no more eerie experience than to be on a boat with nothing running, in a thick fog, and the foghorn going all the time. It really strikes fear into your heart. We did that for three days. It took us eleven days to make the crossing.

Because the ships to Canada were booked up for two years ahead, Audrey Margaret Hetherington's mother gave her a plane ticket to Montreal as a wedding present. Like so many others, Audrey recalls what it was like to be free of the restrictions of food rationing:

My little boy John, from a previous marriage, was five when I married Joe and he'd never seen a banana, ever. And he ate bananas all the way from London to New York. The stewardess thought it was so neat.

Then we flew to Montreal and there was a real bad storm there and we were holed up in Montreal for a night in a hotel. I will always remember a girl coming around and saying, "How many eggs would you like for breakfast?" I said, "How many?" We'd had one egg a month in England and often we didn't get that. I thought I'd never get tired of eggs. I stuffed myself with eggs for about a month and then, ugh, I couldn't stand them.

Betty Taylor had married Don, a Newfoundlander, in 1942, and they travelled to Canada on the same ship, although they were separated on different decks:

As we were coming towards the Nova Scotia coast, we heard that the Halifax dockers had gone on strike. The next news we got was that we were going to New York, then we heard that the New Yorkers had also gone on strike. So the captain of the ship got on the Tannoy and said, "We are going into Halifax and I'll take this ship in myself, tugs or no tugs." And he did. He got her in the dock just as sweet as anything.

Of course, everybody rushed to the side and the old ship was tilting and people were throwing papers from the dock and there was money flying everywhere.

We got to St. John's, and it was the most beautiful sight to see the narrows. The sun came out the morning we arrived, and the colours of the granite cliffs and Cabot Tower — it was beautiful. We went through the narrows and saw the circular harbour and the city just rising in the hills all around. It was gorgeous. It was one of the most beautiful memories I have.

Since Rita Williams's crossing was during the war, they travelled in convoy. She had not seen her husband for almost two years and was understandably anxious to get to Canada:

There were many people from many nations coming to America to set up the United Nations. The next day we had news of F.D.R.'s death. I remember the memorial service for the president on board the ship.

We landed in Toronto on 20 April. On VE Day, soon after, I was a lonely, homesick English girl imagining myself back in dear old war-broken Liverpool.

Joan Georgina Weller had been softened up by a jar of Noxema, which her future husband Claude had used to relieve her sunburn. Two weeks after their wedding he was repatriated to Canada, and she had not seen him for ten months:

I sailed on the *Aquitania* from Southampton on 24 April 1946, along with hundreds of other war brides, with and without children, plus a contingent of returning servicemen. One girl attempted suicide, as she had learned that her husband was seeing another woman, but she was determined to go to Canada to see if she could sort things out. Another bride was armed with two children plus a large suitcase of dirty laundry. She said it was time her new mother-in-law found out what it was like with two unruly tots. I have often wondered what became of her marriage!

I vividly recall a man in first class named Gold who was in the entertainment business and knew we were homesick. He took the time to organize a show on board, using the talents of the brides and the returning servicemen. As I sang in those days, I was part of it and enjoyed filling the days with rehearsals. At the performance, one of the brides gave a moving rendition of "My Yiddish Mama." I'm certain we ran out of hankies that night — there was nearly as much water on board as there was swishing at the sides of the ship! Believe it or not, the military police wanted to lay charges against a number of us, both brides and servicemen, because about thirty of us went out on deck with Gold to get a breath of cool air after the show. After several threats and name dropping, Gold prevailed and we heard nothing more about it.

As the ship slowly edged its way into the dock at Halifax, a number of Haligonians called up, "Go home, war brides! We don't want you here — you took our men!" In later years I'm sure some of us wished we hadn't! When we arrived, a few of the brides were not allowed to land but were returned to England as "undesirable aliens," having been found in the lifeboats with returning servicemen.

I was already apprehensive, since the total time I had spent with my husband before our marriage was about five weeks. When I arrived at Union Station, Toronto, to be met by this stranger in civilian clothes, I almost panicked, but was determined to give it the old college try. I'm still trying after forty-six years of marriage!

Stories of war brides mingling with crew members spread. Pamela Woollam remembers the fate of some who were on her ship:

During the voyage the girls were asked to go to parties in the officers' cabins. Some accepted, but found on arrival in Halifax that their names were announced over the loudspeaker, telling them that they would not be allowed to land as they were deemed "undesirables."

War brides travelling with young children found the voyage particularly trying. Maureen McDonald sailed aboard the Brittanic, *which took two weeks to cross the Atlantic — an arduous time for herself and her baby:*

There was no special food for infants and so we had to feed our babies whatever they could eat from our plates, mostly potatoes and gravy. The babies all got sick; we lost one at sea. The doctors said to just feed them milk, but the stewardesses said not to, as it was nearly two weeks old and not very fresh. However, we survived!

The transportation system on the Continent had been devastated, so war brides coming from there had to endure an even longer and more frustrating journey. It was especially hard for Joukje Will, a Dutch war bride, since she had her baby twins with her on board the Lady Nelson:

We waited for six days for the brides from Belgium and Holland to board before the ship embarked. Like the *Lady Rodney*, our ship was a coast boat, not meant for ocean travel, but due to the great demand by the returning soldiers and their wives for passages, they were pressed into service as transport ships. Because of this, they were very rough and the voyage was hard on all the passengers.

I had the babies hung by my bed in a basket-type bassinet, with a mattress and blanket. Since I was so very sick myself, I was barely able to look after the wee infants. Two hundred war brides and one hundred and ten babies were aboard, attended by three Red Cross nurses and one doctor. One of the girls, so badly dehydrated after the eleven-day voyage, died in Halifax after leaving the ship.

Lily Mann, who sailed on the Letitia, *says that the wives and babies were "packed in like sardines":*

It was a ghastly fourteen-day trip. Many of the women were so seasick that they never left their bunks. One of my vivid recollections is of clutching my son, who could not stand or walk at that time, as I tried to lean over the ship's rail, expecting to die at any moment. It has taken a long time for me to forget the terrible smells that filled the ship.

Marjorie Whitworth had served in the WAAF *for four years and knew how to take care of herself, but many of her shipmates had never been away from home before. She recalls the problems to be faced by those who, like herself, had small babies:*

The powers that be, for some inexplicable reason, decided that all babies must be weaned. I can't for the life of me think why this ridiculous order was made. Almost all English babies were breast-fed at the time. I was most fortunate. The ship was the *Letitia*, a former hospital ship, small but spotless. Those with small babies under six months drew A deck, the best position on the ship. That was the good part. Our room was about half as big as my present living room. It held twelve double bunks — the uppers for the mums, with a string hammock suspended from the side for the babies. The lowers were reserved for twelve expectant mothers, who were not supposed to be over four months pregnant. Some had cheated more than a little here!

We had twelve newly weaned babies, and the time difference meant gaining an hour each night, which played havoc with the feeding schedule, so they howled their way across the Atlantic, for the most part. My baby was a pet; I think he liked the rocking of the boat. I was a seasickness victim, but I just couldn't be sick. The nappies had to be washed, and we only had four very small enamel bowls between us. There was nowhere at all to dry them, and I'm afraid the highly polished mahogany rails in the corridors suffered.

Toddlers were supposed to be on reins the whole time. I never heard of one falling overboard but witnessed a few near misses.

Gwyneth Shirley crossed the Atlantic in January 1947 on the last war-bride voyage of the Aquitania:

The Red Cross nurses did not approve of dummies, called soothers or pacifiers in Canada. "Those filthy, unhygienic things," they said. "No wonder the English have prominent teeth!" I had a three-month-old son and, as you can imagine, there was a real need for soothers in our crowded conditions. There were forty mothers and as many babies in our section—you couldn't call it a cabin. When one baby awakened in the night and cried, it set off a sympathetic chorus!

We were given Red Cross parcels, baby clothes, and, best of all, Canadian nappies. The British kind, made of terry towelling, took ages to dry and, when washed in salt water, eventually dried like a bed of nails. No wonder the babies screamed and they all had raw, red bottoms!

A terrible storm hit us, and the Red Cross nurses were very caring but worked to a state of exhaustion. I suffered a concussion early one morning trying to make up a bottle feeding in the ship's galley, and a Red Cross worker had me moved to a better cabin.

Baby bottles were in short supply, as some were smashed in the storm. So we used ginger-beer bottles instead. Italian war brides nursed their babies until they were toddlers—something to do with food shortages in Italy. When their mothers were seasick, they lost their milk and were unable to nurse. What a commotion! Try to imagine one- and two-year-olds screaming their heads off at this sudden deprivation! The poor Red Cross nurses had to cope with many such emergencies.

I remember a Cockney sailor in the ship's galley. It was his job to supervise the sterilizer, etc., for bottle feedings. He was so disgusted. "I joined the blank, blank navy to see the world and 'ere I am lookin' after bloomin' war brides and their brats!"

We had an outbreak of gastric enteritis among the children. They went down like ninepins. Fog held us up when we were almost within sight of Halifax and every minute counted. As soon as the ship docked, my son and other babies were rushed by ambulance into HMCS *Stadacona* in Halifax. The nurses there were very toffee nosed and made us war brides feel like dirt. We were not allowed to visit the sick children, and there were armed sentries at the gates. The Salvation Army came to our aid—thank God!

As Nancy Wolliston tells us, British pounds were exchanged for dollars on board ship, but many of the war brides found the Canadian money difficult to understand:

When we docked at Halifax, the bands were playing and everybody was cheering us. Two soldiers escorted me down the gangplank. Would you believe I gave them each a $10 bill! My husband almost flipped.

Travelling on board the Queen Elizabeth *in peacetime, Beatrice Lillie, the famous British actress and comedian, had been heard to ask a steward, "What time does this place get to New York?" Grace Gough felt the same as she stepped aboard the* Queen Mary: *"It was like a floating city." But it was a city with strict rules:*

All the war brides were informed if they were to fraternize with the crew they would not be allowed off the ship at Halifax, unless their husbands paid their way. I might add, a couple of brides didn't get off the ship.

There were many, many times in Canada that I wished so much I *had* fraternized!

Considering how young and venturesome the passengers were, it is not surprising that friendships between the sexes did take place. Ruth Delmage shared a cabin with a young woman who made the mistake of "fraternizing":

She had been misinformed and I know she was deported back to England, but that was through her own doings. You were warned about certain rules and regulations to follow before you got on the ship. The troops were on one side of a barricade and we were on another, and there were certain decks we could go on and certain decks were off limits to us.

If you did something wrong and if you went before the ship's captain, that was a mark against you. Depending on what happened, they could deport you back. I knew this girl was the first off the ship and she was deported.

Audrey Pratt was from Eastleigh, a town near Southampton, so her family had been able to see her off on the Lady Nelson. *As well, she was expecting to be met by her husband in Halifax:*

We arrived in Halifax on 19 August to clear, sunny skies. I was immediately sent to a big shed on the pier to wait for my husband. One of our companions was told upon arrival that she was "not wanted" and, therefore, would be returned on the next boat. As the minutes ticked by, many of us wondered what our fate would be. Imagine my delight when my husband arrived to "claim" me. Apparently, he had had car trouble and was therefore an hour late.

Like many other war brides without children, Ellen Tinney helped seasick mothers take care of their young ones during the voyage. She remembers the Aquitania *arriving in Halifax:*

Our first impression of the surrounding area was that it was drab and grey. But on a platform there was a silver band playing "The Maple Leaf Forever." We could see cranes hauling our luggage out of the ship's hold. Many of them fell in the water; others were badly damaged. Luckily, my two trunks were intact.

Gertrude Savage sailed to Canada during the war, urged on by her family, who were concerned for her safety. She had grown so tired of the repeated air raids in wartime London that she had stopped taking adequate precautions, even though the windows of her house had been blown out:

I just couldn't take any more. So my parents would take my baby to the shelter and I would stay in bed. My mother told my husband he'd better talk to me, so he made all the arrangements for me to come to Canada. I came over on a hospital ship. There were twenty war brides in my cabin and twenty-four babies. In peacetime that cabin took four people. I was sick from the day that I got on.

The other girls were so good to me and fed my baby and looked after her.

My husband was in Germany, and he didn't even know that I'd arrived in Canada until some of his friends had gone to a show and seen a newsreel of a boat landing in Halifax and saw me and my baby walking down the ramp.

Because Vera Davison was not yet married to Earl, the Canadian government would not pick up the tab for her travel to Nova Scotia. She set off a year after Earl, on the Ile de France, *which was bound for New York:*

The liner had been used as a troopship during the war and had yet to be refitted. I slept in an open dormitory, with about fifty-nine other passengers, on the bunks the troops had used. The passengers were of several nationalities, quite a lot of Americans going home.

It was quite a thrill coming into New York harbour and seeing the Statue of Liberty. I had teamed up with another English girl coming to Canada, and she was rather unhappy and afraid. She was leaving a blind father to go to a possibly rundown farm and two elderly in-laws. She was not a young girl herself. She was ready to turn back at New York, but other passengers urged her to keep on.

Peggy Richardson, who had become engaged to Cal after knowing him only a week, left her home in Worthing in 1946, bound for Raymond, Alberta. She travelled on a hospital ship:

The wounded men were out of bounds for us. We could wave to them. I heard that two war brides couldn't land in Canada because they had fraternized with the men. Some of them messed around in the lifeboats.

When we got to Raymond, Cal's mother came running out and she put her arms around me and she said, "I'm going to try to take the place of your mother." And she did.

Pat Heath had a dreadful crossing. Her cabin had six bunks, with wire baskets attached to the sides for the babies:

The floor was covered with two inches of water through the whole journey, and the bathroom had only salt water in it. The morning before we landed, the ship's doctor and an army officer checked us out in our cabin. The doctor took one look at the water on the floor and the condition of the babies and said we were lucky we didn't lose the babies coming over.

Three girls were shipped home from Halifax, as they were found in the soldiers' quarters making pin money.

Pamela Parsons remembers that after eleven days at sea, the sight of land brought everyone up on deck. Was it? . . . Yes it was! It was Canada! That was a magical moment for Pamela:

We all ran to the side of the ship and our first sight of land — the white, white snow with the sun shining gloriously down from such a beautiful blue sky. I shall never forget that sight.

The Red Cross men and women took marvellous care of us on the ship, and they also met us in Halifax and helped us to disembark and then saw us onto the trains that took us across Canada to our new homes. Ed met my train in Montreal. He looked so nice in his navy blue pinstripe suit, as I had only ever seen him in his uniform before. We boarded our train, which was to take us to Smiths Falls, a small town in the Ottawa Valley. He kept teasing me that a dog team would be meeting us, as he could see how apprehensive I was looking out at all that snow.

It turned out that because we arrived at two o'clock in the morning there were no taxis available, so we had to walk on ice-covered streets — me with no boots on, just my English shoes, slipping and sliding for what seemed like miles. What a wonderful welcome waited for me at my husband's family home! They had every kind of food on the table. I hadn't seen so much food in one place ever before.

Naturally, I was very nervous meeting Ed's mother, father, and four sisters. I felt their eyes looking me over and sizing me up, as it were. They made me very welcome, and over the following months we got to know each other and I felt right at home in my new country.

As each ship nosed its way towards Canada, the captain and crew kept the women fully informed of their location and their expected time of arrival in Halifax. Hours before they were due to dock, the war brides crowded the decks, searching for the first sight of land. Most were expecting a cold, vast land, inhabited by Eskimos and Indians. As the ship carrying Jean M. Chartrand stirred the waters of Halifax harbour, she had her first taste of a Canadian winter:

We awoke to a snowstorm. We were not allowed to disembark right away; the troops had to go first. I was determined to be the first war bride to become a Canadian citizen, as we had been told that we would be full citizens when we touched Canadian ground. Nothing loath, I trotted down the gangplank and onto the dock, only to be confronted by a burly military commandant who, in no uncertain terms, told me where I'd land if I did not go back up that so-and-so gangplank. I did not need any persuading. After what seemed like a lifetime, we were allowed to disembark and made our way to the huge sheds where our trunks were to be found. Then we were met by the Red Cross, who gave us coffee, tea, and cookies, and bunting bags, baby clothes, and other baby needs for the wee ones. Our next stop was to obtain Canadian currency for our pounds sterling. Then it was "all aboard" the trains, according to a specified plan.

The war brides found a new world waiting for them, a nation that seemed almost untouched by war. The music, too, was different. The voice of Vera Lynn was now behind them, replaced by Canada's own brand of country music. To Connie Ellen Burrill, as she sat back and listened on the Duchess of Bedford, *it was a sign that her life would never be the same again:*

Suddenly, strains of a different kind of music came over the ship's loudspeaker system. This seemed to cause a buzz of excitement amongst the Canadian Red Cross and other personnel in charge of shepherding us war brides to Canada. As we wondered about the music, we heard cries of, "We are home free," "Almost to home plate now," and other remarks. One person said, "Good old Don Messer and His Islanders," and another, "That means we are almost there." We became clued in that the music was being transmitted from Canada and that we were close enough to get reception.

On going ashore, I had mixed feelings and many thoughts, one being, Where are the bands? We had heard that bands had played to welcome war brides ashore from other ships, but none for us lot. Uneasy, timid, but eager was I, as we found ourselves in a large, shedlike building. Many tables/desks were singly spaced over the floor. I remember sitting at one of these desks being questioned. I must say, I was treated very well, made to feel welcome everywhere. I was given an envelope which contained free meal tickets for use on the train journey to Yarmouth. Inside this envelope, to my surprise and delight, was a newspaper clipping of my husband in uniform. I remember thinking how very thoughtful of someone to go to all that trouble for me when they were so busy with so many war brides to be processed through customs and immigration.

Some of us were taken to the local Salvation Army headquarters/hostel (I think it was). We were given bed and board until we were due to leave by train to our various destinations. There we received loving care: hot baths, *two* boiled eggs for breakfast. We were allowed to have a walk about Halifax streets under escort. We felt like fish out of water. We could not believe all the food and fruit we saw through shop windows, in particular huge bunches of bananas! We asked, "Are these real?"

Breaking the last ties with other war brides and home, a pleasant Salvation Army captain escorted me to the station and saw that I was safely on the train and seated. Wishing me godspeed and good luck, he turned to leave. As I watched his retreating back, a sense of aloneness overwhelmed me. Homesickness for England and my husband overran my resolve to "keep a stiff upper lip" and a "staunch British heart." Tears slid unbidden down my cheeks. For some reason, the captain swung around when almost to the door and, seeing my distress, hurried back to give me a hug and a "God bless you." He said, "Now, now, you will be fine. Keep your British courage up high"—and left.

Winnie Fougère's first impression of Halifax surprised her, since several sailors on the ship had said to her, "Surely you're not going to live in Halifax!":

We anchored in the middle of the harbour for some reason. It was dawn on a beautiful summer day, and the whole place had the appearance of the tropics, with the sun rising behind McNab and Georges islands and the lights of the city still twinkling in the distance.

We were so glad to get off the crowded ship and meet our husbands on the dock, with bands playing and "Welcome" banners blowing in the breeze. I felt sorry for the girls who had long journeys by train ahead of them, some as far as Vancouver.

Everything seemed new and strange in this big country of Canada, and at first I missed my mother and home dreadfully. One thing I did like, though, was to go shopping and actually see *real* fruit and chocolates in the stores, instead of cardboard pictures of them!

Along with the parents and loved ones who met the ships were a number of young women who were also happy to see the servicemen return. Margaret Lindsay remembers the greeting the men received from them:

They were, of course, loudly cheered. When they saw us, they very loudly booed us. Needless to say, we stood our ground and behaved like ladies.

The end of the war did not lead to a happy reunion for all couples. Doris M. Richards had been widowed in 1944 and had later decided to come to her husband's family in Quebec. She says, "I've never had cause to forget the warmth and love and welcome extended to me":

As the *Queen Mary* approached Canada in June 1946, there was a heightened sense of excitement and joy on board the huge ocean liner. It was packed with hundreds of war brides, most of them having one or more very young children. They were all eagerly anticipating reunions with their already repatriated Canadian husbands. The thrill of a new life, new home, and meeting new relatives awaited them. The chatter and excitement was intense as we drew near to Halifax.

My baby daughter Alcida and I were amongst them, yet not of them. My heart grew increasingly heavier and my tears fell in the secret confines of my cabin. I was sad and had little to say to anyone. For I had indeed been a war bride for just three months. My beloved twenty-two-year-old French-Canadian husband had been killed in action during the final battle fought at Arnhem in September 1944. He was never to know our baby, born seven months later.

Patricia Enright-Howlett made her debut on Canadian soil in grand style:

First sight of Canada — sailing into Halifax harbour, seeing little white houses dotted on the hillsides. (I had never seen wooden houses before.) My husband was at the dockside to meet me. I trotted daintily down the gangplank, waving goodbye to my new friends who were cheering me on — tripped and fell in a heap at my husband's feet!

At last, the war brides and their children had set foot on Canadian soil. For those who were met in Halifax, their long journey was over; but the majority still had hundreds or thousands of miles of railway track to travel before they reached their new homes — and the beginning of a new life.

4

Across a Land of Whistlestops

YOUNG WOMEN *who were thousands of miles from the land of their birth, some clutching the hands of their children, were now making their way across a strange country to find a new home. During the past hundred years, many other women had done the same — but with one major difference. They had travelled as a family. These wives travelled alone. They reached out to one another as their trains sped across Canada, but once darkness arrived and heads began to nod in their berths, each felt the pang of homesickness and a keen sense of anxiety, which grew as the trains brought them nearer to their new homes.*

The Canadian government had done its best to help. Many people had worked late into the night, organizing a disembarkation program with bureaus across Canada. The Red Cross went hand in hand with the CPR and CNR offices. After the final destination of each bride and child was listed, the information was teleprinted to the Embarkation Transit Unit Movement Control in Halifax.

A medical officer was on each train to ensure that first-rate medical attention was available if needed, and the Red Cross was also on hand with a crew on each train. Typically, a doctor, a nurse, and four attendants occupied two rooms, one at the front and one at the back of the train. As well, there were quarantine facilities on each train to house children who came down with measles or other infectious diseases. The Halifax Herald *reported that those who accompanied the brides had strict orders to "be ready to stay awake the full time of the trip if necessary. If the baby cries in the night, the Red Cross volunteer is to be on hand to look after it so that the mother, tired from her trip across the Atlantic journey, may sleep."*

A movement-control officer was present to handle all matters of trains, baggage, tickets, reservations, meals, and the like. There was also a train liaison officer, whose job was to ensure that the passengers were well cared for so that they reached their new relatives in as relaxed and happy a state as possible.

Doris Paterson had watched the land getting closer as she leaned on the rail of the three-funnelled Aquitania, *and like so many others, she had a train journey ahead of her:*

Our papers are checked, stamped "landed immigrant," and our money changed. I wave goodbye to my friends, as they are to catch a different train. Some of us are taken to the train station. My God, what an immense monster this engine is! My heart lurches. I want my dear little British trains. A soldier helps to carry my cases and holds out his hand for a tip. I look through my new money. He pokes at a $5 bill. I give it to him but later learn they were not supposed to accept tips. I climb up into the monster and am pleased with the comfortable surroundings.

I only have to stay on the train for two days and I will be in Montreal and Ted will be waiting. The other girls in the compartment are excited, as am I. We seem to be stopping at a small Quebec village. One of the girls asks a porter, "How long are we stopping here?"

"About an hour or so," he says.

Geraldine is the adventurous type: "Let's go and see what the shops are like here. It will give us a boost to see all the good things we have been missing."

We climb down the steps, and a wave of feeling rushes through me when my feet reach the ground. This is the New Land. This is to be my home. We go into a shop. What a delight! Geraldine is squealing with joy, "Look, Doris, what a selection of makeup!" I buy some face cream, really just to make a purchase in Canada. We gawk at all the items on display.

Time is ticking away and I am getting nervous about returning to the train. Geraldine is still debating what to buy. Finally, she makes the decision and we go outside. We can't believe our eyes! — our train is leaving the station! It's going without us! What in the heck are we going to do? The train is too far away for us to catch even if we run. We see one of the girls in our compartment hanging out of the door. There is a massive screeching of the brakes. She must have pulled the emergency cord. We run and run and climb aboard. We wait, hunched up with shame and regret, thinking we will be scolded or fined for the delay. But no one comes and we are relieved.

Finally, we are nearing Montreal. Lineups for the bathroom so we can put our makeup on and look our best for the men. Excitement wells up in my throat. We chatter without making much sense. Everyone is collecting their baggage. The train is slowing down and a city is emerging; it looks much like London really.

Now the excitement is turning into panic. Good Lord, it's been three and a half months since I've seen Ted! I've only seen him in civilian clothes a couple of times. What will his choice in clothes be? I dislike flashy wear. Will I even recognize him? When one is separated, one conjures up images that may not be true.

The train is grinding to a stop. We are all at the windows, straining for a glimpse of our loved ones. And there he is! But, oh, my goodness, he has on a ginger-coloured suit — how awful! And his tie must be at least six inches wide with gaudy colours. But his eyes find me and my heart melts. Those eyes are the bluest in the world, and clear and honest and lovable. It's okay — he's still my Ted. The feel of his arms around me is indescribable. His voice is saying, "Dody, Dody, you're here! You're here!"

We go to the hotel and climb the stairs to our room. Everything fades into the background as we shuck our clothes to feel each other in entirety. Love for each other rises with such intensity that it seems the room cannot contain it. My head spins. The first part of my move to Canada is over. Now I have Ted beside me, nothing will be so terrible. His hand closes over mine. Such wonderful hands. Everything will be all right.

Monica Lewis Hale recalls disembarking from the Queen Mary *and setting out on the next stage of her journey:*

After going through Immigration in one of the ship's saloons, we were again helped by Canadian soldiers as we went from the ship to the enormous Canadian train, so different from the English ones. There were small boys begging souvenirs and men selling newspapers as we were helped up into the coaches and shown to our berths. Again, I must pay tribute to those railway employees who coped with this female horde so patiently. As the train pulled out with that mournful whistle, we looked back and saw the *Queen Mary* silhouetted on the horizon and felt that now we really had left all that was familiar. Someone started to sing "Gonna take a sentimental journey . . ." and we all joined in.

The train trip to Toronto was good and bad. We couldn't keep the babies or ourselves really clean because of the smuts from the coal-fired steam engine. After two days we pulled into Union Station, Toronto, and here occurred what to me was the highlight of our trip. We got off the train and dear, wonderful ladies from the Red Cross took the babies, having inquired what formula they were on, and led us weary wives down into the bowels of the station, where lunch was provided and tea was being served in *bone china cups!* I remember thinking, Thank God! Civilization at last! For so many years we had used mugs, the good china having been packed away in case it was damaged in the air raids, and replacements were impossible to get. The sight of those cups and saucers was a real tonic! Dear Red Cross ladies!

After arriving on the Letitia, *Marjorie Whitworth and her baby boarded the train for Toronto. Like most other mothers making the trip, she found that the facilities were inadequate. This was understandable, since Canada's trains had not been built to transport thousands of young mothers with babies in diapers:*

The girls who were going to the West Coast naturally were given what air-conditioned coaches were available. Our coaches had seen better days; they were very dirty to start with and, of course, got worse as time passed. There was nowhere to heat water for the formula-fed babies and nowhere to wash nappies. We did the best we could in the washroom and hung them where we could find a spare spot.

By now, almost all the babies were suffering from diarrhoea. We had a porter who was furious with us and called us "dirty English pigs." By contrast, the porter in the next compartment spent most of his spare time walking up and down with fractious babies, singing them folksongs.

The train made a short stop at Quebec City, and they allowed us out on the platform. It was a beautiful summer day. The Chateau loomed above us; it was quite spectacular. But at that moment, for the only time in all the years that have followed, I wanted to turn around and go back! It was so hard boarding that train again, but in a few minutes I heard my name being called. A Red Cross volunteer, a good friend of my husband's cousin, was looking for me. She asked if she could help in any way, and she certainly could. I got a pile of the very first disposable diapers I had ever seen. In my years in the WAAF I had blessed the Red Cross many times, but never more fervently than then. It gave me a new lease on life! I felt someone really cared.

About an hour out of Toronto the word went round that we were almost there. Clean dresses for us, high-heeled shoes, and even hats! All the toddlers were dolled up to meet Daddy, with frills and white socks, etc. Then they held the train for two hours just outside the city because we were early! By this time, there was no running water for drinking or toilet flushing and it was the middle of August!

We were a sorry-looking lot when we staggered up those steps to be met at the top by all these strangers! We didn't recognize our husbands. They looked so funny in those garish suits with wide lapels, huge shoulders, and fedora hats — all clutching large bouquets of flowers and larger teddy bears. But they were certainly glad to see us!

Certainly, the reception that Margaret C. Haggerty and her companions were given when they arrived in Halifax was just the tonic they needed. With the sound of music in the air and with ladies

*handing out candies to the children, they felt very welcome as they
followed the military officer who was conducting them to the train:*

The porter assigned to our coach spoke only French, and some of
us who had taken French at school tried our best to talk to him. I
made an effort to ask him if I could take the lower bunk instead of
climbing to the upper. This conversation appeared to make him
very embarrassed. The next day his wife came on board with a
basket of fruit for all those on his coach. She could speak English,
so I told her about the switching of the bunks. She started to have
a good laugh. Unbeknownst to me, her husband had taken over
the lower bunk, and in my broken French I had asked if I could
sleep there too!

*Pat Heath had endured terrible conditions when crossing the Atlan-
tic, and she could not enjoy the train journey either:*

We left the boat and boarded a train that went across Canada. I
saw girls get off in the middle of the night at little whistle stops,
get into horse-drawn traps, and go off into the darkness with no
lights in sight. I've wondered about these girls many times. The
first night on the train they only had enough boiled water for two
ounces of formula for each child, so the babies cried most of the
night from hunger. I was so glad to hit Ottawa!

*Joyce Horne recalls that Canada appeared outside her train win-
dow like a travelogue as she watched the villages and towns of
Quebec race by. Then she was "almost stranded" in Montreal while
searching for another woman's straying child:*

We just made the train as it was starting to roll. Northern Ontario
seemed all rocks, forests, and rushing water. It was so cold at White
River, and there I got my first glimpse of post-office boxes. I remember very little about Manitoba, except having my shins kicked black
and blue by a very bored child sitting on the seat opposite me. I
have since wondered how the mothers were able to keep diapers
and clothes clean on that trip. As far as I saw, there was only one

sink for each carriage, and English diapers were made of heavy terry towelling—no Pampers in those days.

One very young mother cried the whole trip, holding her year-old babe as though he was the only link with all that was familiar. She was very homesick. One other poor soul had lost her husband in action and was bringing her two girls to Canada so that the grandparents might see their dead son's children at least once.

As we crossed Saskatchewan, I stayed up that night so I might help a girl off the train. She had a baby in a basket and lots of luggage. As we pulled into a very small and lonely station at three o'clock in the morning, I thought how far from home we all were. Forty years later I met a war bride at my granddaughter's wedding and she was that girl I had helped off the train in Saskatchewan so long ago. A small world. We reached Calgary the next morning, and it was wonderful after being met to sit or walk on something that did not move.

As the trains made their way across Canada, women who had begun the trip by pressing their noses to the windows gradually turned to make friends with their travelling companions. The country they had left could be crossed in only a few hours. Their present journey would take several days. These strangers who had been thrown together had one common thread—they were all travelling thousands of miles to begin a new life.

Each time the train slowed and the guard's voice announced an approaching station, brief friendships came to an end with hugs and best wishes for the future. Holding their children and grabbing their bags, those who were leaving climbed down onto the strange platform. Noses were once again pressed against the windows as the women on board anxiously evaluated the husbands on the platform. As the train slowly puffed its way from the station, the women still on board must have wondered about the reception awaiting them.

At every station on her way to Moose Jaw, Saskatchewan, Helena Hammer watched fellow war brides being met by husbands and in-laws. One young woman was crying as she waved goodbye, having been met by a silent mother-in-law in a horse-drawn wagon:

Another girl collapsed when she met her in-laws and was brought back onto the train by her husband, at the insistence of the Red Cross. Her new relatives meant well, meeting their daughter-in-law in full Indian regalia. It was unfortunate that her husband hadn't told her beforehand that he was a native.

Beryl Haines Ward had felt numb when she left Southampton, unable to summon up any emotion. But once she was on the train in Canada, things soon changed. As she rattled her way across the country, she felt a deep concern for some of the war brides:

I remember the ones who got off on their own in the middle of nowhere, with no one to greet them! Once I was so upset I went to the steps and yelled at the girl, "Come on back!" She just made a helpless gesture. On that journey I remember the women's faces, their ignorance as to what they were coming to, and comforting themselves with the promise from their mum or dad that if they didn't like it they could come home. I didn't have that cushion, nor did I want it.

Finally, Ottawa! From the train I could see the station packed with people and bands playing. It was so organized! There were the Red Cross workers who came aboard and asked for the war brides by name and escorted them to their husbands and families. My turn came, and the Red Cross person told me that my husband, his family, and friends were waiting. I then came to life and freaked out! It all came to full realization. I told the poor soul that I was not getting off that train! When she asked why, I said, "For one thing, I can't remember what Archie looks like! And secondly, my knees have gone to water and I can't walk!" Well, bless her, she talked to me, assured me Archie was very nice and all would be well. By now the train was empty. With my wobbly legs and the Red Cross lady's strong arms, I found my group of greeters — Archie, his parents, aunties, and old friends with flowers and gifts. There was much hugging, and they were wonderful!

Most of the husbands of these war brides were now civilians. The romantic uniforms they had worn as servicemen had been replaced by suits and ties. Many a young wife wondered whether she would recognize her man dressed in civvies. Some, like Joan Cutting, had other worries too:

We pulled into a siding in Toronto and waited for the word to alight. Having only been married one month before Bob was repatriated to Canada, I was somewhat nervous to meet my husband again after a nine-month absence. We were all in line, and I remember it was like being herded into a corral. As our names were announced, each husband would step forward to collect you, as if you were up for auction!

Never seeing Bob in civilian clothes before, it was a bit of a shock to see him wearing a Homburg hat and long, fitted overcoat. It reminded me of the Untouchables!

After almost a month of travelling, Joan S. Oakes had felt lonely as each new friend left the train on her long journey from Halifax to Edmonton. But at last it was her turn to leave:

A group of husbands and in-laws were waiting at the train station. As the small crowd dwindled away, imagine my dismay and shock when I realized I was alone except for two Red Cross volunteers who had come to greet us! They were truly "angels of mercy," taking me under their wings. One was Mrs. G. R. A. Rice, who took me to her home, where I stayed for three days until the Red Cross people tracked down my husband, Thomas, in the Christie Street hospital in Toronto, where he had undergone surgery for a serious head injury.

By this time, the limited amount of money which we were allowed to bring out of England had dwindled away and I was almost penniless. Once again, the wonderful Red Cross Society came to my rescue and paid my train fare back to Toronto to be with my husband.

The first people that Doris Rhindress saw waiting for her on the platform as her train pulled into Amherst, Nova Scotia, were her in-laws:

I recognized them from the many pictures we had exchanged. What beautiful people! I adored them from the start, along with my two new sisters-in-law and brother-in-law. They showed me in so many ways that they liked me, too. On 5 March 1944, our fears were put to rest and a happy telegram was sent to Bob in Italy that he was the proud father of an 8¾ lb. baby girl.

When Della Crossman had left for Canada on board the Franconia, *her relatives and friends had repeatedly told her that cowboys and Indians would be there to meet all foreigners. These thoughts were on her mind as the train approached her new home:*

The trainman asked me who was meeting me in Sackville. I told him I wasn't sure, as my mother-in-law and sister-in-law had both been sick. He told me not to worry, that the Red Cross would meet me and look after my two-year-old son and me. As we were slowly approaching my destination, the same trainman asked if my husband had a red patch on his tunic. I said yes and he said, "I think he is right here to meet you." I looked out the window and saw him. I started yelling, and pandemonium broke loose in the car. My husband had been home for just a week and did not know when I was arriving, but he had been asked if he would assist the Red Cross that afternoon.

The trainman took our son and handed him down to my husband, but he wouldn't go to his father, as he didn't know him. I can't describe how happy I was, as my in-laws were also there as well as other town people. (No cowboys or Indians and lots of good food.)

After Myra Mirka arrived in Halifax, she boarded a train for Saskatchewan:

Sleeping in berths was a new experience for us and the crew was very kind and helpful. I think it was 19 August when we got to Yorkton, Saskatchewan, and I literally fell into my husband's arms, as I tripped over the large water hose snaking along the platform. He was accompanied by two of his sisters and two nieces. Luckily, it was early morning or they might have thought I'd been tippling!

The Salvation Army was waiting to help the war brides as they arrived in Saint John and soon found a hostel for the night for Jean Margaret McArthur:

What a night! I think I would have preferred an air raid. The kiddies were upset and had nightmares all night, and all I could do was cuddle them and cry with them. We thought the cute little wooden houses were nice, the prams we saw were very strange, and all swore that our husbands would absolutely never wear one of those red plaid jackets. Remember that none of us had seen our men in civvies and had no idea what to expect.

The next day we travelled on to our destination, and my mother-in-law was there to meet me. I recognized her from snaps, but there was a man with her who I supposed was my husband. He looked like him and, to tell the truth, I was beginning to panic about that because who was this guy I had married? I hadn't seen him for about eighteen months. Would I recognize him? I certainly didn't like the look of this man in civvies, but it turned out to be my brother-in-law.

Six months later my hero arrived home, and when I saw him it was like nothing had happened. We still had the crazies!

Even though Peggy Moir had to take the train only from Halifax to New Brunswick, she found the experience awesome:

I will never forget the miles and miles of woods we passed, with small wooden houses and even smaller wooden buildings, which I found out later were outhouses. Never in my wildest dreams did I imagine that Canada was so vast and wild looking, and kept wondering what was ahead. But I was young, in love, had a beautiful daughter, and was anxious to be with my husband.

Ruth Delmage had a similar impression of wilderness:

Coming across Canada on the train, especially in Quebec and parts of Ontario, some of the girls got off and you really wondered where they were going to because there was just nothing but trees.

Sybil J. Parkinson had personal cause for concern because of what she was told in Halifax:

The army clerk asked me where I was going and I said to a small place called Baljennie in Saskatchewan. He had a map in front of him and he looked at me and said, "It's not even on here." That really worried me.

As her train rattled its way across the great expanse of Canada, Marjorie J. Crawford could be forgiven for any impatience she may have felt:

Would this train ever arrive in Winnipeg? How many more lakes could there be? Every time I looked out of the train window, we were going past water. So many of the friends I had made on the journey had already arrived at their destinations.

How could I know when I left Brighton how vast this country was, how rugged and desolate in some places? Earl had tried to tell me before we were married but, oh, it couldn't be that bad and I was so in love with him. Oh, another question and answer. Earl had been in a hospital bed the last time I saw him. That was six months ago. Will I recognize him in civilian clothes? Oh, yes, he is on crutches. How could you not know your husband?

Someone is calling, "Next stop Winnipeg." What's the date? I must write it down. May 5 — it is my birthday. I'm nineteen, married just over a year. What am I doing in this unfamiliar place?

There he is smiling. His arms go around me. All the questions have been answered. I'm home.

For many war brides, the trains provided a great relief from the constant seasickness they had experienced on their Atlantic crossing. Barb Warriner, who, with her two daughters, was heading for Big River, northern Saskatchewan, had suffered terribly throughout the voyage:

I, for one, didn't give a darn what land it was so long as it was holding still and not moving from side to side or up and down. I had never been on the sea before and I never intend to go again.

I've had all the sailing I need or want. Thank God, we were here. Another week on the train and we were in Saskatoon. My husband was there to meet us. He looked a perfect stranger. I had never seen him in civvies before.

After staying in Saskatoon a few days, we caught the train for Prince Albert and were met there by a dear old lady, Mrs. Mary Lamb. She was English also, and probably knew how I was feeling so far from home. Someone said later that she met every train carrying war brides from England to their new homes around Prince Albert and district. She was a great ambassador and did a truly great job. Before leaving on the "Muskeg Express" for Big River, she presented us with goody bags of books, candies, and fruit to while away the hours it would take to get to our northern home.

As the child of a World War I bride, Joyce Hassard had spent her early years in Saskatchewan before her family had moved back to England:

Twenty-seven years after my mother had travelled the same path, coming to a new country with a baby girl, I followed in her footsteps, also with our baby girl Lorna. We landed in Halifax on 18 September 1946 and boarded trains for our long journey across this vast country. I remember a train stop somewhere in Ontario, and there were ladies who met the train and passed around baskets of peaches. Delicious peaches—what a treat!

Lorne met us in Winnipeg, and we set out on the train for Frobisher from there, arriving first at Alameda, Saskatchewan, where I'd lived as a child. A very dear lady came on the train to meet me. It was Mrs. Art Best. She said she'd come to meet my mother and she wanted to do the same for me. It was so good to be welcomed back.

A whole new world began to unfold as the wives and their children gazed through train windows at prairies encircled by a huge sky and at a magic kingdom of mountains. Olive Warner remembers it vividly:

Such vast openness, such space. I had a wonderful sense of freedom. I was wearing a hat, one of the little hats that perched on the side of the head with a little fluff of a veil. I took it off and threw it out the window — rather as a symbol of throwing out the old and looking forward eagerly to the new. I am now living in the USA, but each time I cross the bridge into Canada, I still have that wonderful feeling of freedom.

Stella Chudleigh was on her way to a farm in Alberta, travelling from the rugged coast of Halifax to the prairies of western Canada:

The country seemed so vast with such varied scenery, and the air outside the train at the various stops was so fresh and pure. At some places we were given a very warm welcome at the station by local residents, which gave us all a very nice impression. Being late March, the prairies looked very bare and barren, so I was greatly encouraged to see some trees as we approached Tilley and Brooks in the irrigation district.

The army officer in charge of the trainload of wives appeared satisfied with the enthusiastic welcome that I received from Rufus, his mother, and sister, and said, "Yep! That one's okay." There were a few wives who were not met for various reasons, and these were taken to a collection depot in Calgary, pending investigations.

Lilian Anderson was amazed at the vast distances one could travel in Canada:

I don't think I will ever forget the train trip. Who would ever have thought you could spend three days and nights on a train? My husband had written and told me this, but I thought he was pulling my leg. I couldn't get over how friendly the Canadian people were when we would stop in different towns. The people would come over, shake our hands, want to know where we were going and give us lots of advice.

After an eleven-day Atlantic crossing with a sick baby, Cecilia Knight was also surprised at the distance she had yet to go:

The train trip was an endless journey. We couldn't believe that it could last so long. Five days on the train—you're never five hours on the train in England to get to your destination. I was going to Winnipeg, and I knew that was a city, but I used to feel so sorry for these poor girls who would get off the train in these godforsaken spots. The train would stop and people would get off, and there wouldn't even be a station in the middle of Ontario, among all the tall trees. But I ended up on a farm which seemed to be a million miles away from anywhere anyway.

Sylvia E. Richardson recalls her trip after she boarded the train for Montreal:

The sleeping berths were made up and we soon settled down, only to be wakened through the night by the train's whistle. Even now, when I hear a lonely train whistle, it reminds me of the war brides' train.

My first real glimpse of Canada was the next morning, very early, from behind the shades of our sleeping berth. We were passing through a village looking so clean and bright in the early morning sunlight. Throughout that day we were to experience something we had not really thought about before—humidity—and we really weren't dressed for the Canadian summer.

At stops along the way we would watch as the girls were met by husbands and families, thinking of our turn to come. We arrived in Montreal in the early hours. Most of us were asleep, and we were not told we had reached our destination as it was too early for our husbands to meet us anyway. I'm sure had our husbands known we were on a siding just outside Montreal, there would have been a stampede.

Well, the big moment arrived. For me, the whole journey had been an ordeal, and every once in a while I had had to remind myself why I was going through it all. Nearly a year had gone by. Would we seem like strangers? I was excited, nervous. Then my name was called and my husband was there, looking nervous too.

Jean M. Chartrand had a "hair-raising" experience when her train stopped in Montreal:

It was nighttime and we had been told to go to the dining car for the evening meal. The Red Cross nurse, a red-haired Irish colleen with a tongue to accompany her red hair, would look after our babies while we were gone. That was about the time that the railroad in its infinite wisdom decided to split the train, with one section going to Toronto and the other section to go west to Winnipeg. We finished dining and were surprised to find that the dining car was about a mile away from the rest of the train on a side track. The dining-car staff had quite a time with a bunch of "kidless" mothers. After about an hour, the train was connected together for the trip westward. When we got back to our car, there was one very frustrated nurse and one very large group of squalling babies!

As we travelled through Ontario, some of us had a longing for some fresh fruit. Two of the girls sitting across from me decided they would go to the little store across from the station when we stopped. They asked another war bride to babysit their two little ones. The crowning touch was that they arrived back at the station just as the train was pulling away. Later on it was discovered that they were not on board. As a result, we had to go back fifty miles to pick up the girls; their babies needed their mothers.

At one point I had to take money out of my bra and, not having the time to put it back, I put it under the dirty diapers in the suitcase under the seat and went for lunch. Imagine my shock when I returned to my seat and found that all my money was missing! I arrived in Winnipeg with only a nickel in my pocket. The girl who was babysitting across from me went to wash her hands, took off a diamond ring, and had it stolen as she turned her back. The railroad police came aboard at North Bay, but they did nothing as they said it was too late at night, 10:30 PM, and they could not disturb sleeping people. Being ignorant of Canadian laws, we did not know what to do, so we let it ride. Then it was on to Winnipeg.

What a dreary looking station! Only a few of us were getting off the train, most were going further west. I looked around but could not see Wilf. Then a blue parka-clad figure came to greet us. What a welcome sight! Together at last!

Although the war brides could hardly wait to get ashore in Halifax and begin the last leg of their journey, none were as eager to dis-

embark as those who had suffered from seasickness. Doreen Joyce Heminger had travelled on the Queen Mary, *but even that luxury liner had not been stable enough to prevent her from getting seasick. She thought her problems were over when she and her five-month-old son at last boarded the train in Canada:*

I was coming to Keewatin, Ontario, after we left Halifax. I was so ill I didn't know what was wrong with me. I vomited all night and couldn't get up the next morning. I tried to go to the washroom to get my little boy washed up, as he had diarrhoea so bad. I just got to the door when one of the other girls called out, "Catch her!" The next thing I knew was that I was back in my bed and a doctor was with me. He said he thought I had appendicitis. When we came to a stop, the doctor made a call and after a while a big army ambulance arrived and they rushed me sixty miles to Montreal. They wanted my son to go on to Ontario, but I wouldn't let them.

After we arrived in the hospital, they took my son and got me into bed. I wondered where I was, as they all spoke French. I thought I was coming to Canada, and here they all spoke differently. I had an English-speaking doctor come to examine me, and he told me I had to be operated on right away. He wanted to know where my husband was and how they could get in touch with him. All I knew was his address and that he was going to meet the train. They eventually had to operate without my husband's consent, as my appendix had ruptured.

It was three days before I came to. Sitting next to the bed was my husband. I did not recognize him, as he was not in his uniform and he had put on a lot of weight. He asked me where our son was, but I couldn't remember that we had a son or where I was. All I did was cry and wish I had never left home.

We found out that our son was in a Red Cross hostel. My husband went to visit him, as he had never seen him. He came back to see me and said he was all right and that he was really proud of his son. After twelve days in the hospital, I was able to get our son and travel on to Ontario.

It was a trip I will never forget. They told me I would never have made the Ontario border had I not had the operation.

Once in Canada, the war brides felt a step closer to the men they loved. Pat Janzen had watched as officials hurried up and down the gangway. She was packed and ready to face immigration:

We were placed on trains according to our destination. I was going to Winnipeg. It was now 27 June and the weather was extremely hot. It took four days and three nights to reach Winnipeg, with the stops along the way to let passengers off. We watched girls being met by civilian husbands and wondered how ours would look out of uniform.

As usual, the food was lovely on the journey, but it was a hot, tiring trip with no hot water. We could only have quick washes with no privacy, as there were always people lined up. I remember the time I most looked forward to was when the porter made up the bunks in the early evening and I was finally able to get some space to myself, with a curtain for privacy.

When the train pulled into the Winnipeg station, my husband and his parents were waiting for me. It was true. I hardly recognized him in civilian clothes, but their smiles and flowers made me feel very welcome. It was 1 July, Canada Day, which has always since then had a double significance for me.

When Kay Garside's ship finally pulled into Halifax harbour, what struck her most were the curious duck-bill caps that the men on the dock were wearing—and the fact that although the war brides were anxious to disembark, this time it was women and children last:

Troops disembarked first, then we were each assisted by a soldier to the huge baggage area at Pier 21 to claim our suitcases. Then on to the odd-looking trains waiting to carry us to our destinations.

My tummy settled down and I was ravenous. My first taste of turkey was in Moncton — scrumptious — and the snowy white tablecloths were impressive. The food was marvellous, and I ate steadily to Regina. The lakes and forests of Ontario stretched interminably on and on. Much of the country was just a blur, a tired blur. On arrival in Winnipeg, we detrained and spent the day as guests of a women's group. They kindly took us shopping and to see the sights. I recall one Scottish girl who spent the entire day getting her hair dyed a vivid red. She barely made the train when we left. I wondered if her husband would know her!

Regina was getting near and I tried to make myself presentable to meet my husband's family. Not easy after travelling for twelve days. A huge crowd was at the station. Fred's parents recognized me from my picture and made me welcome, as well as his aunt and a neighbour who presented me with a bouquet of gladiolas. They asked if I would like something to eat. I decided to have bananas and cream. Hadn't seen a banana for years. What a disappointment! — it wasn't the thick, clotted cream I thought it would be.

Doris M. Richards, a widowed war bride, had to be even more courageous than most, for she did not have a happy reunion with her husband to look forward to:

As the train from Halifax conveyed us to different villages and towns across Canada, we were witness to numerous joyful scenes as men and women were reunited and children acquainted with their daddies. Viewing this increased my personal sorrow and secret dread of meeting strangers in a strange land, speaking a strange language. When the time came at the station in Trois-Rivières, Quebec, it was necessary for Red Cross officials to introduce us to our newly acquired family of in-laws. Emotion was high on both sides and tears flowed freely. But to this day I have never forgotten the incredible loving feeling that immediately surrounded us.

Despite the differences in background, culture, and tongue, I felt I had arrived "home." Cousins, aunts, uncles, brothers, and sisters, of all ages, welcomed us wholeheartedly and took us home to meet my ailing mother-in-law. It had been her wish to see and hold her English baby granddaughter, the legacy of her son who was destined never to return.

Ida Moreau had not fully realized the implications of leaving Britain until her ship pulled away from the dock and her daughter began to cry for her grandmother. Now that she was on a train in Canada, England seemed very far away, yet she was no longer miserable:

It was a never-ending train journey across Canada to Saskatchewan to my husband's auntie. As we arrived at railway stations along the way, girls got off the train to be met by loving husbands and their families. It was fun to watch the girls get ready, dressed in their best utility wartime outfits.

There was a sad/funny happening when 'we were about to pull out of Winnipeg. One lovely young girl had started her toilet — hair in iron curlers, face covered in cream — and just as we were about to leave the station, a most handsome Canadian officer came dashing in. Her husband had come to Winnipeg to surprise her, along with all his family, who were waiting for her on the train platform. The poor girl departed the train looking like a blob of grease in curlers! The train compartment was in hilarity.

Daphne Arnott had made friends with the rest of the women in her compartment and, like all brides at each stop, looked out of the window to see what the in-laws of her new friends looked like:

One "girl" had married an Indian. Not knowing much about tribal life, she was horrified to see real-life Indians, complete with native costumes, at the train to greet her. She was scared to get off! They were honouring her, but to her it was terrifying.

The Canadian countryside was very different from the rolling hills and green fields of Britain and continental Europe. Ann Gurdon's train raced through the countryside at such a speed that she began to wonder who was at the wheel:

The train driver must have had a heavy date in Toronto, or he hated women. Our train rocked sideways so much that we had to hold onto our food, etc., and our stomachs. Boy, was I glad when that ride was over! When my name was called and I saw my husband come to "claim" me, well, all the bad things were forgotten. It was all worth it, to know we could now be a family.

What of the volunteers who gave their time to welcome the war brides? There were thousands of them, and to this day the war brides remember them with deep affection. Helen McGrath was

one, a Red Cross transport worker who drove wives without trans-
portation to their new homes in the Toronto area:

About 90 percent of the couples clicked fairly well, but there were
those where you just couldn't help but wonder. Some little girl
would come and the family really didn't match. He was probably
a real hunk in uniform over there, but when you saw his family
and who was meeting whom, there were times when we kind of
shook our heads. It kind of hit me how some of these would
work out.

Margaret Yorgan Mace was one of the greatly appreciated Red
Cross nurses who met the war brides' trains and was on call no
matter what the hour. She was assigned to greet the weary travellers
when they arrived at Bonaventure Station in Montreal:

Each Red Cross VAD was assigned a batman, who was usually a
very young private or corporal who had been confined to barracks
for some very minor misdemeanour. Those lads thought it was
great fun, and we Red Cross girls were saluted and warmly greeted.
Their duty was to help carry any luggage the brides had from the
train into the station. We stayed in a little group — war bride,
children, if any, VAD, and batman — while the family name was
called over the loudspeaker. Then the great reunion and introduc-
tions would start. Our duty ended when the husband and the
relatives took over.

   Needless to say, we Canadian girls were looking over the many
girls from overseas who had married so many of our Canadian
boys! We all agreed that our armed forces had shown very good
taste in choosing wives over there. With very few exceptions, the
girls and the children were lovely in every way.

To arrive anywhere in the sunshine helps one take a positive view
of a place. The weather that greeted Sarah Smith in Halifax was
not so obliging:

I don't think I will ever forget the journey from Halifax to Montreal. It was one of their many big snowfalls which made our

journey so hectic. The train ran out of food and water. We washed our faces with snow and had to run to a store wherever we found one to pick up something to eat.

Ronnie Fleming had suffered from seasickness during the Atlantic crossing, but it was all worthwhile when she arrived in Toronto:

On the train from Halifax to Toronto the bunch of us shared our hopes and fears and spoke so openly of how we loved our men. On arrival at Union Station, I know there was music and flags and lots of people, but I was just looking for those blue eyes. And as if by magic, I was lifted off my feet—Jack was there!

Some of the first Canadians to be in a position to help were the railway porters. Most of them were kind to these young wives and their children. Doreen Derkach remembers one porter well:

We had a French-Canadian porter—Frenchie, we called him—and a couple of other girls and I were bugging him about when we were going to see some cowboys and Indians. Well, the next day he said that if we set our alarm clocks for 3:45 AM, we would be coming into a station where the cowboys herded their cattle into boxcars. Lickety-split we set our clocks, and when they rang we got up, got dressed, and waited for the train to pull into the station. When it stopped we all got out. . . . The engineer came over to us and asked why we were up so early and out of the train. When I enlightened him, he burst out laughing: "Ain't no cowboys or Indians here. This is Montreal station!"

Needless to say, the time came when we arrived at Toronto station, and I nearly died when I saw the big round ring that you met your husband in. Being as I've always been a bit shy, there was no way I wanted to kiss anyone in front of all that group. Just before my name was called, I saw this woman with three kiddies sitting with a Red Cross nurse, crying, and I asked if there was anything I could do. Because she had been waiting so long, they checked on her husband and found out that the blighter was already married, and they probably would have to send her and her children back to England. I can't tell you how I felt for this lady.

Grace Chollet was another who had a difficult arrival. She was the only war bride to get off the train at Quebec City:

There was no one at the station to meet me. I felt so lost and people all seemed to stare at me. I felt really terrible and felt like getting back on the train and going home. A Red Cross nurse came up to me and said not to worry, that she would find out what went wrong. Apparently, the telegram had said I would be arriving the next day. The nurse couldn't find my husband's relatives, but said she had an army captain who would drive us to my sister-in-law's address.

By this time, it was getting quite late and I was wondering what would happen to me in this strange country. At last the captain found the house, and I waited in the car with the nurse until we were sure it was the right place. Yes, this was it, and my sister-in-law came hurrying out to greet me, but in the dark she mistook the nurse for me. Well, that did it and I really felt like crying. I said in a very small voice, "I'm Grace," and then she took me in her arms and brought me in the house. From then on I was made very welcome.

Isabella Low enjoyed the good food and the kind porters as her train made its way right across Canada to Coquitlam, British Columbia:

On the fifth day of our journey, after being thrilled with the great distances of the prairies and the beauty of the Canadian Rockies, my confidence grew as the train pulled into the Coquitlam railway station on a beautiful, sunny, warm day. My heart was beating very fast while I waited for the train to come to a stop and get my first glimpse of my husband, Scott, whom I hadn't seen for seven months.

Yes, there he was, waving. We spotted each other about the same time. I could hardly contain myself, and finally we were in each other's arms — together again! He had looked handsome in his uniform, but it was good to see him now in civilian clothes and to know that we could look forward to a peaceful life and put the uniform in the closet.

Audrey Roberts had been so happy to sail into Halifax harbour with a band playing "Roll Out the Barrel" and to put all her sea-sickness behind her. She believes that none of the war brides really understood the vast distances they would have to travel on the train. But finally, on 5 March 1946, her long trip was over:

Our train pulled into Union Station, Toronto, and a check was made to ensure that someone was there to meet us. Our names were called alphabetically and, as my surname was Roberts then, I was way down the list. I was totally unprepared for the next phase. As our names were called, we walked out to a large roped-off area in the station to be claimed (rather like a cattle auction). The crowd roared and cheered, and all 5 ft. 107 lb. of me felt and wished that I could disappear!

There was my husband, dressed in civvies, wearing a large-brimmed fedora and looking like someone I had never met! We hugged (or *he* hugged, being 180 lb.) and kissed, and were urged on to more and longer by the onlookers. I was mortified!

Completely overawed by this most public welcome, I was relieved to learn that we were going to stay overnight at the Royal York Hotel before going on to meet the rest of the family. However, on reaching our room and praying for a little privacy, I discovered relatives and friends, who made it their business to stay as long as possible and toast my safe arrival!

Like many others, Cecilia Knight had been heartsick at leaving her loved ones in England, but she was excited about meeting her husband again and starting her new life:

You always had high hopes that everything was going to be all right. We all had a great determination to make a go of it because everyone in England would say everything was stacked against us, that we'd never succeed. So we all came over with this great desire to make it work, and most of us did.

5

First Impressions

NEIL ARMSTRONG'S *first step on the moon was an historic moment that the world will never forget. And war brides will never forget the day they first set foot on the railway platform of their new home town. But there were no gallant speeches for them—just a nervous glance as they searched for those who had promised to meet them. And there he was! Their man, the one they loved so much that they had left family and friends to start a new life in Canada.*

Evelyn Buzzell's husband was there to take her in his arms and whisk her to his mother's apartment:

She was the best thing that ever happened to me — a lovely lady. However, she insisted that her son carry me over the threshold! Poor Ross. Let's say he staggered over!

Leaving her parents had been such a traumatic experience for "Lady" Solomon that most of her trip to Canada had been a blur, and her newfound friends on the train were no great help. As the train pulled into Winnipeg, they made a rope noose and hung it out of the window. Then they pulled away, leaving her alone on the platform as they leaned from the windows:

Soon the train moved off and my companions called out all kinds of things like "Maybe his wife won't let him out!" "They have him in the lockup!"

So, there I was, no Tony in sight. Just imagine what was going through my mind! After an hour or so waiting in that now-deserted

CPR station, the bold boy races into the waiting room and, between hugs and kisses, etc., tells me the Mounties had stopped him for disturbing the peace. The muffler on his old Chev had fallen off during the 400-mile washboard-road trip from Red Lake to Winnipeg.

"Will his family like me?" was the question most war brides asked themselves as they stepped from the train. On arriving in Regina, Margaret Lindsay was all prepared, despite her nervousness:

Even the birth of my son in an air raid did not scare me half as much as meeting all my husband's family, who were all there at the train station to meet me when I arrived. Coming over on the *Mauretania*, I had a chance to buy a suitcase full of chocolate bars, and, believe me, I was most welcome.

After meeting her future husband in Nottingham, Betty Hleucka had been married in July 1944, and she moved to Alberta in December of that year. Like many other war brides, she was naive about life in Canada:

I arrived at my husband's folks' farm in southern Alberta at 11 o'clock Christmas Eve. It was quite traumatic to come from a Welsh mining town to a farm in Alberta. My in-laws spoke Ukrainian and ate so differently. On the way to the farm I noticed these large odd-shaped buildings, and when I asked my husband what they were he said, with quite a straight face, "Oh, they are houses for large families." Of course, it was dark and I believed him until I saw them in daylight and was told otherwise—that they were grain elevators!

All war brides had a testing period of jokes played on them in fun, but which we took seriously. I was so dumb that my brother-in-law told me that gophers stood on their hind legs by the roadside to thumb rides into town, and I believed him!

One of the biggest shocks awaiting the brides was their husbands' clothes. These men had swept the young women off their feet not only with their charm but, let's be honest, with that dashing uni-

form. Many had never seen their husbands dressed in anything else. Now that their men were on Civvie Street, would they look as handsome?

Renee Murray, a native of Edinburgh who was completely unfamiliar with life on a farm, felt very fortunate that she had such a loving family of in-laws to welcome her to Manitoba. But it was still a shock to see her husband without his uniform and in these different surroundings:

My husband during the war had been Flt. Lt. Donald L. Murray, DFC, so it was all rather strange to see "my hero" out slopping the pigs, milking the cows, or riding the tractor with such gusto.

On arriving in Halifax aboard the Mauretania, *Ivy E. Clark was greeted by a husband who had travelled back to Canada six months ahead of her:*

He seemed like a stranger in his trilby hat and long topcoat. I'd only seen him in uniform. Nighttime cured me of that shock.

I had quite a laugh, seeing the men in big red-and-black plaid jackets, heavy boots with their pants tucked in them, and fur hats. It reminded me of a movie I'd seen with Robert Preston in it. I nearly froze on my first sleigh ride.

I soon lost my liking for sugar in my tea. There was no sugar on the table, and my new mother-in-law was a very tall, straight woman and I was 5 feet, 2 inches. I didn't like to ask for sugar, so that's how I acquired a taste for tea without it.

When I first arrived, we stayed at my mother-in-law's for a couple of days before having a honeymoon. She made me use a covered bucket in the shed, as the outhouse was across the field. The first time I attempted it, his two small sisters assisted me, one on each side. I let go of them, thinking this was a piece of cake. The next thing I knew I was flat on my back on the ice. It sure was hard.

Every time I went to the supermarket I'd get a headache. There was so much food to look at, I didn't know where to start. The rows of fruit and vegetables were unbelievable. I had so many banana splits I got sick of them.

Although Audrey Margaret Hetherington had waited five years before marrying Joe, she began to question her judgement when she first saw him at the station in Moose Jaw:

He was a nice-looking young man in a uniform when he left England. When I got over here, I met this guy in a pinstripe suit and spats — he looked like a gangster! I thought, What have I done?

Janet Paton had crossed the Atlantic on the Swedish liner Drottningholm. *She was fortunate that her husband Jim had arrived in Glen Ewen, Saskatchewan, two days before, so he was there to meet her. He had promised to wear his uniform so that she would not have the shock of seeing him in civilian clothes:*

How he must have suffered, as it was a very hot day in August 1945 and those outfits were not made for Canadian heat.

The crops hadn't been cut when I arrived, and I can remember how golden and tall the grain was. Jim's parents' stone cottage had a beautiful view of the river valley that helped eliminate some of the culture shock. No more going for walks in well-groomed parks or a pleasant stroll in a leafy country lane. The mosquitoes nearly chewed me up! I had bites resembling hives those first few months.

The deep blue sky, the expanse of the horizon, and intense heat of the sun took some time to get used to. The beautiful sunsets made up for any discomforts the strange climate caused me during the day. The wonder of the size of this new land and different lifestyle left no time for pangs of homesickness — I was where I wanted to be.

After enduring a rough crossing on the Empire Brent *in December 1946, Joan Schnare was excited yet apprehensive when her name was called over the intercom and she was told to go to a cabin to meet her husband's family. They gave her a wonderful welcome. As they came off the ship at Pier 21, she was surprised to see a familiar face on the dock. It was a war bride who had worked in the same government building where she had worked in Westminster, London. When Joan and her new family arrived in Chester, Nova Scotia, she asked the obvious question:*

I asked where the city was. The reply, said with great astonishment, was "You are in it." It didn't look a bit like London. I'll never forget the first thing my eyes alighted on back at my new home — a great big black stove, fancy as all get out, with little shelves here and there and a few chrome fenderlike pieces, well polished. I came to hate that monster! It was fueled with wood, and if it didn't go out when I was attending it, the blasted thing burnt everything up. My mother-in-law ruled it, and it behaved like a good child for her.

My husband had never hidden anything from me, but then he hadn't told me too much either. When I had dispensed with my bags, coat, etc., had a small meal and chatted a bit, I was asked if I wanted to use the bathroom. The thoughts of a nice warm bath and then to bed cheered me. Boy, was I shocked when I was handed my coat and given a flashlight and shown to the outhouse! Talk about freeze your assets! I'm sure I ran the four-minute mile in one. I had visions of bears hot on my trail. The next day we had a steady stream of visitors. Talk about the Olde Curiosity Shop! I felt I was the curio; the English bride had arrived. They were intrigued to hear me say the word "pork," and if I said pork chop once, I said it a dozen times.

After moving to Halifax, things brightened up for me. We had a family, and life was taken up with raising them. My homesickness tamed down, much to my husband's relief. I think he was getting fed up with coming home to a snivelling wife. When I look back on those first months, I must admit I wanted to go back to "jolly olde," but I had married a good man and he was an excellent father. We weren't prosperous, but we managed and were happy, so I have no regrets and I love Nova Scotia.

Since most of these women had lived in large towns, it is easy to understand the shock they must have felt when they arrived in rural areas of Canada. "Tiny Red Head" Campbell describes what greeted her at her new home in Arthurette, New Brunswick:

No inside plumbing, no electricity, no gas, no facilities of any kind, and a little hand pump outside the house. The outhouse was by the barn, 300 feet away. My sister-in-law had an ugly rooster, Jimmy Duke. I guess he didn't like or trust an English accent, as every time I went out the door he came trotting. Therefore, I had to have someone escort me to the toilet and wait for me. It just stayed around and waited for me.

Jessie Still had brought her small daughter Rosalie with her from London to live in a village in northern Ontario, Hilton Beach:

Even though I had been warned, it was with shock and dismay that I arrived at our log house, isolated and off the beaten track. Upon entering, two oil lamps were lit. It was late, we were tired, so up to bed. I walked up a narrow, creaky flight of stairs and into an attic room. The bed looked comfortable covered with a patch-work quilt. I had never seen one before; it had thousands of tiny stitches all over it in a symmetrical pattern. It must have taken hours to complete.

Rosalie fell asleep immediately in a crib that was much too small for her. I thought about her crib in England; it was larger and comfortable. I thought about my bedroom back home, with big bay windows and bathroom close by. I lay wide awake long after my husband Mark slept. I looked at the tiny window near my bed. Flies were buzzing on the window shelf—hundreds of them, ugly black things.

My thoughts turned to all the hardships during the war — the lack of food and clothes, the bombing — and I thought, I have tolerated all that and I must be brave enough to accept this new life . . . and finally I fell asleep.

Daye Plowman came to Douglas, Manitoba, in 1946, and on seeing her new home, her first thought was "Oh, my God, what have I come to?" It was certainly a change:

From a large city to a little village of ninety-eight people. But what it lacked in size, the people made up for—they were the friendliest people I had ever met and they helped me in every way they could, like canning and baking, which I couldn't do.

My funniest moments included trying to take a bath in the little round tub in the middle of the kitchen floor (I never did find out how to bath right in that thing). No bathroom or running water. I tried to milk cows when all they wanted to do was put their foot in the pail or hit me in the face with their dirty old tail. Plucking chickens — now that is another story. These are just a few of the things I had to learn, but I loved it all and have a lot of happy memories which I wouldn't trade for the world.

Pat Miller had moved from London to the small town of Bear River, Nova Scotia; but with her husband Reg beside her, life was what she had hoped for:

Wooden homes impressed me vividly, though I still long for a home built of durable solid brick, as I have always feared fire. Incendiary bombs had such a hard task penetrating and burning brick homes during the war, so perhaps that's the reason. Oh, such large homes here, so clean, and such wonderful cooks lived in them. But how odd to see a wood stove or cooking range sitting out on the floor! Stovepipes were another oddity. It didn't seem safe to have a hot wood fire in the middle of the floor.

And why didn't these Canadians have tea every two or three hours? I was going to have to change this right early. And why did I shock my mother-in-law by saying that I thought she had a very homely kitchen when I was complimenting her on its cosiness? What was a "mess of greens" for supper? A mess — my gracious! A mess back home was definitely a mess. Supper was a light snack we partook of around bedtime back home, so who wanted a mess of anything then?

One evening, upon answering a knock at the door, I was confronted by a tall, uniformed man; his suit was brown and he wore a peaked hat. He reminded me of the dry cleaner's delivery man back home. He inquired of the address of a near neighbour and drove off. I thought, how grand that Bear River has the same service here. When Reg arrived home that evening, he said that the Mounties had been around Bear River checking up on radio licences, and wondered if by chance I had seen them. I blushingly confessed that one had called and I had almost handed him my two-piece suit to clean and press!

What did I miss the most? No cinemas — dear old Catford had two big cinemas and a variety house, stores of every kind and, believe it or not, a public house every hundred yards, where people spent a very friendly evening over a piano or a game of darts.

Just a few more differences offhand: Why the meat market and not the butcher's shop? Drugstore and not chemist? Sidewalk instead of pavement? And trucks where lorries always sufficed?

Katherine Biggs had every confidence that she knew what she was getting into when she came to New Brunswick. After all, she had worked in New York before the war, and her Canadian friends had said that where she was going was quite a city:

We got to Moncton at one o'clock in the morning and there wasn't a car on the street and the station was just like a little whistlestop and I thought, Where have I got to?

Her first medical experience in New Brunswick was also rather disconcerting:

I had a pain in my shoulder and, at the village store, was looking for liniment for the complaint. The storekeeper handed a bottle to me and on it was printed "Good for man and beast." I was shocked and remarked that in Scotland we were not so tight fisted that we had to share the cure with the horses!

Having come from Glasgow to Seaforth, Ontario (population 2200), Margaret Bannon could not wait for her husband to give her a tour of the town:

He took me "up town," as they called it, to show me around. I couldn't believe it, as it was so small compared to the big city of Glasgow, with so many theatres, dance halls, and picture halls and so much transportation. The dance hall in Seaforth was above a jeweller's store and there was one picture hall. I told my husband that I could never stay there, but here I still am today!

I remember meeting some ladies in the community who asked if I could speak English! I was mortified to think that person didn't even know what language we spoke in Britain.

Eunice Partington had met her Reg in the village of East Horseley. They had married in 1945, and the following year she set out for her new home on a farm in Evesham, Saskatchewan. During the train journey, she heard stories of husbands who had deserted their new wives, and these were little comfort to her when she stepped down onto the platform at Saskatoon:

To my utter dismay, there was no husband to greet me. Five, ten, fifteen minutes passed and my heart was in my mouth. Surely this can't be! My mind sped back to those stories we had heard on the train. I cannot describe my feelings, just utter despair. I wondered how I could get back to England; I had no money for a return trip. I was just about to reboard the train bound for Edmonton, where I was told I would be housed until contact could be made with relatives, when my husband Reg appeared. Oh, what relief I felt! And, needless to say, I was overjoyed. An incorrect time had been given to him for the arrival of the train.

Two days were spent in the city getting to know one another again, purchasing a few pieces of furniture for a home, sightseeing, and marvelling at all the unrationed foods and clothing. Then it was back on the train again, bound for the final destination of Evesham, a small farming community west of Saskatoon. All the family was there to greet us. We travelled to my husband's home and there were served a lovely "lunch." It took quite some time to get used to the term "lunch," which seemed to imply a snack at any time of the day. A cake with sumptuous icing had "Welcome to our family and to Canada" written on it, and welcome they all made me feel. The family was of English origin, and I am sure this made my culture adjustment easier.

Of course, there was no electricity or running water, and outdoor toilets were commonplace, but these inconveniences didn't seem to matter to me at all. Now the coal and wood stove was a different matter, and it took quite some time to be able to cook something in the oven that wasn't either half cooked or else burned to death!

Soon after my arrival the village put on a shower for my sister-in-law, also a war bride, and me. What a lovely gesture! So many useful gifts and a good introduction to many new friends. Everyone was so friendly, but how nervous I was!

Lilian F. Noble arrived at a log house in Lloydminster, Saskatchewan, the first she had ever seen:

My first question was, "Where is the tap?" to which my husband's young brothers took me outside and I discovered the tap was a tripod plus a pulley, with almost 200 feet of rope and a bucket. You removed the heavy wooden lid, lowered the pail down to touch water, and then the long haul up. When I lost the pail and rope, I wasn't very popular.

Molly (Malinowski) Rollins had travelled to Canada on the Aquitania and had arrived at the Ukrainian-Polish settlement of Wishart, Saskatchewan:

It was so far removed from my British upbringing. According to Polish custom, I was met by the family bearing a bottle of wine. It was a very warm and happy welcome. Two weeks after I landed, threshing time came on the farm and I went to the homestead to cook for the threshing gang. I had never used a wood stove before and had a really bad time remembering to put wood in it to keep the oven hot.

Betty Vine's first impressions were not so positive. She was from Coventry and found herself in a small Nova Scotia town living with a strait-laced Baptist family:

My family was fairly easygoing so it was quite a shock when my mother-in-law greeted me with, "I suppose you smoke." Luckily I didn't. Then, on my first Sunday, I turned on the radio and she charged into the room and switched it off, saying, "The radio is never to be played in this house on a Sunday." I wondered what I'd got myself into.

I'd been in Canada about a month when I went to visit a friend, also from Coventry, whose husband was working on a farm in Kentville. She was living in a house with a pump for water and a wood cookstove, no bathroom, and the toilet at the end of the garden. She wasn't enjoying farm life at all. We were standing by the window when her husband went by, driving a horse and cart, dressed in his work clothes. The tears poured down her face and she said, "Oh, my God, and he looked so handsome in his uniform!" She wound up back in England.

Audrey Pratt faced some tense moments when her husband was an hour late meeting her ship at Halifax, but there was more in store for her in the Nova Scotia village of Belmont, her new home:

Never before had I seen so many Christmas trees! Of course, I wondered what I had gotten myself into just to be with my handsome Canadian soldier. Our home was very rough, with no electricity and a hand pump for water. I can remember many a night in the winter when the frost would stand out on the walls and we would huddle around the wood stove. Of course, the biggest shock of all was the outhouse, which, after I had become accustomed to it, I decorated as prettily as possible.

My second meal in Canada consisted of salt codfish in sauce and potatoes boiled with the skin on! It certainly did not appeal to me at the time. However, I have since discovered that it is quite good. Many other Canadian foods have come my way over the years, but I have not mastered a taste for molasses or cranberries.

Coming from a suburb of London, Kay Garside found the immensity of the Saskatchewan countryside breathtaking, though she longed for some gently rolling hills to break the monotony. Back home, so much had been taken for granted—like electricity, inside toilets, and running water:

What a shock! My parents' flat wasn't large, but right then I would have given the world to be in it. My husband Fred arrived four days later and we drove into Regina to meet him. His parents hardly knew him. He had been gone for five and a half years, had a moustache, and had become a man. His mother fainted with all the excitement. It took Fred a long time to settle down, and I couldn't understand why at the time. I was so busy getting everything sorted out in my own mind, I didn't realize how hard it must have been for him. For five and a half years he had been told what to do and how to do it, and now suddenly he had many decisions to make and responsibilities to handle. It was a hard time for all of us.

My mother told me she couldn't believe someone like me who loved to go dancing, to shows, and walking could ever settle down to life on a farm. She knew that I couldn't knit, but I tried. I sewed three dozen diapers by hand—a labour of love.

Grasshoppers were bad that year. I had never seen one in my life. They were huge ugly things, flying in the open windows of the car when we went anywhere. My father-in-law thought it was funny that I should be scared of them. I sat with my coat over my head to keep them from landing on me.

My first experience of that highlight of summer on the prairies —the sports day—was a revelation. Sitting out on the bare prairie with no shade anywhere, watching people play what looked like cricket but wasn't. Eating a picnic lunch, sitting on the ground in the shade of the car didn't turn me on either. During the hottest part of the afternoon, all the men adjourned to the beer parlour— no women allowed in that hallowed place. The women sat in the car and ate very inferior ice cream. I was disgusted.

Myra Mirka from Glasgow took an immediate liking to the prairies:

Being the month of August, the vegetable gardens were at their peak and the chickens ready to be plucked. It seemed like we ate chicken everywhere we went. I tasted corn on the cob for the first time, homemade pickles, fresh baked bread, canned fruit, and pies with fruit filling. Then there was the thick fresh cream, which was poured on just about everything or else whipped into potatoes. I weighed 102 lb. when I left Glasgow, but I must have gained 10 lb. in the first couple of weeks in Canada.

In 1946 most of the farm homes were quite small and had no modern conveniences, so the loo was the wee house out at the back. Some people drove old cars or tractors, but many still used horses. I really enjoyed going to town with my sister-in-law with a couple of horses pulling the wagon box and the dog running behind.

Everything was so different from Scotland. The scenery, the wide-open spaces, the vast ever-changing sky. I was amazed at the distance between small towns and asked my husband why they didn't build more houses in between. The roads were rough and very muddy when it rained. I must say that most of the people I met were very kind and friendly. Sometimes they'd have trouble understanding what I was saying. One fellow finally would pull a pencil and notebook from his shirt pocket and say, "Here, write it down."

It was a really exciting time for me, but I have to admit I had moments when my thoughts would be back home and I would wonder what my mother and sister were doing and I'd long to hear their voices. We wrote back and forth faithfully and, as their food was still rationed, my husband and I would send food parcels to Scotland quite often.

Being in a new country, it was easy to make mistakes. Customs were strange, and even expressions were different. Pauline Elizabeth Ament was met by her husband Lloyd at the train station in Saskatoon, and she soon made several bloopers that must have had her husband wondering:

Well, my first mistake — ladies do not smoke on the street, which was fine. Then we drove to Kindersley. It was sunny, warm, everything was green and I made my next mistake. I said, "Lloyd, why don't people in this country cut their grass?" It was wheat! He must have felt like sending me back! Well, we arrived at a town. The wind was blowing and there was so much dust. I said, "Where are we, Lloyd?" He answered, "Home." I remember thinking, my God, what have I done?

Anyway, we arrived at my in-laws, who seemed very happy to see me. There was one twin sister in the kitchen, and after a few minutes another one appeared from a hole in the floor, which of course was the trapdoor to the basement. We had a beautiful dinner and I was passed a jellied fruit salad, which I politely refused and said, "I'll have it for my afters, thank you." They all ate it with their chicken, which I thought was horrible and so strange. Then I had to go to the bathroom to "spend a penny" — down the hole in the floor. My mom would have a fit. I had my first bridal shower and I remember thinking that someone had ruined the cucumbers. We were eating dills!

Well, I had one friend here. Lil Acker was from Sydenham, London, so I was lucky. We had lots of fun shopping. I asked for a reel of white cotton. The lady got a huge bolt down. I said no, I wanted to sew with it and she replied, "Oh, a spool of thread." I said, "Oh, no thank you. That's what tailors sew buttons on with." But we sorted that one out, and then we asked for a joint of beef and not a roast, mince instead of ground beef, and tins instead of cans. Oh dear.

I might add I had never cooked because of rationing. I could make a great pot of tea but, oh, the cooking — how I hated the wood and coal stove! I actually treated Lloyd like a god. I gave him burnt offerings nearly every day! No wonder he loved to get to his mum's on Sundays (me too)!

Well, I think I cried every day for the first three months. I was so homesick. The people here were good to us. We had teas and showers. We were always very welcome in their homes. Then the rains came. Oh, my goodness, no sidewalks except wooden ones and no paved roads. Lil and I were out one day, both under her lovely British umbrella, and our little puddle boots full of mud. I had never seen mud like it. But Mom used to say to me, "Life is what you make it, wherever you are." How true.

When Margaret Lancaster arrived at "a wide spot in the road," she discovered that it was her new home, Rathburn, Ontario. Like so many other war brides, she made an embarrassing mistake by using British jargon:

Shortly after my arrival, my husband Joe and myself had to make an early departure somewhere. As I wished to be wakened, I said to my mother-in-law, "Please knock me up in the morning."

Horrified, she replied, "I don't think I can do that. That's Joe's department!"

*Nancy Wolliston also made quite an impression. She and her hus-
band felt very lucky to get an apartment three days after she arrived
in Halifax, but right off the bat, Nancy made her mark:*

I put a note in the milk bottle and wrote a note to the milkman
saying, "Knock me up in the morning and I will pay you." That
note went all round the milk depot!

*Magazines and newspapers prepared their readers for the arrival
of the war brides and did their best to offset any criticism: "They
will be wearing shabby, dowdy clothes, no doubt the same ones
that had been sent in the form of* CARE *packages during the blitz."
One article suggested they be treated kindly, "since they will feel
uncomfortable and embarrassed when they first arrive. Remember,
just because they aren't used to washing machines and the like
doesn't mean they are dirty people. Also the effects of the war may
make them irritable, weepy, and unreasonable but as Canadians,
we should all try and understand."*
　　*True, many of the war brides did feel emotional and insecure.
The first few months were not easy. Sybil J. Parkinson remembers
the time her husband Tom took her shopping in Saskatoon:*

I went to try on two dresses and when I came out of the change
room I couldn't see him anywhere. I thought, oh, my goodness,
he's left me and taken our son Terry!

*Then there was the weather. Wives who had arrived in summer
might have been lulled into believing that winter could not really
be that bad, but Barb Warriner and her two daughters were greeted
by the full brunt of winter in northern Saskatchewan:*

My mother-in-law was at the Big River station to meet us with the
sleigh box and a team of horses. I think all the blankets she pos-
sessed were in that sleigh, for fear we got cold crossing the mile-
wide lake to get to her homestead. It was so cold that night; I'm
sure it was fifty or sixty below zero. What a night to arrive to what
was going to be home for a while! But that good old English blood

stood up for all of us. We weren't allowed to lift our heads from under the blanket in case we froze our noses. I had heard the expression "freeze the you-know-what off a brass monkey" but had never believed it so much as that night.

When Ida Moreau got her first taste of winter in Edmonton, she realized that she was even farther away from London than she thought:

When we came out of the railway station in Edmonton, our daughter and I were wearing our English wartime utility coats, without interlining, and it was twenty degrees below zero! I looked back and forth, then asked my husband where the city was. He said, "This is it." My heart sank to my feet. There were only four multi-story buildings in Edmonton then — even the Hudson's Bay Co. was only one floor. I then discovered that some of the streets had wooden sidewalks.

After Betty Benn arrived in Edmonton, she realized why all the telephone poles were so short:

They were half-buried in snow! During one encounter to catch the bus to go across to the other side of Edmonton, I slipped on the ice and broke my wrist — this was when I was eight months pregnant. What a sight I was: 108 lb., gaining 40 lb. during pregnancy, with a cast right up my arm. Ken took a photo of me sitting on the step with snow piled high and a German shepherd crossing by, to send to my parents to let them know how great it was with the wolves at the door. I also mentioned to my mum the dreadful long walk to the outhouse, thinking to gain some sympathy. But she said the walk would do me the world of good. Wasn't that typical of dear English mums?

After Ivy Winnifred Ogram's fiancé George returned to Canada, they had planned that he would come back to England to marry her. Instead, she found herself on board the Queen Elizabeth *on her way to George's farm near Lloydminster, Saskatchewan. The voyage was so rough that "everything was battened down and ropes were strung everywhere to help the passengers get around." Twelve days after she arrived, on a bitterly cold day in December 1946, they were married. But it was the time after the reception that Ivy remembers best:*

Just as we were ready to turn in, I was alarmed to hear a terrible commotion going on outside, guns being fired, hollering, and trays and saucepans being banged together to make a dreadful racket. I was unsure as to whether or not we were being attacked or just what was going on. Soon the door opened and neighbours and friends all trooped in, rearranging the furniture so that they could serve up a delicious lunch, much to the surprise of the new bride. I later found out that this was a tradition for newlyweds called a charivari. We were the last in the district to have this custom carried out on us, and we look back on it with amusement.

Unlike most war brides, Phyllis Dykes was able to take a plane to Montreal. She then embarked on the long train ride to her husband's home in Red Deer, Alberta, where she was greeted, much to her dismay, by a welcoming committee:

Five half-grown turkeys. They crowded round the car, gobbling, cackling, and stretching their necks. They scared the life out of me and I really clung to my husband. I guess that did it, as those turkeys made life miserable for me whenever I left the safety of the house alone.

Mom and Dad Dykes were having a new house built with running water and indoor plumbing, but in the meantime we lived in a converted garage and used an outside biffy. Well, those turkeys would mill around outside the window, gobbling and stretching their necks up towards me as I watched through the glass. The minute I opened the door they were right there. Once in a while they wandered off to another area, then I would be out the house and down the path to the biffy in a flash. But it seemed they always knew, and by the time I wanted to leave they were cackling at the biffy door, so there I remained waiting for someone (usually my father-in-law) to come and shoo them away. I must say, the old copy of the Eaton's catalogue was well thumbed through those first few months.

I have never enjoyed turkey as much as I did that first Thanksgiving and Christmas here in Canada — when those darn turkeys were cooked and could bother me no more.

On arriving in Brandon, Manitoba, Margaret C. Haggerty found it an impressive sight:

Our driver, Tommy Riach, a true Scotsman, gave me the grand tour of Brandon. After having lived through the blackout for six years, the sight of so many neon signs was a big thrill. I thought how big Brandon was — that is, until we were stopped on Rosser Avenue by a policeman asking Tommy how come we were passing for the third time!

The war brides were strangers to all but their husbands. When Chris Jackson arrived in Canada, she and her husband moved in with his family, who were rather staid. On the second day, Chris tried her best to make conversation:

At one point during a rather lengthy silence, I very innocently said, "What kind of screw does a stenographer get?" (I did not, of course, know the Canadian meaning of this word; at this time it was a common phrase in England referring to salaries.) The silence was intensified and then everyone started to chuckle. It wasn't until much later that my husband explained my gaffe and the reason for the laughter. I was devastated!

When Peggy Chalkin arrived in Toronto, she did not think much of the food the family served:

After all the greetings were over, I was very nervous. We proceeded to have dinner. Corn was being served, but I would not eat mine. I was insulted — they fed that stuff to pigs at home. Well, you can guess my life in Canada was off to a bad start. What with some very cruel remarks, I was all set to go back to England. I made a booking twice, but my husband wanted me to stay and I did.

Eileen Bruguiere-Taylor arrived in Guelph to a house full of people and a wonderful party to welcome her. Her culture shock began with a trip to buy groceries:

On my first visit to a supermarket—Loblaws in downtown Guelph —I stood inside with my mouth open. Never had I seen so much food in one place. There were even items I had never seen before and some I hadn't seen for the six years of war. Honestly, I thought I would go crazy and wanted to buy everything in sight. But my stomach wasn't used to so much, and I had a hard time keeping anything down for quite some time.

One exciting day I went shopping for clothes. The stores were so lovely and the selections so great. Again I went crazy. I had received quite a bit of money when I was demobbed from the ATS and I was determined to splurge.

The thing that bothered me most on my arrival in Canada was the central heating. The train was stifling with the double windows that didn't open and the steam heating, and the private homes also had double windows and coal furnaces. It took me a long time to get used to it. In England everyone is a fresh-air fiend, and windows are open day and night, winter and summer.

Although Dot Ford's arrival in Kuroki, Saskatchewan, was a very quiet affair, things picked up when the neighbours decided to invite her over to help butcher a hog:

When the train stopped I got off onto the railway tracks. The train pulled away and I was left standing, with a nine-month-old baby on my hip and a bag of nappies in my hand. Gazing around I saw a man way down the tracks, wondered if it was someone looking for me, and headed in that direction. Sure enough, it was my husband Larry. What a shock, seeing him for the first time again in over a year! Also, it was the first time I'd seen him in civvies, after remembering him as a young officer in air force blue. We were strangers for a while, but things soon changed.

That day our neighbour Jim asked us if we'd come over and give them a hand butchering their hog. When we got there, the fire was lit and water was heating in a barrel to scald the hog. I was sent in the house to visit with his wife, but first thing you know Jim comes in and says, "Come on out, you women. We need help getting the hog out of the water." Now remember I was a city lass bred and born and had only seen pork as a roast on the table. Well, we four got pulling on the ropes and up came the biggest hog I ever saw. It must have weighed 300 lb. After we got it anchored, I guess you'd say, Jim handed us gals a butcher knife each and said, "You might as well help scrape the hair off," which we did.

One year later, to the very day, we were invited over to butcher again. Quite an anniversary present of my arrival in Canada!

Canada is largely made up of immigrants and the descendants of immigrants. The war brides were merely the latest wave of new-comers, and they were generally welcomed in a warm and friendly manner. When Gloria Brock arrived in Abernethy, Saskatchewan, her husband John was not yet home to meet her, but she found that her in-laws were lovely people who tried to make her feel comfortable:

My father-in-law was a bit brusque, but he was a very kind man. When they showed me my little bedroom, just inside this little cupboard there was a pair of moccasin-type slippers and a pair of nylons tucked inside. I thought, what a lovely thing to do. My father-in-law wasn't the kind who would say, "I've brought you a present." He wasn't like that. He'd set up a gift someplace where you'd find it and then he'd watch your reaction.

Kay Bleakney had to wait quite a while at the Moncton station for her husband Ken, but she did not regret having come:

After driving twenty-five miles to Fawcett Hill, a very large building appeared and I said, "That's a very big house." Ken replied that that was the barn and that the smaller, lamp-lighted building was our homestead. A comfortably plump lady opened the door and a lovely smell of freshly baked bread reached my nostrils. Her arms went around me and she said, "Welcome home!"

The next day I awoke to find soap, powder, and cologne on the dressing table, and Mum with a cup of tea and cookies. She said, "I was told English people enjoy their tea in bed." A most wonderful lady who, unfortunately, I only enjoyed for nine short years.

Elly Cornish had met Les in Holland in June 1945 and found that, with the Canadians as liberators, it was a wild, wonderful summer. Les had tried to describe what Canada was like, but after being away from the country for five years, he had been seeing the prairies through rose-coloured glasses, as Elly recalls:

The glasses got more and more rose coloured! When I got here it was a *little* bit different. Les picked me up in Regina and the next day we were on our way to Girvin, one of those prairie towns you're past if you blink. Now, apparently the country around Regina was, at one time, a lake bottom, and it is as flat as flat can be. At that time, around 30 May, the wheat was just starting up and no green was visible.

And there I was, every mile we travelled sliding farther and farther down in the front seat of our '35 Ford, looking desperately around me and wondering what I would do if I didn't see a tree soon! At last, hurrah, a farmstead with large trees came into view. So I sat up straight again, ready to face whatever the future would bring. And I've never regretted any of it!

Even though Betty Taylor had travelled all the way from Brighton to Newfoundland, she could not easily shake off her wartime experiences. Shortly after arriving, she found that she still had an automatic response to sirens:

I took the streetcar down Water Street in St. John's and all of a sudden I heard this siren, and the next thing I knew I was flat on the floor in the streetcar and everybody's looking at me, grinning like crazy. Here's me about eight months pregnant. It was an automatic reaction to a siren; you just flattened yourself. Of course, when I got home and told the family, they were absolutely in hilarious hysterics because they thought it was funny. And here's me, white as a sheet. They hadn't experienced sirens in England. I didn't know what it was. They had to tell me it was a fire truck.

If the brides from World War II were surprised at what they found when they arrived in Canada, so, even more so, was Daisy Horn, a World War I war bride, when she alighted in Tisdale, Saskatchewan:

When I arrived at the station I said, "Where is your bathroom?" and a man pointed to a little building in the bush. The door was stuck wide open, off its hinges and embedded in the gumbo, which was just like cement. Well, I thought that if this is what people in Tisdale do, they shouldn't mind me. I could see people walking by, but what could I do? I was so sick that I hardly cared. My first impression was that Canadians sure liked fresh air.

Then we drove forty-five miles in an old Ford over ruts and mounds and dead trees, etc., to get to my in-laws, who farmed at Nipawin. There were five buildings there and I thought it was a farm, but no, it was the town itself. While eating lunch there, somebody mentioned the bread was getting low and I asked innocently, "What time does the baker call?" When I was told they baked their own bread I thought I'd die, yet here I am at ninety-one still baking my own bread.

We never left home without an axe or a gun, as we only had trails then and no good roads. Often a tree had fallen over the trail or we'd get a chance to shoot some game, a deer or a partridge. Those were the good old days, but I wouldn't want to go back to them now.

Elizabeth Smythe's husband had rented an $8-a-week Toronto apartment as the first home for themselves and their daughter. When Betty arrived at Union Station in Toronto, she was ushered into a large waiting room, along with the other war brides. But what she most remembers was seeing all the Canadian men waiting to meet their loved ones with bouquets of flowers and big teddy bears:

Then I spotted my husband—empty handed—but I didn't care. In the cab going home I asked him where my flowers were, and he said he was afraid I'd think he was a sissy. There was much more at home than flowers. He had made a real home for us, but I remember that it was very humid and I was dying with the heat. I was lying down on the bed and he was going around mopping up everything, so proud of all the new things and all. He had been saving up red salmon and Snow Flakes soap powder and whatever else had been rationed. There hadn't been much rationed in Canada, but he had saved it all because he had been back for a year. He had them all lined up on shelves in the kitchen.

Pat Heath was met in Ottawa by her mother-in-law. It was a shock just to see the way she was dressed:

She was in striped bobby socks, a feather in her hair, and an old shawl around her shoulders. She thought it was funny, but it scared the heck out of me until I saw my father-in-law, an elderly English gentleman very much like my own dad. He accepted me the first day he saw me, but my mother-in-law took a little longer. I think it was because I was the third daughter-in-law to live with them and they had had problems.

I was the envy of the neighbourhood with my beautiful English carriage I had brought over with me, except for a neighbour's daughter who accused war brides of stealing the Canadian boys. I soon set her straight when I reminded her of the RAF boys who brought Canadian girls to England after their training in Canada.

Eileen M. Barkwell's father had moved his family from Manchester to Jamaica in 1938, and it was there during the war that Eileen met her future husband, an Irish Fusilier from Vancouver. She travelled up from the Caribbean to join the women's division of the RCAF, but her fiancé Jack had to stay behind. A disconcerting coincidence awaited her:

They signed me up in Hamilton, Ontario, put me on a train and said that a girl from Rockcliffe Air Station would meet me and escort me to the barracks. She did, and when I said I was engaged to a Canadian, she wanted to know where he was from. I told her and she said, "Oh, my parents have a cottage on the lake up there and I have a summer boyfriend there by the name of Jack Barkwell." How small can the world get when there were at least a thousand girls on that air station and they had to send one of my fiancé's old girlfriends to meet me? She was as shocked as I was.

Jean McGoey's knuckles were white after suffering through a high-speed ride with her fiancé's sister and her boyfriend from Dorval to Ottawa: "My stomach felt the way you do on a very fast elevator!" Cathie Rosenplot had a calmer arrival. She had first met her Canadian husband-to-be when he jumped off a tramcar before it stopped, and landed at her feet. Her first impression of Canada was one of puzzlement:

Upon arriving in Halifax we knew Canadians did drink, but found it hard to believe the sign in the harbour that said "Drink Canada Dry."

Misconceptions about Canada were abundant, and the naive war brides were frequent targets of friendly teasing. Maureen McDonald was determined to use caution when she first arrived in Ottawa:

I left England at the age of nineteen, and before we left my husband George said, "Did you know that at night the wild cats come down from the hills and perch on lampposts and signs?" My first impression of Ottawa was the lights, after leaving England and its blackouts. I arrived in Ottawa at midnight on 24 May, and as we drove through the main streets, the streets and stores were alive with lights.

Canadians believed they had been deprived during their wartime rationing, but, to most war brides, Canada was a land of plenty compared with the scarcity of goods in Britain and on the Continent. Irene Turner, from Newcastle, found her first Christmas in Milton, Ontario, almost too much to bear:

My sister-in-law Chris took me to Eaton's in December. I couldn't
believe my eyes and felt like Alice in Wonderland. All those dazzling
lights after the blackouts in England seemed like sacrilege to me.
People buying like crazy seemed much too much for me, and I had
a good cry.

Christmas in Milton — the family gathering, the biggest turkey
I had ever seen, and the table groaning with food — was my undoing. I was terribly upset when I thought of my family and friends
in Britain with their meagre rations. It was like another world, and
the heartache of loneliness and homesickness set in. Oh, what an
ache that can be!

*Joan Johnson arrived in St. Catharines, Ontario, on Canada Day
1946, and immediately noted the differences in fashion between
England and Canada:*

My first impression was the extreme heat and also the teenage girls
with their low-necked peasant blouses and the older ladies' bright
cotton dresses. Having been brought up in a very strict Baptist
household where all older ladies wore dark clothing, plus the wartime restrictions on clothing purchases, I found the colours
entrancing.

*Although her French-Canadian husband had been warned by his
family not to marry an English girl, Joan Poirier was thrilled by
the welcome they gave her:*

When I finally arrived in Montreal at Windsor Station, my husband
Gérard was there to meet me with about thirty of his relations,
only one of whom spoke English. Luckily, my high-school French
was good enough to carry me through, and my welcome was overwhelming. At his grandparents' home, a table was piled high with
wedding gifts and toys for the children. Another table was decorated with ribbons reaching to the ceiling, and a huge feast ensued.

What a wonderful welcome from these warm French Canadians
to an English girl . . . and a Protestant at that!

Charlotte Farrow's husband Ken had purchased a 300-acre farm in Dobbinton, on the Bruce Peninsula north of Toronto. Her first morning as a farm wife remains a vivid memory:

Next morning, up before the birds, pail in hand, with soothing words from Ken, we headed for the barn to milk the cows. Good Lord! I had never seen such a large cow that close. Well, here goes. Needless to say, my first attempt was catastrophic.

I sat down, pail between my knees, and started to pull, squeeze, pull. I was not getting much milk, but as long as the cow was quiet I was happy. Suddenly, the cow decided to switch her tail, a tail that had been in the gutter. Smack! I got the full force of the tail—manure and all—round my forehead and face. I couldn't see a thing. My knees relaxed; down went the pail with what little milk there was in it. I saw all my work and effort trickling away. It was quite a while before I tried that again, and the cows were not sorry.

We are still on the farm—500 acres now—and there are *no* cows!

Unfortunately, every war bride did not receive a warm and heartfelt welcome. In the real world, one's hopes and dreams often end in disappointment. After Constance McKenzie had watched all the other reunions at Union Station in Toronto, she realized that her husband Art was not coming to meet her as planned. He had decided it would be more convenient to wait for her at St. Catharines. And when she and her two children finally arrived there, they were not received with open arms:

I did expect more than a peck on the cheek from my husband, whom I hadn't seen in over a year. His greeting to the kiddies was a hello. The children were miserable and tired, but Art expected us to go to a party. I put my foot down on that. I'm afraid that my temper went and we had a row. That was the last time I had a backbone.

For the war brides and their husbands, the most important factor in achieving a smooth transition was their shared love. This bond would often be sorely tested during the tough times ahead. But, for the time being, they had each other and were sure they could tackle whatever the future held. Most of them were right.

6

"It Wasn't Like This at Home"

*T*HOUSANDS *of miles away from family and friends,
and from all the security they had come to rely on, the war
brides began a new life. This was far from easy. Phyllida (Rickford)
Miller had married an officer of the Royal Canadian Artillery in
1941. Knowing that she would eventually have to adjust to life on
a farm, she had prepared for her future by signing on with the
Women's Land Army. In Canada, she found that she thoroughly
enjoyed rural life and the hard work involved. But she faced difficulties nonetheless:*

I thought I had the world by the tail, as the saying goes. Adjustment
to life on our prairie farm wasn't as hard as expected. The secret,
perhaps, was that there really wasn't anything in this new environment with which I could make comparisons and say, "It wasn't like
this at home." I was *all* completely different from what I had been
used to. Here there was no electricity, no running water or plumbing. The roads were ungravelled dirt roads, unpassable after heavy
rains, and often blocked by snow in winter. There were no next-
door neighbours, no cultural life, no holidays.

But there was a lot to learn. I settled into it with a will and the
self-reliance born of a British upper-class upbringing: "Make the
best of it" . . . "You've made your bed, now lie on it" . . . "Keep a
stiff upper lip" . . . and all that! Young, energetic, and in love, it
was all a challenge and an adventure. But, oh, the loneliness and
the homesickness!

I had envisioned farming as teamwork, a truly shared lifestyle.
I very soon discovered that the roles of husband and wife on the

141

prairie farm were rigidly structured. Though I had learned in the WLA to milk cows, pitch hay, make stooks, and even drive a tractor, I found that here these were all the farmer's business. The chickens were my job. And, of course, the housework, gardening, and raising the children. In farming and financial matters I was not consulted, though I am a well-educated and intelligent woman who had handled her own bank account since age sixteen. On arrival in Saskatchewan, I had turned over my savings into what I thought of as "our" bank account. But it was not a joint account and I didn't have access to it. My husband always paid the bills, and it was quite some time before I really became familiar with dollars and cents instead of pounds and shillings. The children were all given a weekly spending allowance. I was not.

I think the hardest thing then was having no real friends: people who could share my interests, my viewpoint, my memories. I am an only child and both my parents are gone, so being alone is nothing new to me. But this was something different — a kind of spiritual isolation which followed me even after we had left the farm. In the various little prairie towns where we subsequently lived, there were no other English people. Indeed, it was not until we moved to the city of Regina about twelve years ago that I first met fellow war brides.

When, finally, we moved to Regina there were many changes. The outbreak of war in 1939 had put an end to my hopes for a university degree and perhaps a career in journalism. But now, in my late fifties, my husband urged me to study full-time and earn credit for the classes I was taking. To work for a degree was a challenge indeed, and I accepted it. Just three years later, and shortly before my graduation, my husband left me with a parting note on the dining-room table (just like a scene in a corny stage play). So I ended up alone, with a double major in psychology and religious studies and a B.A. with great distinction!

Housing was a major problem in postwar Canada. Consequently, many war brides lived with their in-laws until they could find, or afford, a place of their own. When Joan Georgina Weller first arrived in Toronto, she and her husband Claude had to live with her in-laws, including three sisters-in-law:

From the start, my mother-in-law was difficult and rigid. According to her, Claude had no right to select a wife without her prior approval. Over the years she mellowed somewhat, and some years later recklessly admitted to Claude that he "could have done a lot worse"—faint praise indeed!

When I had been in Canada for about a month, I had a visit from a woman from the Church of England. My mother-in-law was rather put out when the visitor asked to see me alone, but she was trying to ascertain if I was happy or if I wanted the church to send me home. She said there were some dreadful stories of war brides' experiences. . . . Those officers' uniforms were deadly, I can tell you! Had my parents not cast the die, I think I would have opted to return at that point, but I have always been a fighter and hate to admit defeat.

As soon as possible, I phoned around to find a flat, either above a shop or in an apartment building. At that time, returning servicemen were having to pay "key money" to get a place to live. One man, who was advertising three rooms, inquired whether I was English, and when I replied that I was he spat out, "We don't want any damned English here!" and hung up. Finally, a kindly Englishman offered us a two-bedroom flat in a building at Church and Wellesley (now the Toronto-Dominion Bank), in the basement of which he manufactured Gray's Balm, a pleasant smelling chest rub which permeated the building. I might add that in the three years we lived there, none of us ever had a cold! However, we were awakened on many occasions with the "women of the night" haggling over prices. One night my husband called out the window, "For God's sake, make up your minds so we can get some sleep!" It was all a far cry from my home in Enfield, Middlesex, in a rather large semi-detached house in a quiet neighbourhood.

The nationwide shortage of housing also affected Marg Pallot in Montreal:

After the excitement of being able to shop for clothes without coupons, eat a banana split for the first time in five years, and marvel at the meats and groceries available in food stores, homesickness set in with a vengeance. We lived in downtown Montreal, where the only visible grass was the dusty variety in the city parks.

In 1947, partly due to the influx of war brides and so many marriages happening when the boys came home, housing was very scarce and rents soared. This meant that we were forced to share a small two-bedroom flat with my husband's mother and sister — an arrangement that was difficult for all, as you can imagine. The government was attempting to remedy the housing shortage with its wartime housing program, but even that was on a point system depending on the size of the ex-serviceman's family. Our second daughter was born in June 1947 and our chances of a home increased. However, it was only going to the housing authorities and threatening to go home to Scotland that our case was finally investigated by an official, and we were given the keys to our first little house. It was located in the boondocks of Montreal East, surrounded by fields. I remember it with deep affection — at last, my own home.

Wives who had to settle into their new environment without a husband at hand to help them found things especially tough. It was difficult enough getting to know one's in-laws and making new friends, without having to do it on one's own. Connie Ellen Burrill found this very hard. She lived in Yarmouth, Nova Scotia, for three months before her husband came home. The most common occurrences drove her to panic:

I would dive under the kitchen table from pure reflexes in heavy thunder and lightning storms. It sounded like gunfire, etc., to me. The first time I ever walked "downtown," it struck me that everyone spoke Canadian, even the children. Then I laughed at my own foolishness, but I longed to hear a British accent.

After arriving in the village of Chaplin, Saskatchewan, Veronica J. Moore, like other war brides, had a lot of new experiences to get used to. Cooking with a coal and wood stove proved to be a challenge to many of the brides, Veronica included. Bathing in a laundry tub was also a skill to be acquired. Yes, it was all very different from England:

The dance hall became a popular meeting place for many future war brides and their Canadian husbands.

There is much to learn about Canada. At home in Brixton, little Anne Rae, her mother Elizabeth, and her grandparents are all interested in seeing an illustration of Toronto, soon to be Anne and Elizabeth's new home.

Anne Rae, two-and-a-half years old, watches with interest as her mother finishes packing the last item of clothing for the trip to Canada.

The bags have been sent on ahead, and Thomas Bratten and his wife say a last farewell to Elizabeth and Anne, February 1946.
National Archives of Canada/PA 175795

Anne Rae and her mother wave goodbye as their train leaves a London station.
Art Cole/National Archives of Canada/PA 175803

Mrs. Rae's passport is stamped at Liverpool dock, the last stop before boarding the *Mauretania*.

Art Cole/National Archives of Canada/PA 175802

A small face in a big space: Anne Rae waves goodbye to those on deck from a porthole high up on the side of the *Mauretania*, June 1946.

Art Cole/National Archives of Canada/PA 175801

Abvian Bumby and her son take a last look at England from the train, on their way to Bronte, Ontario.

K. M. Hermeston/National Archives of Canada/PA 17506

The first large draft of war brides and their children, eating on board the train to Liverpool, February 1946.

K. M. Hermeston/National Archives of Canada/PA 175799

War brides and their children leaving the station in London en route to their ship to Canada.

K. M. Hermeston/National Archives of Canada/PA 175798

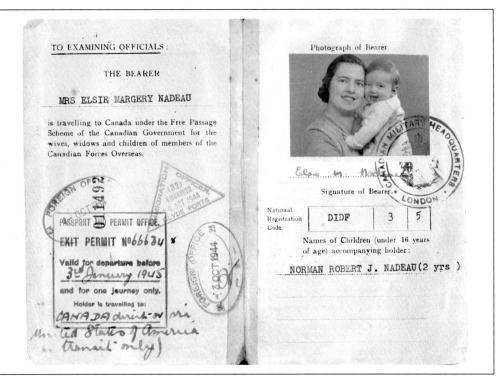

The Canadian travelling certificate of Elsie Nadeau and her son Norman. These documents were issued to the war brides by the Canadian government and were valid for one trip to Canada.

With her full load of war brides and children, the *Mauretania* is finally under way, pulled from the dock by tugboats, February 1946.

Art Cole/National Archives of Canada/PA 175804

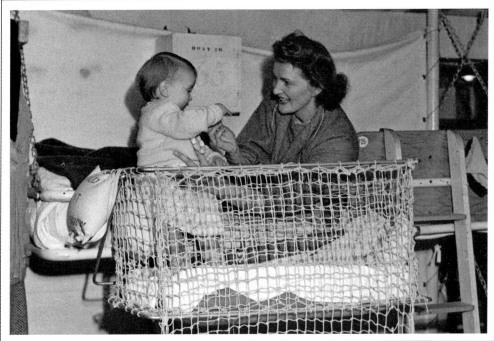

Taking care of the children on board the *Letitia*, April 1946.

The Canadian Red Cross was on hand to help on the long journey. Here Sally Cuthbert of Calgary is serving Mrs. Ivan McArthur and her son Robert, who are setting out for Perth, New Brunswick.

K. M. Hermeston/National Archives of Canada /PA 175786

The *Letitia* finally reaches Canada, April 1946.

National Archives of Canada/PA 175793; PA 175794

Having grown up in the city and being used to classical music, ballet, and the theatre, etc., to say it was a culture shock was putting it mildly. Even after all these years, I still yearn for a little of the arts. My first winter, 1946, was one of the worst on record for snow. We were snowed in all winter and could walk right up over our house and come down the other side. We had to move into one room, that's all the old stove would heat, and we had to tunnel out the snow to the window to let in some light. As I look back now, it didn't bother me at all. We were cosy and we had a radio. I was so thankful to be safe after all those years of air-raid shelters.

Jessie Still found that her new home town in northern Ontario did have some entertainment to offer:

One cold Saturday night we sat around the wood stove and Bob, my father-in-law, announced we were going to listen to the opera. Opera? Judging from the music I had heard at the house parties, I was quite surprised. Did my relatives really enjoy opera music? Well, I supposed, it was probably a light operetta, *Carmen* or my favourite *H.M.S. Pinafore*. Everyone was quiet just before the program started, and then . . . the unmistakable voice of Minnie Pearl with, "Howdy, folks, this is the Grand Ole Opry!" I had a good laugh. Indeed, it was a happy, cheery program, and I looked forward to it on Saturday nights.

Jean M. Chartrand was trying to settle into life in the small town of Oak Point, Manitoba. Her mother-in-law spoke mainly French, so Jean had to brush up on her rusty French. It took a while to adjust to her new circumstances. But like all war brides, she found that Christmas Day was the worst:

I felt very lonesome for my parents and my sister who were so very far away. There was no such thing as phoning them. Sure, I had a husband, but I had to get to know him all over again and learn the Canadian ways of living.

My first winter in Canada had many of the folks in Oak Point smiling. I wore a kilt, sweater, tweed jacket, knee socks, and brogues, and I was still cold. The following winter I wore ski pants, doeskin shirt, a parka, and snow boots!

I still vividly remember my first trip across country on a sleigh trail to my mother-in-law's home. We were travelling in a double wagon box and sleighs pulled by a team of horses. I was very comfortable on a bed of hay, wrapped up in blankets. My baby was fed and was sleeping, so I decided that I could snuggle down and sleep, too. Suddenly I felt a sharp slap on my cheek, and my husband was telling me to wake up as this was no place to sleep. I began to wonder what kind of man I had married. When we arrived at Mother's, she could see I was a little upset, but I was not going to let on about the type of son she had. Finally, she got me to tell her what was bothering me. Then she burst out laughing. By this time, I was beginning to regret ever having left the comfort of my own family circle. Then Mother told me I should never sleep out in the cold in winter as it might be a very long sleep—death.

Joyce Hassard recalls that times were tough and she missed her family in England terribly. Nevertheless, the spirit of Christmas triumphed that first difficult year:

Our first Christmas together in Canada, we didn't have much. Ninety dollars a month didn't go far, even that long ago, and we decided as we'd had to buy so many winter clothes we couldn't buy each other anything. But on a nail behind the tree on Christmas morning was a chenille dressing gown for me and for Lorne a cribbage board. We had both disobeyed orders.

And so my life in Canada had begun. It was eighteen years before I got home to see my family again—eighteen long, lonely, heart-breaking years. But our lives have grown better and it's been a wonderful life in Canada.

Joan E. Landry had first met her husband-to-be, Conrad, when she was only fourteen years old. Things almost went no further because "he decided he wasn't going out with school children." Yet they later married, and she followed him back to Canada. Joan came from the East End of London, and her new home was on the Magdalen Islands of Quebec, so she not only had to get used to a rural life but also had to adapt to new food and, especially, a new language:

When I arrived on the Islands there was quite a difference from the East End and Islington, and even though my husband had told me whatever he could about them, I don't think one is ever quite prepared. I knew, for instance, that the Islands' population was made up of 95 percent French-speaking Canadians, also that there was no electricity or running water, or many of the amenities or conveniences, or even any public transportation. However, there were things that did help me, for example, the welcome I received wherever I went, the beautiful scenery, etc.

My husband went back to fishing while I stayed with my mother-in-law all day, speaking with sign language. She did her best and so did I, but it was not a very satisfactory situation. I made mistakes and there was some misunderstanding but, taking everything into consideration, we got on quite well. I was eighteen and a half when I arrived here and had had to do my share of chores in the houses where I had been in foster care and also at home with my mother. It must have prepared me somewhat for this new life, as I would try anything! I did not have much choice.

I remember the first morning I arrived here, seeing a huge sauce-pan cooking away at around 8:00 AM and my husband telling me it was the noon meal. I said, "Not already cooking?" I found out later that it was a boiled salted meat dinner. I had a difficult time getting used to it and, in fact, am still not fond of it. The tea would be made in the morning for the whole day and left to stew on the stove. No need to tell you how I liked that! I finally bought my own teapot and would make my own fresh tea whenever I wanted some, which was considered a terrible waste of perfectly good tea.

I had been a bookworm while in England, and when I arrived here there was little in the way of reading material in French, let alone English, which was nonexistent. That was one of the most difficult things for me to accept, and I wrote to whomever I knew to beg them to send me something to read, also sewing and knitting patterns. I would read everything from front to back, even the advertisements.

When Tony Solomon first popped the question to Margaret, she had said, "No, I hear it gets very cold in Canada," to which he replied, "Naw, it only lasts a few days then warms up." But the weather wasn't all that Margaret had to get accustomed to:

After a month's vacation with Tony's parents (who made us a banquet that lasted about three days), we were chased out of his home with a straw broom. This was for good luck. I thought this was a strange custom. I figured they were mad at us!

We headed north to Red Lake, Ontario, where if you wanted running water you picked up a bucket and ran for it! My first winter "up north" was full of learning — blundering, blubbering, and lots of homesickness, writing home cheerful letters so the folks wouldn't worry about me, taking a picture of the best house in town and telling them it was our place, going to the post office twice a day for mail (especially silly, since the mail truck came just once a day). Our postmaster used to shake his head sadly at me but would wave the blue airmail form at me when one came.

Shopping in our one store, the Hudson's Bay, was a real headache at first. Asking for a half-pound of gammon that was in front of me in the display case and being told, "Oh, we don't carry that stuff," then finding out from a friend it was called cooked ham. Or the paperboy asking for two bits for the local paper. At the drugstore I asked in a whisper for sanitary napkins and was told by the clerk that I would have to go to the linen department of the Bay for them. And here I was facing a towering stack of the damned things, but called Kotex. Or my husband wanting a wrench when he only had to say spanner.

My 1946 shopping list of items not to be had for love or money: oleomargarine, self-raising flour, potato, raisin, or buttermilk scones; crumpets, Capstan cigarettes, tea biscuits, Yardley products, Pears soap, Ovaltine, Horlicks, English draft beer, Tizer (soft drink), fruit wine, Evening in Paris perfume, fresh ocean fish, Danish butter.

As I closed the door when my husband left to work the 7:00 PM to 3:00 AM shift (at 78 cents per hour) at the nearby gold mine, that's when the tears would flow. Pregnant with our first child, and there was no one to talk to or ask advice from. Dark winter nights with only a tiny mantel radio to listen to.

Things I missed: fish and chip shops, fishmongers, chemist shops, newsstands, Sunday dinner at Mom's after church with all the family, Big Ben striking nine on the radio, BBC news announcers, BBC comedy shows (Tommy Handley), Bebe Daniels and Ben Lyon, Vera Lynn, English big bands (Charley Kuntz), Joe Loss, Wednesday market days, sheep blocking the roads, doubledecker buses and streetcars (especially the jolly conductors), wet cobblestones, mist on our cheeks, the smell of the sea, going down Clyde River on the old steam side-paddle boats to Rothsay and Dunoon, winter pantomines, Devon cream toffee, newspapers on Sunday, daily papers, local jokes, train stations, friendly accents, and, believe it or not, rain.

Jessie (Dick) Wood was one of the war brides who travelled ahead of her husband, having sailed for Sydney, Nova Scotia, on board the Letitia *in May 1946. She was out for a drive one evening with her in-laws when she heard a strange chorus of singing:*

I did not like to ask the nature of the noise as I was not yet on very familiar terms with them. However, after some time my mother-in-law said, "My, the frogs are loud tonight!" I had never heard frogs sing before or even knew that they did!

A good attitude made all the difference. In November 1944, Janine Thompson arrived in Canada with her fifteen-month-old daughter, and pregnant with another child. Her husband had bought a farm in Nova Scotia, and Janine had to struggle to learn the ins and outs of farm life:

I was nineteen years old, full of hope and adventure, quite certain of a glorious future in this land I had always wanted to see. In the winter I would not get out for three weeks or a month to see another neighbour, or no one could get in through all the snow. What a different life I had now than what I was used to in England! My dad wrote to me every week and my sisters and brothers also wrote, so I was lucky on that point. Of course, I still got very homesick at times, but life was really too busy to be worrying over that. I had made my bed and was going to lie on it, come what may.

Homesickness claimed many victims among the war brides. Ida Moreau, who had moved from London to Edmonton, knew all too well what it was like:

I was so homesick, it was like a dreadful sickness. Some dear old well-meaning ladies at the uptown YWCA started a war brides' club, which used to meet every Tuesday afternoon. I would go, then return home and cry all day Wednesday, Thursday, and Friday, feel a little better on Saturday and Sunday (maybe because my husband was home), I'd be much better on Monday, then on Tuesday I'd be off again.

I was uptown one very cold March day when homesickness swept over me, bad enough to drown me. I don't know how I got to the immigration office but there I stood, holding my little girl's hand, crying. I wanted to return home to England. I must have looked a pitiful sight. One gentleman asked me if I'd married an Indian, and I replied no. The next question was, "Does your husband beat you?" No, he didn't. I was told that I couldn't go back because war laws were still in place and civilians were not permitted to travel overseas. Oh, my, what a sad young woman left that office!

Barbara Warner tried in vain to get used to her new country:

I followed my husband to Regina, where I have always found it to be the loneliest place in the world and still do. We returned to England after five years. Healthwise, I couldn't hack the heat or the cold. Our six children were raised in England with many trips back and forth to Canada, promising ourselves that we would retire in Regina. The time came and we returned to Regina, only to have my husband pass away with a heart attack six weeks later.

For Jessie Still, seeing a photograph of an English garden on a calendar brought on an agonizing bout of homesickness:

What is homesickness? It is a malady for which there is no medication. It attacks you and then goes away, and then returns. I missed the smell of the sea. In less than an hour from a London terminal, I could get to the seaside. Homesickness hits you below the belt. It sneaks up on you in a song or a smell or a line of poetry. You confine it to the back of your mind, but it comes back again and again.

Beryl Smallwood had spent ten years in a convent school in Belgium and then four years away from home in the WAAF, and felt that this cured her of any homesickness she might have otherwise felt in Canada. Her husband Tony was going to university in Vancouver:

We eventually got housing with other veteran students at UBC at a converted ack-ack site where the barracks were remodelled into housing. We were all poor but made our own fun and, of course, home brew.

During the time between semesters it was necessary for the men to get jobs for the summer. Tony and I, plus baby, travelled to the Cariboo with another war bride and her student husband. The men got jobs felling trees for a mill. We lived in the woods in an old log cabin, sans water or toilets, and for mattresses we used spruce boughs (somebody said that was supposed to be good!). Then the boys decided they would try their hand at panning for gold. The next day the people in the village were very upset at all the mud coming through their taps. Our husbands had panned the water supply! There was great teasing about us city slickers!

As so many who have immigrated to Canada have found, the tug to return home, if only for a visit, can be hard to resist. Pat Heath's homesickness for Surrey persisted until she was able to take a trip back there:

I joined the English-Scots-Welsh-Irish Club (ESWIC) in Ottawa, but after about five years I gave it up, as I felt so homesick every time I went. I had to make the break and become a Canadian. After ten years, I felt if I did not see my family in England I would die. So I took a job for one year as a cashier and saved every penny, and home I went for six weeks. My husband would not allow me to take our two boys in case I did not come back.

For some, the homesickness would not go away. Pamela Parsons felt welcomed by her new family and really enjoyed life in Toronto, but she had to see England again:

In 1949 my father offered to pay my fare home for a holiday, so I went for six weeks. My family in England really made me welcome. They gave me the royal treatment to the extent that when I got back to Toronto, I just couldn't stay. My trip home had really unsettled me, I'm afraid, and nothing would do. I begged Ed to take us back to England, which he did, and our first son was born over there. But Ed was so unhappy in England that we came back to Canada when my son was eleven months old.

Vera Davison thought she had escaped the misery of homesickness, but it was to strike her many, many years later:

An unexpected thing happened. When I left home and came so far away, I had not gone through the normal homesickness that many people have. In spite of leaving so much I loved behind — family, city life, theatre, etc. — to come to a place and people so different, I was not homesick. The only reason I can offer is my sense of adventure and interest in learning so many new things and beginning my own family.

When recovering from a brain aneurism in 1977, however, homesickness hit me so severely that it almost floored me. Perhaps it had been pent up inside me all those years.

One would think that the beaches of Vancouver would remind someone from Brighton of home. But Winifred Rose found the majestic setting of Vancouver a disappointment:

Having left my home town of Brighton, where there are plenty of beaches and entertainment, to me Vancouver was quite depressing. The mountains were overbearing. I walked on wooden sidewalks which reminded me of cowboy towns in Western movies. As homesickness overtook me, I wondered if I would ever settle, but settle I did, although the homesickness took ten years to subside.

As the city grew and prospered over the years, the mountains became less overbearing, yet even today I prefer to view them at a distance. I cannot get used to the beaches. They are too untidy, with old logs and, in recent years, large boulders and cement dumped there in the wake of progress. I miss the amusement piers of Brighton and walking the promenades. These pleasures I still enjoy on my return visits to the country of my birth. I love both countries now.

I resided with my in-laws for the first few months I was in B.C. One day my sister-in-law asked if I would bake a cake while she took her mother out. In the kitchen was a huge monstrosity — a wood and coal stove. I decided to give it a try and managed to bank it up. The recipe they gave me called for shortening. I just didn't know what it was and looked everywhere for something that read "shortening." Anyway, I mixed the cake without shortening and baked it. My in-laws had a good laugh over that. They ate the cake anyway, so it was a feather in my cap.

Homesickness still made me feel lonely even after a year had passed. With my husband working on New Year's Eve, I went to my mother- and father-in-law's for the evening, feeling down. I was young, I wanted to have some fun. About fifteen minutes before midnight, my father-in-law gave me a drink of rye whisky. I'd never drunk such stuff, but tried some. It was too strong. I felt its warmth, though, and out of the blue I said, "I can stand on my head." I tucked my skirt into my panties and stood on my head! My father-in-law called his wife in from the kitchen to come look at this. He was laughing. My mother-in-law was disgusted and promptly sent me outside on the pretext that it was lucky for a dark-haired person to be the first to enter the house at the stroke of midnight. I knew why she sent me out — the air was crisp and cold. My father-in-law was laughing his head off. Later, he blew up some balloons, then escorted me to the bus stop to meet my husband, a bus driver, finishing his last run on the way to the garage. Pushing the balloons ahead of me through the bus doors, I said, "Hi, honey. Happy New Year!" My father-in-law went on his way, still laughing. I had made his day.

Dorothy Clyne and her three-year-old daughter came to Canada in 1946 from her home in Peterhead, Scotland. Her husband Fred had been born in the same town, but he had emigrated to Canada as a young man. Dorothy recalls the problems of adapting to life in Silverdale, British Columbia:

The mosquitoes must have told each other that good Scottish blood was available, as they came to me in swarms. I scratched and scratched day and night until I was bleeding all over — straight agony! However, soon a baby was on the way and we were blessed with our first son, David, and a few years later were blessed with another son, Roy. So, with three children and my husband, who suffered a lot from sciatica and nerve problems (the result of war), there was no longer time to pine for Bonny Scotland.

Nan Casey was a Dutch bride who had met her husband-to-be two weeks after her country was liberated. She was married that December and left for Canada two weeks later. She arrived in Penticton, British Columbia; but when they could not find a place to live there, they moved to a mining camp five thousand feet up in the mountains:

I was six months pregnant then and, believe me, it was quite a change for me to live in the mountains in a two-room house. I had to learn to cook, bake, can, make pickles, jam, and prepare wild meat. We had a lot of venison, and I liked it, but it was very different from Dutch cheese! I did speak English when I came, but it seemed as if I was living between two different worlds. You're curious about your new world, but still very much attached to the old one.

As Eunice Partington was adjusting to life on a Saskatchewan farm, she had many memorable experiences:

For the first year we lived in a small house perched on a hill in the middle of the prairie, and upon our arrival there found the neighbours had supplied us with a large pile of cut firewood and twelve chickens. We had little furniture, but I soon became adept at decorating wooden apple crates, orange boxes, and even round cheese boxes for use as cupboards, tables, etc. What a family these neighbours were! They had five children who could not understand my accent, and so it became necessary to pronounce words with a short "a" rather than the long "a." I learned so much of the Canadian ways from them, and how good they were to me.

I remember so well enjoying those long summer days helping in the garden, hayfield, or wherever I was needed, picking bowls and bowls of wild strawberries along the railway banks, making them into jam, picking saskatoon berries, and the quilting bees, where I was introduced to the art of quilting, a pastime I continue.

Summer soon turned into fall and harvest time. I was quickly introduced to threshing crews. Our neighbour cooked for two crews and she asked me to help. What enormous portions required preparation and cooking! It was a good experience, and at that time I learned to bake bread, churn butter, the ins and outs of the cream separator, the old hand-crank washing machine, gas lamps, and sad irons. Rationing in England had curtailed any extensive baking experience, so I was in need of some supervision, especially with that wood stove.

Like so many other war brides, Ivy Winnifred Ogram had to face the hardships of rural life. She had much to learn about helping to run their farm near Lloydminster, Saskatchewan:

Life in Canada was very different from the lifestyle I had been used to in London. Rural versus city life was quite an adjustment. The house was heated by a pot-bellied stove in the living room, which gave good heat, and a wood cookstove in the kitchen. In the mornings the water in the pail would be frozen. My husband would get up and light the stove before I ventured out to dress.

There were many chores in those days—lamps had to be cleaned and filled, firewood split and carried indoors, water drawn up from the well by a pail on a rope and pulley and then carried up a steep incline to the house. I'd get two pails of water at a time, and being less than five feet tall the pails weren't far from the ground. Several times when it was icy, I'd slip going up the slope and end up getting very wet.

When I first arrived, I wore dresses or skirts doing the chores, but after freezing my knees climbing over the fence to feed the pigs, I soon learned to wear pants. There were also chickens to feed and eggs to collect. I liked milking, except the cows would swing their tails, sometimes slapping me in the face or treading on my feet. A far cry from the London office that I was used to!

My husband separated the milk and I washed the separator. When we had enough cream, it had to be churned into butter, a slow job. I baked bread in the wood cookstove. Making bread was a lot of work but, oh, the smell of fresh-baked bread — better still, the taste of a thick slice with golden syrup—yummy! When I cooked my first Christmas cake, I sat in front of the stove with a piece of wood in one hand and a dipper of water in the other—my method of regulating the heat. And, oh, that wooden washing machine! It had a wooden dolly operated by a handle on top which was moved from left to right, back and forth, back and forth. Bath night was a tub in front of the stove when everyone else had gone to bed. Different but adequate.

Although May Meekins and her son thought they were settling in rather quickly to life in Truro, Nova Scotia, there were still a few tricks to be mastered. For one thing, there was a new jargon to learn, as she discovered when visiting the grocery store:

I asked for pot head and a loaf. The grocer had to call my mother-in-law to find out what I wanted! It was headcheese and a loaf of bread. Another time, I decided to go to the post office to pick up the mail. I borrowed a bicycle and took off (I always rode a bike back home). All the way there and back, people were waving and yelling at me. I thought, what a friendly lot! My in-laws were frantic. I indignantly informed them that I was very adept at bicycle riding. But I felt foolish when my father-in-law said, "Yes, but not on the wrong side of the road!"

Many war brides did not wish to worry their parents during those early days of hardships and avoided mentioning their struggles in their frequent letters home. Some, like Peggy Rogal, did not even tell their mothers that they were coping without the convenience of running water:

In the winter I would mention in my letters how cold it got. My poor mum would write and say, "I do hope your pipes won't freeze." No worry there. We didn't have any pipes to freeze, even if it did go down to forty below!

Evelyn Nicholson was living near the small hamlet of Edgeley, Saskatchewan, which had a population of around fifty — quite a contrast from London! Most people in the community were very friendly, and to show their kindness they presented her with a chest of silverware as a gift. But she had a lot to learn:

They talked about bushels to the acre, combines, and, of course, the Dirty Thirties. This was all new to me. On the other hand, they did not seem to know much about London. Some thought it was a wicked place where you were likely to be murdered walking in a park. Others said that one city started where another had ended, as though there was no open countryside. How wrong they were!

My mother-in-law encouraged me to do the cooking, and I mastered the big, black, wood-burning stove. Water was collected in rain barrels, and in dry weather it was hauled by the men from a "dug-out" on a "stone-boat." The drinking water came from a well some distance from the house, and it was useful in the hot weather as it kept the butter and other foods very cool. Also, some distance from the house was the outhouse, near the "bluff," another new word for me. How I hated going out there in the dark! I especially missed electricity. The light from the coal-oil lamps was not the best to read by or write letters or knit by.

I vividly remember taking a bath one evening in front of the stove, and I had carefully removed the leaves, dead spiders, and other bugs from the water in the tin bathtub before relaxing in the warm water. Suddenly, there was a knock on the kitchen door. "Don't come in," I yelled as a neighbour entered the room. I screamed and crossed my arms across myself, and he retreated very quickly. I don't know who was more embarrassed, but doors were never locked in those days.

The radio was the main entertainment and there were "soap stories" to listen to, like "Ma Perkins," and the men enjoyed the hockey games. People also rubber-necked on the party-line telephone, and I could often hear a neighbour's canary singing as I used the phone. Everyone was very interested in everyone else's business, and what they didn't know they made up.

I missed my family very much, and I missed London and England. As I had lived above my father's shop and worked in a bank, there were always people around. Life was so different. I missed the underground and theatres, and being able to go to the sea. It was not the best thing for us to be living with Nick's parents either. They were pleased that their son had chosen an English girl to marry, but our backgrounds were very different. My husband did not settle down to the farm life, and he had become allergic to cows, reacting with swollen eyes and lips. Arguments with my mother-in-law became frequent, especially when we began to make plans to return to England in the summer of 1947.

We sailed at the end of September and stayed for four years. We were lucky to get two rooms at Southfields, near Wimbledon, to live in. Our first child was born in December 1948 and before our little girl was a year old, Nick was already talking of returning to Canada. I felt sick at the thought, and resisted the idea for a long time. He did not find life in peacetime England as he had expected. My blood pressure was high, and the hospital could find no physical reason for it but suggested it was the worry of returning to Canada.

One of us had to give in. It was very hard having to tell my parents, and this time we were taking their only grandchild with them. Sadly, my father died in 1959 after a short illness. The family said he was never the same after I had decided to stay in Canada. My passport had expired so I was unable to see him or attend the funeral. I have been very careful to keep my passport up to date ever since.

For Janet P. Bulloch Paton, there was quite a contrast between life in Scotland and settling into the small town of Glen Ewen, Saskatchewan. Nevertheless, she seems to have maintained a positive attitude and she learned to love the prairies. Everyone was extremely friendly and helpful and on a first-name basis. It helped that the community was made up of different nationalities:

It seemed to me the menfolk worked continuously, and I realized that was how it had to be on the prairies. The reward for their labours were the fields of grain and the huge haystacks. Everything seemed to be done on a grand scale, even the hailstorm in August 1946. That was a terrifying experience. I learned very quickly what the phrase "maybe next year" meant. It was demoralizing to experience what hail could do to the land and the pocketbook.

I also learned some new words that first fall. "Shower" meant a gathering of kindly folk with gifts to help brides get started housekeeping. The Glen Ewen ladies organized such a surprise for the war brides, and I was also given one by the Auburn ladies. The beautiful lunches served at such events soon made us forget wartime rations and unsweetened goods. I became aware quite soon of the importance of friends and neighbours in the West, and very often they became closer than family.

The first winter was like looking out at a fairyland. The trees in the valley and yard wore lace shawls after every frost. I couldn't believe it was possible to be able to walk on top of snowdrifts without sinking out of sight. I will admit the pot-bellied heater was a more efficient way to keep warm than the fireplaces. The melted snow water was nice to do laundry, etc, in. Tap water was forgotten.

The first year I was introduced to baseball and hockey, where men tried to kill each other with what looked like giant boomerangs to me. I didn't understand how the locals got so enthused about a sports day. All I saw happening were the spectators racing around eating and men in queer outfits trying to hit a ball with a stick. Everyone seemed to be enjoying such outings, and I realized it was a chance to relax from everyday chores that always somehow seemed to be there and had to be taken care of somehow.

There were lean years, also bountiful ones. Despite the hard times and work, I learned what being a farm wife meant. I was never sorry I lived on the prairies. Some of the early experiences of making do and doing without material things made me a stronger person and caused me to realize it was indeed God's country.

But not everyone was friendly. Peggy Chalklin had a frosty reception when she arrived in Toronto:

We English war brides were treated horribly in the middle forties. We were jeered at, spat at, cursed at, and called dreadful names. I guess they were trying to break our spirits, but they were dealing with the wrong people. They hadn't come through what we had. It made you tough. I'm a very sentimental and emotional person, and those days will live with me forever.

For some, the struggle was just too much. On 11 January 1944 the Halifax Herald *reported that one war bride, Mrs. Briggs, had decided she would "rather be back in Britain, despite the danger and shortages. They have far more fun in England than you do over here. Everybody laughs and everything, even with falling bombs they're still living." She was not the only war bride who decided to return, although the numbers are astonishingly low — approximately 10 percent.*

Elsie Beattie, a former member of the WAAF, *was one who decided to stay. She had met her husband Dave at Topcliffe in Surrey, where they were both stationed. She came to live in Anerley, Saskatchewan, which consisted of one store, a school, and three elevators:*

We had no running water, and it was quite a thing climbing over the snowbanks to the outside toilet. We planted a garden and grew lots of pumpkins, as my husband wanted pumpkin pie. I had never seen a pumpkin until I came to Canada. I ended up using just the stringy part of three big pumpkins — it took me half the morning taking the seeds out — then I threw the rest out. My husband had a fit when I said it took three pumpkins to make one pie. It was not all that bad either!

Renée Bell's baby was seriously ill throughout the journey to Hamilton and had to be hospitalized on arrival. On top of this, there was more trouble in store for her:

I received a very poor welcome from Cliff's mother, as he was expected to marry her friend's daughter; also, I was a Roman Catholic and she was a Presbyterian. We had to stay with them for seven weeks, as apartments were so hard to find. Cliff's mother did all she could to make me unwelcome, and the only places that seemed familiar to me were church and Woolworth's.

I think those seven weeks were the most unhappy of my life. Every day we would rush down to the *Hamilton Spectator* office as soon as the paper came out and scan the apartments to rent section, then rush off to try to be the first to apply. In the end we got one — a dark, dreary place where we had to be the janitor to get the apartment.

I joined the war brides' association, and every time I came home from a meeting I would cry and beg Cliff to send me home.

"Where shall we go tonight? How about a movie or the theatre?" That was a choice that could be enjoyed in most cities of Europe or Britain. But even in the larger centres of Canada, the war brides discovered a lack of entertainment, as May A. M. Wright remembers:

I grew up in south London, Brixton, moving to Balham at the beginning of the war. I was accustomed to the classical music, ballet, Shakespeare, theatres, museums, etc. There was no transport where I lived in Saskatchewan, except by team and sleigh for the four miles to town to catch the train to Regina, where there were some of these things. My husband's younger brother was a country-and-western music fan — this was a culture shock.

Loneliness was another story. My husband Les was the only one whom I could talk to about the life I had left behind. I didn't understand the new life I was living. I wrote many letters but did not receive many replies. I don't think I have ever got over the loneliness.

Peggy Moir found that in New Brunswick the highlight of each week was Saturday night. It was a rough-and-ready lifestyle, and Peggy had a lot to get used to:

On Saturday nights we'd go to the nearest town, which was sixteen miles away, on a school van — a truck with long wooden seats down each side and a heater stove at one end. It was 25 cents return. I thought the town was like the Western towns I'd seen at the movies. People still travelled with horses then and hitched them to posts in front of the stores. Most men seemed to wear red checked jackets and the children looked poorly dressed. It was not unusual to see men standing on the corner passing a bottle around. We would usually go to a movie and do some shopping. The stores stayed open as long as people wanted to shop. How different from England it was!

We eventually moved to the city and I joined a war brides' club. I feel like we were pioneers, getting used to a very different culture, the weather, and strange-tasting foods like fiddleheads, clams, pumpkin pie, and buttermilk.

Because housing was so difficult to find in the postwar years, Jean Margaret McArthur and her husband decided to build their own home in Fredericton, New Brunswick:

Of course, there were no building materials to be had, but we had heard of a building for sale which had to be torn down. Our bid was accepted and we were off. After work, my husband toiled on the big building, tearing it down board by board. Every nail had to be removed and all the clapboards tied in bundles and everything transported to our lot. My husband had help from family and friends, even me, removing nails and such. It was a huge job and we both got very slim, which was good, for I had gotten a bit chubby from all the bananas, patty pans, and ice cream I was eating.

So finally we moved in. Oh, heaven—alone at last! Now I felt my life was really beginning. We had lived in crowded conditions and it was good of the family to keep us for so long, but we were more than ready for our own space. We had the privacy most young marrieds need—I could sit on my husband's lap or kiss him good-bye without people making snide remarks. I could work on my kids' manners, which was an uphill battle because I never heard Canadians instilling them into their offspring. Books and magazines appeared in our house, which we hadn't had before. After living through the war in London, I always felt that living in Fredericton was like being buried in a backwater. Having been a child in London and having a delightful time playing in the streets, I

162

always felt sorry for my children because all they had was a huge yard and all the woods to run in.

Lilian Pearson, who stepped off the train in Birsay, Saskatchewan, received a wonderful welcome from the villagers and local farmers and their wives, which made her feel special. Yet she longed for the day they would have their own home:

Having very little money, but being young with plenty of spunk and energy, we hitched one of the horses to the stone boat and pulled up to a one-room building on the farmstead and began hauling out horses' harness, barrels of grease, cans of nails and, oh, lots and lots of junk. Then we scrubbed and cleaned, put down a new floor, and papered the walls, bought some curtains and rods from a farm auction sale—and we were ready to move in.

One room—our palace. We had a front door and two very small windows, a chesterfield to sleep on at night and sit on in the daytime, an oil heater, one chest of drawers, a brand new cookstove, a washstand, an enamel bowl for washing ourselves and the dirty dishes, and a pail of drinking water. We also had a wooden table that Reg had made, plus four wooden chairs, a pressed cardboard wardrobe, and a kitchen cabinet. There was a hook in the middle of the ceiling for the coal-oil lamp, and a trapdoor in the floor where there was a dirt cellar for storing potatoes and other things. The first time I saw a lizard down there, I shot up out of that hole like a jack-in-the-box.

How cosy we were! — Poor, but very happy and very much in love. I was a farmer's wife, so had to plant a big garden. Which way up do you put the onion sets? What a duffer I was! I would only gather eggs from empty nests, for I didn't trust those beady eyes and sharp beaks. Once I stuck the hayfork through my foot when I was riding on top of a full load of hay. And when I tried to harness a workhorse, one look at those big yellow teeth and I dropped the harness and ran like a streak of lightning, leaving my husband laughing.

Perhaps I was one of the lucky ones. I had spent four years in the ATS and had got used to being away from home, so I wasn't really homesick. I just cried twice — once when someone played

"Home, Sweet Home" on the radio at Christmas and again when shelling peas for hours, wondering what I was doing it for; after all, I had been a shorthand typist.

And then my dad died a year after I came to Canada. That was sad, as I didn't see him again after the time he kissed me goodbye at the railway station in London. Somehow he knew, as he remarked to my mom, "You'll see her again; I won't be so lucky."

Henriette Reid and her husband settled in Ottawa, where he was the director of publicity for Veterans Affairs. Although she did not suffer from the primitive conditions many war brides had to face, there was still an adjustment to be made:

We managed to get a two-room flatlet — no bath or kitchen, and we had to use the sink for washing ourselves and the dishes. We cooked on a two-burner grill. And me from a home in Bruton Street, Mayfair, where our present queen was born!

Laura Lillian Burris, who was one of the first war brides to come to Canada, in 1943, had quite a time while in the hospital giving birth to her daughter:

The birth of our first child taught me many things. One doesn't automatically go to the hospital on the due date. You wait for the pains. If you are overdue, the doctor prescribes a four-ounce bottle of castor oil with oranges. After all this, if you survive, following the birth you will receive a castor oil and orange cocktail. Make sure this is recorded on your chart or the next day you will receive the same little treat.

In my weakened state after the delivery, much to the delight of my room-mates, I told the nurse that my husband had gone overseas in 1941. Result: cold shoulder, until I explained that I was a war bride! But a good time was had by all.

The years after the war were not easy, but we persevered. Now, as I think back, it comes to mind how very young and naive we were in thinking that having survived the war and the bombing, everything else would be a piece of cake.

Joan Collins had met Slim at her grandfather's pub in Gosport. She came to New Brunswick in April 1946 and says, "My early days in Canada were interesting to say the least":

The ice box was almost my undoing. You probably know what I'm talking about—a lead-lined cabinet with a place at the top to place a block of ice. At the bottom there was a little cubbyhole with a door on it to place a bowl to catch the melted ice which ran down a connecting pipe. In other words, a fridge without electricity. Oh, horrors! We were staying with an aunt who lived above another aunt, Aunt Janie. Aunt Janie was a tall, thin, austere lady, held very much in respect by the family. Guess who forgot to empty the bowl when entrusted with that duty! Yours truly. Aunt Janie's ceiling was stained! My heart quaked and my knees knocked. But, bless her heart, she forgave me, seeing I was not used to the beastly thing.

Forest fires were quite a hazard in those days as there were no planes to water bomb. I helped my in-laws and neighbours fill enormous puncheons by bucket brigade from the nearby river to truck into the woods. At this time I also learned to give skunks a wide berth! My outings in the summer with my English pram and canopy was an episode that caused many stares and comments. I felt like I was Barnum & Bailey.

War brides from Europe who could speak neither English nor French, like Maria Ouellette from Ravenstein in Holland, found adjustment to life in Canada a particular challenge. Maria can now look back at her early life in Bathurst, New Brunswick, and laugh:

Married life began with our moving in with my new in-laws. As no one else spoke my language, we resorted to signs. I'd go to the store, hold out my hand with the money I had, and have the salesperson take the required amount. I thought food habits were very strange; for example, bread was burnt to make toast, people ate corn while in my country that was food for chickens, and lobsters were disgusting-looking creatures that Canadians actually ate.

As my English vocabulary improved, I am now reminded by my family of some of the comical sayings and expressions I used. My husband arrived home from work one night saying he had muffler trouble. The word *muffler* is Dutch for earmuffs. I told him not to worry, but that I would knit him a new pair. My next-door neighbour was showing me the radishes he had planted in his garden. Mixing up words like I did, I told him I thought his sardines were doing very well and growing quickly. I was making bread one day and after my husband had opened and closed the kitchen door once too frequently, I said, "Please close the backside door. How do you expect my bread to lift?"

A neighbour and close friend was being treated in hospital for a prostate problem. I proceeded to inform my family and friends that "George has problems with his frustrated glands." When I wanted to inform my doctor of heart palpitations, I told him, "Doctor, I have populations in my throat."

My children grew up knowing a lot of my Dutch expressions that would not have made sense to others, like "broom," the floor; hang up your coat on the "Kapstok"; or "lekker," food. When travelling past many different brasseries and seeing the outdoor signs, I mentioned to my husband that I hadn't been aware that so many merchants in Canada sold bras. My girlfriend had a breast biopsy. In my concern for her welfare I telephoned her the following morning in the hospital, asking, "How do you feel after your autopsy?"

For Robin Beatteay, the trip across the ocean had its own problems. She was seven months pregnant and had to be carried off the Stavangerfjord *in Halifax. "I guess the new baby didn't like the boat trip." After her arrival in New Brunswick, she heard nothing but compliments — which unfortunately were not for her:*

Everyone I met would tell me how lucky I was to have married such a fine boy. I appreciated the fact, but after two weeks of hearing the same thing, it got a bit sickening. When my father-in-law once again said how lucky I was, I responded in my very best English, "Well, Dad, I think Bill is *damn* lucky to get such a fine girl as I." Dead silence. Then Dad said, "Yes, you must be sick of hearing how wonderful we think he is, and I agree, he is damn lucky."

My daughter Kathleen sang on a children's program called "Uncle Bill's Radio Show." Uncle Bill would talk to the children as he introduced them before they sang. He asked Kathleen, "Who is the smartest in your family?" Without hesitation she said, "My father knows more because my mother is English." Just imagine how many people heard that over the air! It took me a long time to live that one down.

Barb Warriner, caring for her very large family in Big River, northern Saskatchewan, found that life was full of new experiences and a lot of hard work:

One morning at the well, I said to an Indian neighbour of ours, "Gee, Eddie, I'm sorry to hear your wife is knocked up again." He looked at me with big brown eyes and said, "Gee, lady, she only had a baby last week!" Was my face red! All those old sayings from home, like "keep your pecker up," were damned out here.

We lived in a three-room shack for a few years. How we managed that I hate to remember. I know the kids kept arriving until there were eight of them. Talk about wall-to-wall beds in one of the bedrooms and wall-to-wall bed and cribs in the other! Wow, what fun trying to make them every day! But we managed, no complaints.

Then one day we got a letter from my mom saying she was coming out for a visit. What a rush that was! The first thing to do was get the crop in, then to build a house, which never did get finished. We finally got it livable on the night I brought her home from Prince Albert. No back door, but a horse blanket was hanging there to keep out the mosquitoes. What Mom thought she never said — she kept it to herself until the day she died. I do remember her asking me before she left if we could afford shoes for our kids. I told her they had a pair for town, plus a pair of rubber boots each, but they preferred to run barefoot. I don't think she believed me.

I have memories by the thousands. Has anyone tried to make an angel food cake in an old wood stove with no temperature controls?

It didn't work for me. That cake came out of the oven like an adobe brick. I threw it out the door and it hit a hen—poor hen, she never knew what hit her.

I have often thought what a cold, bleak country I had chosen for my home. For years I was so homesick, especially at Christmas time. The first carol on the radio would turn the "tap" on. Oh, to see my dear old Mom making mince pies, curd tarts, Christmas puddings and cakes, and everything else that was so traditional at that time of year! Also, my dear old Dad, who was a member of the police choir, singing his favourite carol, "O come," and us trying to join in.

But, all in all, life has been wonderful. I've settled in this great country I now call home. We have raised twelve great kids and we're proud of them all. Wouldn't be without one of them. Although one little one looks down from above, he is still counted among the others. It was a hard job raising them; we didn't have too much money, but always lots to eat and plenty of milk. We hope we've done a good job.

As a young woman, Enid Black had led a sheltered life. She came out to join her husband Walter in April 1946, never suspecting the terrible problems that would follow. To begin with, as Enid left the boat she found herself in the arms of a stranger:

I didn't recognize my own husband! First of all, I hadn't seen him in civvies before and also he had lost so much weight. We didn't know then that he was dreadfully ill. The first thing we did was to go to a restaurant. Walter had promised he would buy me a banana split. Well, you can imagine my eyes popping out of my head when I saw the amount of ice cream. It was lovely, but I couldn't eat it all.

We arrived in Sydney the next morning. It was, I might say, an uneventful arrival. My in-laws acted as if it were an everyday thing having an English girl among them. It was most probably lack of interest. My mother-in-law was an uneducated woman from Newfoundland. She was saying dreadful swear words that I had never heard before.

My husband didn't seem to want to have anything to do with me. To be very frank, he hadn't wanted sex. We had been apart for eight months and I, being very young (nineteen) was very full of love and passion. So I, of course, decided there was somebody else. But little did we know what was in store for us.

It must have been about three weeks later when Walter was building a little house and he was putting the windows in, when he suddenly had a dreadful pain in his chest. It was diagnosed as TB. The doctor told me he would be in the hospital for six months. Well, I was devastated. I couldn't imagine being alone for that length of time. Now you must realize we had very little money. It would take a lot of scraping to get enough money to get a bus to see him. If it hadn't been for the family priest giving me a couple of dollars now and then, I don't think I would have made it. My mother-in-law treated me like I had the plague. She would not go in my room or even go to the hospital to see her son. She wanted me to burn all of our possessions. In those days people were terrified of TB.

Walter got much worse and spent thirty-seven months in the hospital. He was dangerously ill and weighed 93 lb. His hospital was full of veterans with TB—all so young, and lots of them died. But through it all I made some lasting friendships. TB is a sneaky ailment; one gets far advanced without really realizing it. Now when we look back that is why Walter didn't want anything to do with me, poor soul.

When Walter got out of the hospital, we moved to the Annapolis Valley. As time went on, he began drinking away all our money and he became very abusive. He convalesced for four years and used to make home brew and get so drunk he didn't know where he was. He kept drinking until it was the most important thing in his life. He was very hateful when he drank. He used to give me good hidings for no reason at all.

I had had about enough. Walter was being abusive to the children and I couldn't tolerate that, so I decided to leave. God knows where I was going to live. Walter begged me to keep him. I told him he had to do it himself. He did—he called AA, joined, and hasn't had a drink since. That was twenty-three years ago! But today I am living with a man in the early stages of Alzheimer's disease.

Strangely enough, Walter is the sweetest, kindest person now. He is very happy in his own little world and is easily pleased.

The children of these war brides had seen much, young as they were. Those who had grown accustomed to the sounds of gunfire and air-raid warnings before they closed their eyes now had new problems to overcome. Elsie Nadeau travelled to northern New Brunswick during the war, in October 1944, with her young son Norman. It was not easy for him to adjust to peacetime life:

It was quite a while before I could get Norman to go to bed in his crib. He was so used to sleeping under the Morrison table back home that I finally put him to sleep under my mother-in-law's kitchen table!

Some war brides heading for life on a Canadian farm had imagined it would be much the same as in England. Iris Hughes found life in Alberta quite a surprise:

I thought running a farm would be like being a country housewife in England, with visions of a thatched-roof house and white picket fence. What a culture shock! The house was of bare boards, banked to the windows with manure and straw to keep the frost out in winter. I realized why, as the house wasn't insulated and every rail hole was as big as a quarter. You couldn't even wash the floor in winter or the water would freeze before it dried. We farmed with horses. Many a time my husband harrowed and walked behind them with his bare feet, because all he had was his army boots and they made blisters on his feet.

Those who had held important positions found the adjustment even more difficult. Having had a very responsible wartime job as quartermaster with the Red Cross in Europe, Katherine Biggs found it difficult to accept the way women were expected to behave in New Brunswick:

After a few years, my husband became principal of various city schools in Moncton. A little thing I did resent in this country was that teachers or principals must not do anything to upset the community. You must be very low key, whereas in my home town I grew up with the principal's wife being one of the leading town councillors and very vocal. I wasn't used to having to be dumb. My husband would say that I mustn't say this, mustn't say that. I think women were pushed around in Canada. Of course, you must remember I came up through the war and we had progressed forward.

Canadian women who were left behind when their sweethearts went off to war also had adjustments to make. They were upset when "their" men returned with foreign wives on their arms. Gertrude Savage was one of the war brides who experienced their resentment:

A lady came to see me and she said my husband had no right to marry me. I said, "He didn't have to marry me. It was his choice." She said, "But I was waiting for him."

Gloria Brock had a similar challenge in the small town of Abernethy, Saskatchewan:

John's old girlfriend was pointed out to me and someone said, "That's the girl John was going with and he probably would have married her if he hadn't married you overseas." Now this was a strange country and John wasn't here yet, and I thought, Did I break up something? You didn't know what these men had done before they met you. You didn't know if you'd broken up an engagement or interfered with someone else's life. After it happened a couple of times, I got wise to the fact that they were just testing my reaction.

It does bother you and you think about it. You don't have your family there, and if you had a husband who wouldn't listen, who do you confide in? That's why a lot of homes broke up, because of interference like this. But if these people went to England, it could happen there; it's not just Canadian people.

It can be difficult to fit into the close-knit community of small-town life, as Cecilia Knight discovered:

There were two churches and the social life revolved around those churches — and I was the one and only Catholic in the area. So I wasn't in the social swim and I did feel very much on the outside. It wasn't their fault; if I had belonged to one of those two churches, I would never have felt anything like that, I'm sure. But as it was, I felt as though I was missing something all the time.

Unlike many war brides who found themselves on farms or in small towns, Joan Smale had come from a small village and now found herself in a city:

Toronto overwhelmed me at first by its sheer size, which bore little resemblance to the village I had left behind. The summer heat and the subzero temperatures in the winter took a lot of getting used to. Living accommodation was scarce, and living in one room and then two rooms with shared facilities was quite a shock after being used to the run of a house.

My in-laws were very kind to me and the younger boys teased me about my culinary efforts, particularly when I fried wieners in their casings under the mistaken impression that they were some kind of sausage. Everyone was fascinated with my accent, and I didn't have any trouble attracting an audience wherever I went.

My only child was born in 1947, and the following year my husband decided that marriage and fatherhood was not for him and he left us to rejoin the army. I had the moral support of my mother-in-law, even though she didn't turn her back on her son. Lack of money was a problem, so I found a daycare for my son and managed to find myself a decent job. For a year or so it was a hand-to-mouth existence, but things gradually improved and I was able to settle down and really enjoy my life in Canada.

Hilda Maude Mleczko found that coming from England with a strong British accent made it difficult to fit in. She was living in Cape Breton:

Adjustment to my surroundings here came slowly. It took me years because I was an adult when I came to Canada and was already set in my ways. Striving to become a real Caper (Cape Bretoner) and talk like they did seemed to be an impossible task for me. Try as I might, my Limey accent always tripped me up. Also, there were so many expressions I had to drop and train myself not to use, replacing them with good old-fashioned Maritime terminology. Pavements became sidewalks, lifts gave way to elevators, trousers had to become pants, and so on. But the expression that got me into the most trouble was "knocked up." Now, in England that is an innocent phrase that means to wake up.

I remember one time my husband had to go to Halifax and told me he possibly wouldn't be back until the next afternoon. Instead, he arrived back home at 3:00 AM, when I was fast asleep, and awoke me by rapping on the window for me to let him in. The next day a neighbour asked, "What did you think of your husband coming home at that time?" I retorted, "How would you like it if your man came knocking you up at three o'clock in the morning!" Poor woman — I'd given her a cup of tea and she was so startled by my reply she dropped it in her lap!

The transition was even more radical for those who had married native people. Mary Anna Thomas moved from Monifieth, Scotland, to an Indian reserve in Saskatchewan. She says that she had no idea what to expect for herself or her two young children, and that the white community had even more difficulty accepting her than the native people did:

Acceptance by neighbours on the reserve did not come easily because some were resentful that my husband had chosen to marry a "moonias," a white person, instead of one of his own kind and, worse still, someone from another country. Relatives were less of a problem.

My efforts at friendliness were often spurned, but I persisted anyway. After our older son started school on the reserve, things seemed to improve because we became more involved in social activities. But the restrictions which we were obliged to endure irked me, as I had never before been bound by such pettiness, and

173

resented it. One example was if my husband wanted to sell a load of wood or a load of hay, he had to obtain a permit from the farm instructor (a white man), and if it was denied there was nothing that he could do about it. Since such sales were a boost to or sometimes our only source of income, agreement was essential. Then, if a farmer such as my husband wanted to kill one of his own animals for his own use, again he had to obtain a permit.

Living conditions were very primitive—no water on tap, a stove which had to be fed continually with wood, and coal-oil lamps to see by, as well as an outside biffy. Roads were merely trails. Coming from a home with lots of space, indoor plumbing, and electricity, it was a marked change. We travelled to the local village once a week for groceries and mail. Having been used to easy access of travel by bus or train, it was quite an experience to travel by wagon or buggy, and in the winter by sleigh or cutter.

One of the happier times on the reserve was visiting at the New Year. Indians recognize the New Year holiday more so than Christmas, and it was the custom to travel around from house to house. At each house where a stop was made, we were expected to eat, so after a time one learned to take small helpings. A traditional dish served was boulettes, very tasty and resembling meatballs.

We attended powwows and picnics, joining in the fun and giving a helping hand where necessary. At first, the beating drums and chanting sent shivers up and down my spine and gave me an eerie feeling.

Marie Bourassa was only seventeen when she married Red after a whirlwind courtship in Glasgow. Through a misunderstanding, she thought that he would soon get leave in Canada, so she set out for Radville, Saskatchewan, in March 1945, hoping to meet him there. When, shortly after her arrival, she found out that Red was back in Scotland, Marie left her in-laws, but then had serious questions about living alone in this strange new land:

What was I doing here anyway? I had only known Red for two months when we got married! I thought we were going to be together. Instead of that, we not only missed being together in Scotland, but I hadn't heard from him since. The only reason I knew I was married, and had been for almost two years, was the wedding ring on my finger. Maybe what I should do, I thought, was go back to Scotland! I tried to find a way to book a passage on a ship, but I was told that civilian travel was not allowed during the hostilities. Even though the war was over in Europe, it was still going on with Japan.

I was not going to be outdone. I was going to get home one way or another. I went by train, not knowing where to go. I thought the best place would be where I had arrived in this country — Halifax. I met some merchant seamen in a restaurant, and it turned out that two of these fellows were old shipmates of my Uncle Danny! That seemed to be the turning point for me. Suddenly, I didn't feel so alone. I felt hopeful. They were full of excitement when they explained they had a plan. Buying my passage was out, but there was another way if I was willing to take a chance. If I was caught it would mean trouble and they would say they didn't know me. I agreed to go along with their plan. Anything, I figured, so long as it takes me back to Red. The plan was that I would meet them the next morning at eight. I was to bring my suitcase with me, ready to board ship. I was to dress in slacks and a blouse, and wear a turban.

I got up early and met my friends. Only then did I find out why I was to dress the way I did. One of the fellows took my suitcase and handed me a scrubbing pail with cloths, brushes, etc. This, they informed me, was how I was going to get on board ship, as a cleaner. Once on board, I was to mingle with the other six hundred plus evacuee children that were returning home and nobody would even notice. How right they were!

No one even glanced at me. I kept waiting for a hand to pounce on my shoulder and crumble all my hopes, but nothing happened. I was on board the SS *Louis Pasteur* and we were heading for England. The next five days were comforting. Each day I was getting closer to Britain. I had made it, and there was no turning back! My friends had made arrangements to hide me in comfortable quarters. They saw to it that I received adequate nourishment on a regular basis, and during the day I ventured on deck and mingled with the other passengers.

We arrived at Southampton. Two of my seamen friends were going on leave and would be taking the train with me. This, I was to find out, was where I needed their help again. I did not have a train ticket to surrender at London. It was easy enough to hide from the ticket inspector on the train. I just had to stay in the lavatory until he passed that part of the train. I needn't have worried, because one of my seamen friends went ahead of us on arrival and purchased two platform tickets. He then came back and gave me one.

I left London that night for Glasgow, arriving the next morning. I made my way to my home, where I surprised the whole family. I was inundated with questions. Where had I come from? Where had I been? What was I doing here anyway? Then they hit me with it: "Don't you know Red is on his way to Canada? He left a couple of days ago."

In the weeks ahead, I was to discover how foolish I had been and realized that my actions were not only foolhardy but showed a remarkable immaturity on my part. I began to despair. What money I had was gone. I was living with my parents, sharing their food rations. I had no ration book of my own, as this had been surrendered to the authorities before going to Canada. My parents were even supplying me with my cigarettes. I had no identity card, therefore was unable to look for work. I felt as if my life had come to an end. I was here, and my husband was in Canada. And so it was with these thoughts running through my brain I wrote to Red and told him to get a divorce. It looked as if we would never see each other again.

We were now into December and the food rations weren't stretching any further. It was hard enough trying to cope on what each person was allowed, but rations for five feeding six was just not right. I tried once more at the food office and was told to "hop it." This, I felt, was the end of the road. I guess I wasn't thinking too clearly and so in frustration I went to the newspaper — I was hoping to get a ration book out of it. Other newspapers were quick to pick up on this information. Glaring headlines told of how this "slip of a girl" could evade the great British security system, and during wartime at that! How many trained enemy personnel had been able to breach our shores? What a can of worms I had opened!

Finally, in February, I sailed on the SS *Mauretania* looking after a ten-month-old baby whose mother had died under tragic circumstances. Before I knew it, I could see those same bleak shores of Halifax, but this time they were gorgeous, just bloody gorgeous. I felt like kissing the ground. I was finally on the right side of the ocean. Eventually, I reached the familiar open and flat spaces of Saskatchewan, and before I knew it the train was pulling into the Regina station.

All of a sudden it hit me. Would Red recognize me? Would I recognize him? After all, it had been two and a half years since we had seen each other. As I stepped off the train there he was, but he was different. I ran into his open arms. Reporters were there also, wanting a story. Here we were, two and a half years late, but finally on our honeymoon!

Our life has not been a bed of roses; it's had lots of ups and downs. But we've had each other and, no matter what, I'd do it all over again.

When Olive Warner arrived in Toronto, she felt that so much was new and exciting. She had left her home in the village of Mile End, Essex, and was fascinated by what she discovered:

The popcorn vendors on the streets, the ice man that came with chunks of ice to put inside that wonderful invention, the ice box.

The baseball games were wonderful. Just to hear the people cheer the players on (not done at a cricket match) and to see those strange-looking knickers that they wore. We thought baseball was like rounders and, when a player hit the ball out of the field and ran around the bases and then stopped, my friend yelled, "Run around again!" She was mortified when everyone just stared at her, and someone explained that you don't do that in baseball.

A war bride from Jamaica, Eileen M. Barkwell, remembers some of the suspicion that awaited her in Canada:

We married, had a honeymoon on the north coast of Jamaica, and I came to Canada and left Jack down there. I had met his people and stayed with them before I was married, but I got the third degree from one of his sisters. Even after he came back, they were none too warm.

After living in this small village of Campbellcroft, Ontario, I have since found out just what the trouble was. They did not know who my father was! These small villages do not like their kids marrying someone they know nothing about and would rather they married a girl from the village, or the next one at a pinch. They never stopped to think that we did not know them either until we got there. The Canadian women accused us of stealing their men and having our way paid to get here . . . with their taxes yet!

It was quite a change from a more or less even climate in England and a hotter than ever one in Jamaica, but at least there we had servants who did our work in the house for us. My mother arrived from Jamaica to see the winter, dressed in her summer clothes!

Had I the means, I would have gone back to England, where I was born, but also with three children who could not be taken out of Canada it was impossible.

For Winifred M. Pope, coming to a village of only four hundred people, in the Canadian bush, was a terrible culture shock after living in Brighton:

My in-laws were kind enough to me and did the best they could in their own way, but they were very unemotional, and I found it hard to communicate with them. This was hard to adapt to after coming from a fairly gregarious family of seven. Those first months in Canada are very hazy. Such a terrible sense of unreality overwhelmed me, and when I was alone in those early years I'm sure I cried enough tears to sink the *Queen Mary*. When I learned that my mother had suffered a very bad nervous breakdown after we left, it added to my grief. My daughter was just over two years old, but I talked to her as if she were grown. She was my companion and sounding board—a special bond still exists between us today.

Irene Turner had a wonderful reunion with her husband John, having eagerly awaited his return from Europe. But soon she felt a distinct change in the attitude of her mother-in-law:

She resented us going off together. After three weeks of this, she broke down and told me how jealous she was of the time I spent with her son after his absence of five and a half years. We sorted it out together, however, and finally got back to our good relationship.

When Marjorie Whitworth arrived in Toronto, she was fortunate enough to find that a local war brides' club had been formed:

We met monthly in our homes and tried to outdo each other with the refreshments: sausage rolls, Eccles cakes, lemon curd tarts, pickled onions, and, of course, every variation of trifle! Our meetings were terrific bitching sessions, a great place to let off steam. There were over twenty of us and only one girl went back to England. Those girls became the sisters I never had.

As Wynne Brink sped across Canada on her way to Sylvan Lake, Alberta, she was fascinated by the large cars and attractively painted wooden houses. For her, adjustment to Canadian ways was not easy, but she was determined to succeed:

I realize now how fortunate we war brides were. We arrived in Sylvan Lake complete strangers, not only to each other but to the whole community, yet we were never made to feel like outsiders. Everyone was very friendly and went out of their way to make us feel a part of the community. We formed a war brides' club and would meet in each other's homes once a week, to talk, laugh, and compare experiences we were living through. We were all terribly homesick, and it helped tremendously to go through this together. Some of the girls have remained my best friends to this day.

Reflecting back, the first year was the hardest. There was so much to learn and a great deal of adapting to do. None of it came easy, but we were helped along by humour. A sense of humour and laughter can sure help when the going is rough.

I began to realize that I would never be able to completely become Canadian until I stopped comparing England to Canada and vice versa. I had been converting dollars into pounds and pence in my head to get a better idea as to the value of things. I had one foot in Canada and one foot in England, and this would never do. I wanted to become 100 percent Canadian, so slowly but surely I began to shuck off my English ways and began to think Canadian.

It didn't happen overnight and one can never forget the country of one's birth or one's upbringing. I loved England, still do, but after eight years I returned home to England with my son for a visit. It was wonderful, glorious, to be home with Mum and Dad, but this time I was homesick for Canada. It was then I realized I had become a Canadian and longed to return to my husband and home.

Miem Gordon was living in Wychen, Holland, in her family's hotel when the Germans occupied it in 1940. Four years later, the Canadians arrived and Jack Gordon stole her heart. As Jack's wife, she eventually settled in Vermilion Bay in northern Ontario:

My command of the English language was passable, as I took it in school like most Europeans. However, with four new lady acquaintances of Canadian heritage, we ventured to the pub. As the first four rounds were purchased by the ladies, it was my turn. I made the statement, "Dutch treat." They all looked shocked and then laughed. They explained with ear-to-ear smiles that the Canadian term *Dutch treat* meant for all to buy their own. I sheepishly paid for the beers.

On my first New Year's in Canada, Jack was to pick me up after work at eight o'clock and we were to go dancing. I was looking forward to the night out very much. At 6:00 PM — midnight Holland time — I felt lonesome. We had a shelf in our shack and on it were pictures of my relatives. I started to toast my mom, dad, brothers and sisters and, of course, assorted relatives. By the time Jack arrived . . . well, perhaps I shouldn't say anything further. Jack went out with his buddies and I missed my first New Year's Eve dance in Canada. For everyone's information, I have never missed one since.

Even though Gwen Wakeford was not a member of the Red Cross at the time, she was pressed into service to help the war brides in the Oshawa and Whitby areas settle in. One Dutch war bride in particular was fortunate to meet her, as she describes:

I was in a local store when I noticed a young woman, Rita, trying to explain what she wanted. She was speaking in a foreign language, which I took to be Flemish. I phoned another war bride, also from Holland, and got Rita to talk to her. The look on this girl's face when she heard her own language was ecstatic. Her new friend arranged for English lessons, I got her a job at General Motors, and she quickly adapted to her new lifestyle.

As a schoolgirl, Stella Chudleigh had wondered what life would be like on the Canadian prairies. In March 1946, in Brooks, Alberta, she began to find out:

I soon settled into life there, in spite of no electricity, gas, or plumbing of any kind. Rufus had explained how everything was in great detail, so there were few surprises. That first summer I had to learn from my mother-in-law how to wash clothes on a scrub-board, clean coal-oil lamps, separate the cream, churn the butter, cook on a coal and wood stove, iron with a sad-iron, can dozens and dozens of jars of fruit and vegetables, and cook for the hay crews and threshing crews.

Mom treated me just like another daughter and was very patient with the "green" twenty-two-year-old English girl who had been born and raised in town. The neighbours also accepted me as one of them and showed typical western hospitality in so many ways, being very supportive and kind.

Gladys Ludwig remembers that her trip to Kitchener was very unpleasant, though she greatly enjoyed seeing all the city lights after the years of blackouts. But she missed her close-knit family:

My mother-in-law was very kind and understanding, but I was so terribly homesick for my family and home. We had all been through so much together and then the wonderful time we had with the parties in the street when the war ended with Germany.

I was feeling so down I finally decided to ask the Red Cross to help me get back to England. But when I got to their office they were closed for the summer!

For Constance Chippure, the distance from Rotterdam to Barry's Bay, Ontario, was measured in more than miles:

In Rotterdam we had a large home with two bathrooms and hot and cold water in all four bedrooms. I arrived in this little town of twelve hundred people. My in-laws were nice, but treated me as if I were a person from another planet! How many times I wished I could go back to my easy life, but my husband was good to me and I loved him.

My husband worked in town every day and I was left in the woods, not another house close by. I learned to bake bread in the wood stove, but I buried a lot of loaves in the ground before my husband came home! They turned out rock hard. I burned a lot of meals on that wood stove, too. I had never cooked at home, as we had had a live-in maid. So I really learned the hard way!

When Peggy Ward Souliere spotted her husband at Ottawa's Union Station, she "was off like a shot"—and forgot her luggage. Fortunately, it was given to the Red Cross, so she was able to retrieve it the next day. Peggy was much less happy, however, when she found that cultural differences were to be a real problem:

It wasn't many days after arriving that I realized that I wasn't very welcome with my father-in-law or his family. I was not being accepted because they were French and I was English; they were Catholic and I was Protestant.

Through the years we've had our ups and downs just like anyone else, but with my husband being French and I English, there's been some clashes, I can tell you. But it's all come out in the wash, as my old mum used to say.

Edna Squarok says, "After being with approximately fifteen hundred women for eleven days on the Aquitania, *I didn't care if I never saw another woman for weeks!" She describes her experiences in coming to an entirely new culture:*

I had never been told that my parents-in-law came from the Ukraine or that my mother-in-law couldn't speak English. What shocks I was in for! The women sat in the living room and the men in the kitchen. At church I was guided to the opposite side of the room with the other women. No one seemed able to explain why men and women did not sit together. It just wasn't done.

Every Sunday after we got our own farm, we visited my parents-in-law. With no radio, TV, or newspapers, and I not understanding their language, I had a very difficult time adjusting. My father-in-law always spoke to me in broken English, which helped a little. I even found their sense of humour different.

In our small one-street town there were two grocery stores, and I had trouble making myself understood. When I asked for a block of salt—expecting a small 1 lb. block of cooking salt—I thought it funny to be asked if I wanted red, white, or blue. I had no idea Canadians were so patriotic as to have salt the colour of our flag and started laughing. I laughed even more when the girl staggered out of the storeroom with a 50 lb. block, thinking I would have to have a family of twenty to use that up. Someone then explained it was cattle salt!

Beryl Haines Ward received a wonderful welcome from her husband Archie and his family when she arrived in Ottawa. But like most other war brides, she was in for a certain amount of culture shock:

For the first few weeks it seemed to be one long tea party. Everyone wanted to meet Archie's English wife. Gifts were brought, compliments given. Many times the remark was made that I sounded just like our queen! These people were also generous of spirit and most forgiving. I pulled the worst boners. I smoked and it didn't occur to me that others didn't. At the first tea party I automatically handed my cigarettes around. Everyone smiled gently and refused. My smoke seemed to billow and filled the room. I heard my dear

Mummy Ward muttering, "It was the war, you know. She was in the army." Much nodding of heads as if I were afflicted.

On another occasion we were leaving a party and I had a good idea. I said, "Why don't we all go to the pub?" There was a stunned silence. This was Ottawa 1946. My dear Archie said, "We don't go to pubs, darling." Oops, another one!

I also had to get used to the language. I requested two reels of white cotton and the delivery man arrived carrying two bolts of cotton cloth! Also on the order were two cards of press-studs and the clerk wrote that they didn't stock that item. Just try asking for the haberdashery department! Blank stares. My mother-in-law sent me upstairs for a comforter and I came down with a hot-water bottle. Try asking the butcher for a joint! Thank goodness it was before pot was generally known! I noticed mail boxes at the end of the lanes in the country. I asked my father-in-law what happened if one needed more than one loaf of bread! During my first pregnancy, I asked a mother of two how she washed her nappies. She looked puzzled then answered that she washed them in the sink with the dishes, like everybody else did!

There was, however, a dark side to all this. I was never homesick, because I had been conditioned through school and the years in the army. However, I was lonely for the lifestyle I had left behind me. Ottawa was a dreadfully dull city then, a civil servants' town. We wore stockings, hats, and gloves to go to the Bytown market on Saturdays. I baulked, of course, but the rules were rigid. When the fall clothes came out, the light (especially white) clothes had to be put away. No one, except the businessmen, went into the city during the summer. "The city's just full of tourists, dear." Men and women were kept very separate. Ladies did or didn't do this; men did this but not that.

I met with bigotry, which I had never before encountered. My friends had always been a mix; my family had entertained all sorts during the war, including blacks. In Ottawa I was told that being an Anglican was almost being a "dogan." I was told never to buy raffle tickets from the Roman Catholic children who came to the door; that they were taught to cheat and lie, then confess on Sundays! We had some dandy "discussions." I couldn't believe such bigotry.

I received my own share of prejudice. Archie came back to his home town and his old friends. They thought I had taken this man away from this own countrywomen. As with World War I, the young women were left at home to wait, only to have their boys snatched up by the British girls! It was also made clear that the North Americans had *suffered* as well. They, too, were rationed!

Squibs Mercier was widowed at nineteen, when her first husband was killed in action in Italy. Her second husband was a Canadian airman, and she arrived in a small Quebec town, determined to try her hardest to fit in:

It was getting close to Christmas time and we were invited to the cousin's for dinner. On arriving, I followed the ladies upstairs to leave our coats. However, being observant and anxious to learn about this new culture, I noticed that they were also removing their panties and stuffing them down the arms of their coats! I hesitated at this weird custom, but when in Rome . . . I told myself, and did likewise (though I did reflect that my dear mother would not have approved). Regardless, I ventured down the stairs very carefully. I did not have an opportunity to question my husband about this procedure, nor did I wish to chance another ridicule (like over the shower) by asking the ladies, so mum was the word. Later on the local priest arrived, and I had to restrain a giggle as I looked at his stern face and thought of all us ladies sitting around with no knickers on! The evening ended without incident, and we returned to collect our coats and retrieve our panties. It wasn't until later that I discovered that they had been wearing snuggies and had removed this outer garment when I thought they were removing their panties!

I soon discovered that life in this town was not my cup of tea. The language barrier need not have been a barrier at all if only the hospitality of the townfolk had been evident and forthcoming. Their main concern on being introduced was to inquire about my religion, and it was their core of conversation. Did they not realize that there is one God and how we approach Him is personal? This attitude was so foreign and cold in comparison to my own dear mother's way of welcoming strangers.

This town had little respect or affection towards veterans, and I later discovered they had opposed conscription and had harboured anyone wishing to avoid enlisting. We moved on gladly to Winnipeg, a great cosmopolitan city with a heart that welcomed all comers.

Even though Alice Barrett has been widowed for twenty-two years, she fondly remembers how her husband Bill joked with her:

Every time we had an argument, my husband would say, "Get in a boat and start rowing!" One year he gave me a rowboat for Mother's Day!

Although Doreen Murray suffered from seasickness on her way to Canada, she was in for much worse after she arrived in Saskatchewan:

I became very ill and was given twelve hours to live. I had emergency surgery, lost eight feet of my intestines, then a week later lost my baby as a result of the surgery. I spent a month in the hospital and was very weak, but this didn't sit very well with my in-laws, who wrote to my parents in England saying that I was no good as a farmer's wife. I wasn't very welcome.

Several incidents came about and I was so scared that when I broke a plate, I ran outside and hid it under a granary, where it was found many, many years later.

My mother-in-law passed away in 1948 and I had to look after my father-in-law, and that took eighteen years of our married life. It was a nightmare.

Irene Murray walked into a nightmare from the moment she landed at Pier 21 in Halifax. She had left her home in Forres, Scotland, and brought her son to what she hoped would be a better life. She had a long wait for happiness to come her way:

My first few hours in Canada weren't so exciting, as my husband who I hadn't seen for well over a year acted silly and not a bit loving after all this time. I thought, Why did I ever leave home?

We had to catch the train to the Annapolis Valley and got to my husband's home around two o'clock in the morning. My husband's only relatives were his mother and brother. His mother was so pitiful, and his brother was too.

Well, I had to make the best of it as there I was in another country with no one to turn to. I will never forget the first few days. I was told my husband had never been any good and now since he was back home all he did was drink. He was stationed in Halifax with the army and, after a few days of quarrelling, he returned to Halifax and only came home for the odd weekend.

I met a lot of nice people in the community where I was living. I guess they were as anxious as I was to see what I was like. After meeting my son and I, they were anxious to make us feel at home. They gave me a lovely shower and were so nice. But as I hadn't much money, I had to take a housekeeping job so I could have my son with me. I worked for four dollars and our keep for ten months. By this time my husband wasn't coming home any more, so in March 1947 I went to court to see if he would have to pay for our son's keep. He was supposed to pay eight dollars a week, which he did for six months, but then he went to Ontario and stopped paying. There was no family allowance or welfare then, so I had to keep working in different places to stay alive. My family wanted me to come home, but I said I had come all this way to see Canada and now I would see what I could do to make ends meet.

We kept going and at last things looked brighter. I got to know a lot of nice Canadians and they felt so sorry for us they got me a nice job in a forces base, where I got good money as a waitress. I enjoyed this work very much and was able to start living again. I met a nice Canadian man who adored my son and, of course, myself. After going out for about twelve years with him, my lawyer got hold of my husband and he consented to a divorce if we would pay for it and say we committed adultery, which we had to do if we wanted to get married. This we did in October 1961, which was the happiest moment of my life since landing in Canada in 1946.

It was quite a shock for Joan Buan when she arrived in the middle of nowhere in northern Alberta. She was fortunate to have a won-

derful mother-in-law, but sometimes the attitude of the people in the little town of Spirit River was hard to take. All too often she heard the familiar line that most immigrants have heard during their time in Canada: "Well, why don't you go back to where you came from?"

For those who had left loving parents only to find themselves living with an abusive husband, the pain was all too apparent. Peggie says she was "all gung-ho" about starting a new life in Guelph, Ontario. But the reality of her situation soon changed her attitude:

When you talk to war brides, there is lots of tragedy. I was talking to one whose husband committed suicide. There are horror stories. I really haven't met anyone that was happy, not really. None of the marriages, I don't think, has been successful.

Alcohol became a big factor in my marriage. He drank in Britain, but I didn't recognize it. It wasn't just that; he had a mental problem which led to a series of shock treatments and then he had to have a lobotomy. Our marriage ended with that—it subsequently ended in divorce. It was tragic, because he distrusted me with anything or anybody. We went to several psychiatrists, who said he could have been born with this condition; I don't really think it was caused by the war.

When Phyllis McKenzie left her father at the Southampton dock, he said, "Now, my girl, you're of good bulldog stock. Give it a good try, but if it's too tough I'll bring you home again." Well, it did prove to be extremely difficult for Phyllis, but she was determined to stick it out. First, there was the problem of her husband's health:

It was not good and he had major surgery for ulcers. His nerves were shot due to shelling and bombing in Europe. So eventually he sought solace from the bottle and then everything started to deteriorate. I endured abuse but still felt I had to hang in there because of my family. My mental and physical health went downhill through the years. Upon the birth of my seventh child I felt I couldn't manage to raise her in the present situation so, consequently, she was adopted by a childless couple.

I finally got a separation, feeling very guilty, of course. My irate husband caught up with me and I was attacked with a knife. I survived another crisis, and he was jailed for four months. But he saw the error of his ways and stayed reasonably sober for two or three years. Suddenly, he was taken very ill with cancer and cirrhosis of the liver, and I took care of him until he died. He finally apologized for what they said he did to me, but he was not able to remember any of the incidents.

Phyllis says that her life has turned around since then. She now enjoys a very fulfilling life and works on a committee that helps women and children who have been victims of abuse.

When Grace Gough's husband met her at the train station in Verdun, Quebec, and saw his daughter for the first time, their marriage seemed full of promise. But things did not look so promising when Grace entered the house where they were to stay:

It was very, very shabby. After a few days I was to learn we had lice, cockroaches, and rats. In this house lived my husband, myself, our baby, his mother, his two brothers, three children of theirs, and another two sisters, amounting to eleven folk in total. I was devastated and unhappy. My husband had a drinking problem (as did many other returning veterans). There were lots of fights, heartaches and kids. By the time I was twenty-one years old I had had four children (one had died), very little money, and no way to get home to England. That's when I got involved in a religious cult. From that time on I was entrapped in more problems!

Jessie Parcels was taken aback when she visited her in-laws in Campbellford, Ontario, and was shown where she and her husband George were expected to sleep:

It was in a woodshed with just a bed, dirty laundry, and rats! Before I left, the family wanted my money for board. George had sent money home to be kept for us, but it was gone. My trunks had been delivered there. My sister-in-law was wearing my going-away outfit, and it was absolutely ruined with stains. My white kid gloves were gone, never to be seen again.

We moved into our own house, but I used to have to wade through the snow to cook Christmas dinner at my in-laws' house. The last Christmas I did it was in 1948, when there wasn't even a scrap left for me to eat. So I walked home, cooked my own Christmas meal, and never did it for them again.

Audrey Roberts's experience in settling down to married life in Kitchener is another unfortunate reminder that not all war brides stepped into a happy new life:

In due course I became pregnant and thought all my dreams had been realized. Sadly, the dream was shattered when I miscarried and had to be hospitalized. I think this was one of the saddest and loneliest times of my life. The one person that I had counted on was not there for me, and my family were thousands of miles away.

Still determined to have a family of my own, I became pregnant in 1949 and became the happy mother of a baby girl. It seemed, on looking back, that it was when I had to stop working and the charming, happy-go-lucky person I had married was faced with the responsibilities that things began to go wrong.

Unfortunately, things went from bad to worse and after eighteen years of marriage we were divorced. In all those years I kept my problems to myself, thinking that perhaps it would cause nothing but grief to my family so many miles away. I was to learn later that they were aware that things weren't as they should have been, but because I was too proud to admit to any problems they felt they had to keep their own counsel. How silly I was!

When Phyllis La Rocque first came to join her French-Canadian husband in Windsor, Ontario, she, too, found the going rather rough:

My husband's mother and sister were great to me, but the cousins and aunts were not. They would only speak French, even though they could speak English, and wanted to know why he had married "a goddam Limey" when there were plenty of Canadian girls. My husband used to get so mad we hardly went to their houses after that. But I found that most Canadians were fine, although when they asked you if you were bombed over there, they never seemed to believe you.

Liliane Rayen could not speak English when she first met her future husband after the liberation of Belgium. After their marriage, she arrived at his small town near Saint John, New Brunswick, not knowing what to expect and used to a comfortable life in a big city:

I was almost in tears. My mother-in-law didn't welcome me very well. I was her second daughter-in-law who was a war bride. Inside the house it was dirty and very run down, no running water, no toilet. I cried every night for three weeks, but stayed and hoped we could improve our way of life.

It didn't happen. My husband was lazy. We then went to live in London, England, but we were only there a year when my husband wanted to come back to Canada. He had expected to have the same fun he had had there during the war. By then we had a fifteen-month-old daughter.

When we came back to Canada, we lived in Toronto in a furnished room. We moved a lot and finally had three children. Eight years later our marriage came to an end. I had been to a lawyer for advice, and when I came home he beat me up so bad I had to stay in the hospital for three days. I would not put up with that and I pressed charges. We were divorced after twenty-two years of marriage. I have remarried and am very happy now.

The downward trend of Jenny Moyaerts's life began the day she met her future husband while working at the Maison du Canada in Brussels. She became pregnant by him, and he insisted she keep the baby and marry him. When she travelled to Winnipeg to join him after the war, she was informed that he had moved to Vancouver. There, her welcome was less than enthusiastic. Then the real heartache began:

I opened one drawer, pushed aside some of his socks, and saw an open letter addressed to him. I hesitated (forgive me—normally, I am very much against indiscretion) and read it. It was a love letter, signed by a woman. The women we shared the apartment with said she was a divorced Russian woman who worked as a saleswoman in a big department store.

I found the store, and there he stood, smiling and talking with her! I looked at them quite a while, I remember. I left and walked and walked. I stopped on a large bridge and looked down at that new sight for me—hundreds of logs floating in the river. It fascinated me more and more, and the idea came to me to jump over the rail with my baby. There was nobody around; everything was strangely quiet. What prevented me from jumping I'll never know.

Although I had delayed telling my mother what was happening, now I had to. Of course, she insisted I should go back to Belgium. My husband's family said I could stay at their place for ever and wished it, especially his mother, who was very religious and hoped her son would come back to all of us. His father, however, had told his son never to come back again.

I did return to Belgium. At the train station, one of my brothers-in-law said to the others, "I will never forgive him." I remarried in Belgium, to a friend of my brother's. He said he would make me happy, also my child. But he didn't; they all get jealous. My son suffered, and at the age of eighteen he asked me if he could leave me and go back to Canada.

I have been alone for nine years. Finally, I wished to close that distance between us and came over here, close to my son. I arrived last October but find it hard, and I am lonesome. But it does not matter any more. It is late.

7

"Our Husbands — God Bless 'Em"

*T*HEY WERE JUST BOYS. *Most of them had never been away from the area of their birth, and the call to arms had offered them an opportunity to see the world and enjoy life to the full. They had left the Canadian farms and cities far behind and were now on their own. Some who had kissed the girls goodbye with a promise to return to waiting arms were about to break that promise.*

Joe Hetherington left Old Wives, near Moose Jaw, and went overseas with the army in 1941. He says, "It was my first time more than forty miles from home. I'd been forty miles from home once on horseback":

I met my future wife, Audrey, in 1943 at a dance. I took her and her mother home. I was so well loaded that I didn't know until one of the guys said, "You know you made a date with that lady."

LeVerne Haley was a farm boy who had never been away from home when he joined the Royal Canadian Air Force in 1942. All that changed when he went overseas in 1944:

The last base I was stationed at before joining my crew at Dalton, Yorkshire, was St. Athan in Wales, where we trained on advanced types of planes. I was granted ten days' leave before I reported to the next station, so I decided to go to Belfast, Northern Ireland, and arrived there on 6 May 1945.

Of course, 8 May was the celebration of Victory in Europe Day. There was a gathering of thousands of people at the city hall square, so I decided to go. A Belfast native standing beside me saw the Canada flashes on my shoulder and the pilot's wings on my chest and started talking to me. He asked if I knew anyone in Belfast and when I replied in the negative he looked around and said, "There are a couple of nice-looking girls all alone." So he dragged me over to them, spoke to them, asked their names and my name and said, "Now you are introduced and it's all up to you."

I guess the girls, particularly Rita, felt sorry for me, so after we heard Mr. Churchill's speech, they led me around the streets of Belfast and we ended up at the church where there was a service of thanksgiving, so the evening passed quickly. The rest of the week was a holiday off work, so I met Rita on several occasions. My leave was extended, so we got to know each other well before I was required to report back to my base.

We carried on frequent, almost daily, correspondence after we separated. I carried on with training and was finally posted with my crew to a place called East Moor in Yorkshire in late July. My correspondence with Rita was getting serious and rumours of eastern postings were flying about, so I decided I had better inquire whether there might be a chance for us to marry before the year end.

My commanding officer said if we wanted to get married he would grant leave but I had to be back on base by 28 August to go to the Far East. They placed a call from the CO's office to Rita at work. All I could say was, "Can you marry me in two weeks?" She was speechless at first, but did manage to say yes. Then the CO said to her that if she had any problems we could solve them. Rita said, "I have no coupons for a wedding dress." He said, "Can you make a dress from silk?" to which she said yes. Then the CO phoned stores and told them to write off a parachute from stock and bring it to the office. By the time the adjutant had drawn up all the necessary papers for leave and the wedding, the parachute was there. The CO handed it to me, along with all the documentation, and said, "Here is the wedding dress. Good luck. See you on 28 August. Now get out of here and let me get back to work."

I was in Belfast ten hours later. The wedding gown got made, the church got booked, a wedding trip was booked, invitations were sent, and the wedding took place on 23 August 1945. In the meantime, hardly noticed by us, the atomic bomb exploded over Hiroshima and Japan surrendered, so it was a happy wedding. The minister, a close friend of the bride's family, read the following:

The Maple Leaf has stolen the Shamrock away
We wish them joy on their wedding day.
A peaceful journey to the end of this life
Free from trouble, free from strife.
When the Shamrock reaches the land of wheat
May friendly hands be stretched out to greet
The bit of Ireland we gave away
On August 23rd, that memorable day.

Because the war was over, we honeymooned in Dublin, and I proudly wore my RCAF uniform as I escorted my new wife to church that first Sunday of our wedded life. The minister greeted us at the door and heard our story. He asked us for the names of our favourite hymns, and the congregation of that packed church sang them for us as the minister spoke of Canada, the air force, and our marriage. I never felt so humble and choked up with emotion in my life.

LeVerne continues his story in June 1984, after Rita had been diagnosed as having inoperable cancer:

She passed quietly out of this life in her own bed in the house we had lived in for thirty-eight years so happily. So I thank God for what He gave me. I offered my life for my country, but He gave me a lifetime of happiness instead.

When Doug Elliott went overseas, he fully intended to marry the Canadian girl he had become engaged to in Stratford, Ontario. But on his first leave in England, he and a buddy went up to London, and a chance meeting changed his life:

A gentleman with a bowler hat and an umbrella on his arm asked us if he could help us. We said we were looking for someplace to eat. He said, "I'll call my wife to see if you can come home for tea." We did. After a short time, two pretty little English gals came home from work — my future wife Irene and her sister Meg. We took them out to the pub for a drink after tea.

Almost a year later, our company was having a final medical before D-Day. I was dropped from category A1 to F4 and scheduled for return to Canada. It's awful what a pretty little English gal can do to a six-foot, tough Canadian soldier! I had decided Irene was the gal for me some time before. I had terminated my Stratford engagement and Irene did the same with the RAF airman she was engaged to. One day my CO called me in to say if I was going to get married I had to do it right away, as I would be going home very soon. We were married on 8 April 1944.

John Brock has the unique distinction and very special honour of being declared an honorary war bride, on account of his generous help in establishing war brides' associations across Canada, which he did with his wife Gloria. When he first met Gloria, he was not yet nineteen:

We were pretty young. I guess that's the way it works out when one meets somebody they like, that they strike up a nice companionship. I was sent over to the Continent just before we were to get married. So the first thing I had to do was go to my padre over there and ask him to get me a special leave to fly back to England. He did, and on 26 May 1945 we got married and went to Aberdeen for our honeymoon. Of course, I had to go back to Europe again and take up where I had left off with the war.

It was natural to be concerned about whether or not she'd like life in Canada. You hope she'd enjoy coming, but you have to think of what she was leaving as well. I've said this time and time again, and I always jack myself up by thinking, now this lady left her home in a huge city in another country and came to the open prairies to a farm. It was totally different; you can't compare them — not the people, not the land, not the country. Yet we asked the war brides to do this and they did. So, therefore, you have a feeling that, in that sense, they did a lot for you. I check myself up once in a while and think, well, this lady did this for me. I often think of that.

Commitment is the word. It bound us together. You think, now what has this lady done for me? It is a very binding thing. It always struck me that it couldn't be any more different than coming from another country, from a huge city to a wide-open prairie onto a farm. She wasn't used to working around animals or any of that, and she had to get used to it, which she did.

Part of what made it harder for Gloria was that I was still overseas when she came over. So she came here and had to be met by total strangers. That was another thing she went through that made our commitment more binding. She had to get along as best as she could until I came back.

Like John, Les Cornish headed for the Continent. In Holland he met and married a young Dutch woman, Elly. He returned to Davidson, Saskatchewan, to prepare for his wife's arrival. The first line of business was to get a job:

I went back to work for the farmer I had worked for before I went overseas. He had a big house, so we took part of the house over and that gave me a home to bring Elly over to. I had to have an established household, so that worked well for us. After that year, we went to live in a little old shack on the prairie.

Russ Fletcher was just following a family tradition when he married Joan: his mother had been a war bride in World War I. He found himself in Glasgow on leave and strolled into Woolworth's to buy some souvenirs for his sisters in Canada:

Another chap and I were looking around, and all of a sudden this little girl fell over my feet! She was just like a little doll with her long ringlets, dressed to perfection. I guess she'd wandered away from her mother. Her mother got quite excited and went tearing around the store. I picked up the girl and held her in the air, and her mother saw her and was crying and all upset.

Joan was a pretty good-looking blonde. Being the nice airman that I was, I suggested we have a cup of tea. Her daughter Sylvia fell asleep on my knee, and I said to her mother, "Her dad must really be proud of her." She was a delightful little girl. Joan told me that Sylvia's dad had been killed in training when she was five months pregnant. I suggested we might go to a show one night and she accepted. I was pretty cagey. Joan was staying with her aunt at the time, and I took her aunt some flowers. We probably went out two or three times. Then, when I was going back to Manchester to meet one of my brothers, Joan came to see me off and she gave me her last egg. I'll always remember that.

Russ and Joan wrote back and forth, and then she went to London for a visit. Russ had some difficulty finding her, as the telegram company had written down the wrong address:

You know, God has a funny way of doing things—He makes you persist. I was pig-headed enough and she was good-looking enough, and there was no way that I wasn't going to find her. I slept that night in Paddington Station on a couple of big chairs and went back out looking for Joan. I finally found her.

Joan and Russ had only been out about ten times before they decided to get married, which they did in November 1946. After bringing Joan and Sylvia to Canada to live in his aunt and uncle's basement, Russ finally found them a place of their own in Calgary:

It was a garage, cut in two, not insulated, and we had to go to the basement of the adjoining house to use the bathroom. I didn't know this until a few years later, but Joan's uncle had told her that if she couldn't hack it in Canada in two years, he would see that she got home again.

I always felt bad if Joan didn't have enough money to send a little parcel home to Scotland with goodies in it for Christmas. We were really hard up one Christmas. I think we had five cents between us. We'd charged up the kid's toys—we didn't have any money to buy toys. We didn't have a turkey; we got a piece of round steak and that was our turkey. I stuck a branch off an evergreen in a can for our Christmas tree. This uncle of Joan's had sent ten dollars to Sylvia. We took the ten dollars and bought eight dollars' worth of goodies, put them in a parcel, and sent them back to her family in Scotland. Joan didn't want them to know things were that tough for us.

Russ feels that marrying someone from overseas has enriched him culturally. When he met Joan a whole new world opened for him:

Plays, theatre — and she's brought that into my life. I look at my brothers and my sister, and I find that I'm probably the richer, not meaning dollar and cents, but I know that there are more fulfilling things going on in my life than in theirs. . . . Joan gave me new life. My mother never wanted me to go to war, but had I not gone to war, I would not have got my wife or my wonderful daughter, and probably I would not have my life today.

Cal Richardson knew that Peggy was the woman for him as soon as he saw her, but it took a lot of miles before he found her:

I went all the way over to England to find the one I wanted. My brother was going with Peggy's sister, so this is where I heard about her. I started building a house of our own in Raymond, Alberta, before Peggy came over. I never had it completely finished. We had two rooms. It only had the rafters up, no roof. You could see the stars when we were in bed!

Tom Raeside was only nineteen when he met his future wife during an "excuse-me" dance at the Palais de Dance in Aldershot. Although she was only sixteen, it was love at first sight:

I loved Britain the minute I stepped off the boat—the people's sense of humour and courage during the blitz. And meeting my future wife was an added bonus. I wasn't concerned about bringing her to Canada. I knew we would weather it together. Being married to a war bride has brought so much to my life — joy, laughter, four children, fifteen grandchildren, and a wonderful bunch of in-laws in England.

While on leave from Holland, Tony Solomon met Margaret at a neighbourhood party in Glasgow. His description of their first date

— dinner at Margaret's house — reflects how much the Canadian servicemen missed a home life and how much every kindness meant to them:

When I entered Margaret's house (the first time I had been in any house in three years) I felt shy, clumsy, and a little strange. But the aroma of home cooking soon won me over. It was then I noticed a huge pile of meat bones in a dish on the cookstove. I was stunned and thought, these poor people, is this all they have to eat? I was soon reaching into my tunic for the food coupons we were issued before going on leave. I gave them to Margaret's mother, but she kept saying, "You don't have to do this. We have enough."

Soon I was sitting down to a meal that reminded me of the ones in my humble home in far-off Manitoba, where there was always good Ukrainian food in abundance: soup (Scotch broth, if I recall), mashed potatoes, meat, and vegetables. But most prominent in my memory was the custard and rhubarb pie — man, that was good! Later, when I knew them better, I told them about the bones in the dish at that first dinner, and they hooted for a while over that.

Margaret's dad was a British vet of World War I, so we swapped action stories and talked about his stint in India. We really hit it off right away. Her parents were kind almost to a fault. They had a new pair of oxfords and hand-knit dress socks for me on my next leave. What a surprise that was for me after tramping in size 10 studded clompers for five years! Maybe Margaret's sore toes had something to do with that. The kindness of the people over there will never be forgotten by us Canucks. Where else would they let all the armed forces ride free on the city buses and streetcars?

Most of the men who served overseas, wherever it was, were surprised at the welcome they were given by total strangers. George McDonald found this from the moment he landed on British soil:

One of my first impressions of England was the friendliness of the English people. They opened their houses to us young Canadian soldiers and welcomed us into their families. Some of them even gave us their daughters. I met my wife Maureen at a local dance. As I was recovering from a broken leg, it was an effort for me to dance, but one look at her and I knew the effort would be worthwhile. While I had some concerns about taking Maureen so far away from her family, I had great hopes for our future together. She has brought great joy into my life, plus seven children, so you can see it was a very productive union.

In 1985, John and Nan Ponting renewed their wedding vows in the same Birkenhead church they had been married in forty years earlier — and in the presence of the same best man and matron of honour. John remembers the lucky coincidence that brought him and Nan together during the war:

I went overseas in early 1944 as an armoured corps reinforcement officer and was subsequently posted to a reinforcement depot at Inkerman barracks just outside Woking in Surrey. Shortly after our arrival, two officer friends and I visited Staines to see the Thames and the pubs, as well as the Wrens who were stationed a short distance outside town.

We met two Wrens in a pub, and my friends took them to a dance at the town hall while I went back to our room in Staines, a little worse for wear from the British beer. During the dance, my friends arranged for a day's punting on the Thames the next day and also arranged for a companion for me. We enjoyed a good day on the water and tea in the Blue Anchor, where I took a fancy to one of the Wrens — not the Wren chosen for me. However, the Wrens had to get back to barracks and so did we, and that was the last I saw of "my" Wren until many months later. I didn't even know her name. I was quickly embroiled in training and did not visit Staines again before proceeding to Italy. My wife in Canada died in July 1944, and I was not even able to make a visit back to see my young daughter.

In April 1945, having left Italy with the Canadian Corps, I was serving with the regiment in Holland and managed to wangle a leave to England. I obtained a travel warrant to London, obtained quarters in the Maple Leaf Club, and went on the town with an infantry officer. We decided to have lunch in the Ontario Services Club and were served by the beautiful Patricia Medina, a British actress. Having eaten, we were going down the steps when I noticed two English Wrens climbing the stairs. I said to one of them, "I remember you from Staines a few months back." It was the lovely Wren I had taken a fancy to. We immediately returned to the Ontario Services Club and bought them lunch. From there, we went to a pub and then to a cinema on Leicester Square, where we saw *Tars and Spars*, then on to the Park Lane Hotel for dinner and dancing. I made arrangements to visit Staines the following weekend.

We had a lovely (but wet) weekend, during which I proposed and Nan accepted. At the time of my proposal we were sitting on a green park bench on the Thames, adjacent to the Pack Horse, with my trench coat over us to keep the rain from soaking us. The green bench was still there during our last visit in 1990, but a little worse for wear.

We were married on 2 July 1945, and I returned to Holland and was repatriated to Canada in December. Nan joined me the following May. She became an excellent mother to my daughter Lana, though becoming a stepmother was not an easy thing. She also brought up our boy and two girls and did an excellent job. Nan adapted very well to Canada and my relatives. We were able to travel through nearly all the provinces, and Nan was happy everywhere. I just wish she were with me now. My wife is an Alzheimer's patient in a nursing home. She served with the WRNS for four and a half years and with me for forty-six years. She deserves better than she has at the moment.

When serving in Britain, Phil Cottrell returned to Birmingham whenever he could, and with each visit he became closer to his cousin Doris:

It didn't take long before we were telling each other of our love. I finally got up enough nerve to ask her to marry me and, what do you know, she said yes! I used to bring my buddies with me when I would visit Doris. We sure had some good times! The pubs in England were great. Many a time we had great singalongs. My folks back in Canada were great and sent us food parcels. We sure looked forward to getting them! I used to take most of my parcel to Doris. Aunt Elsie would put most of it away, saving this precious food for the wedding. We were married on 24 July 1943.

We spent our wedding night at her brother's. This was a mistake. First of all, they rigged the bed, and the walls were paper thin. Consequently, we spent a very quiet, uneventful night. We then went to London for a week and stayed at Streatham Common. The other guests were quite "mature." Apparently, this was a safe retreat for senior citizens. We were a bit late coming down for breakfast. Talk about stares and snickers! During our honeymoon we visited the highlights of London. One day we were out walking when we were stopped by our provost. I was wearing a tie. My leave was cancelled. So I went AWOL for a couple of days. I sure paid the price when I returned — I was on latrine duty for two weeks. But it was worth it. (Three months later we were allowed to wear ties. Who can figure out the army?)

I returned to Canada in August 1945 and Doris came to me in April 1946. I'll never forget Union Station, Toronto. Her name was called out and there she was, cute in her Deanna Durbin hat and a baby in her arms.

For Paul Dumaine, a Quebecker, going to Britain presented even more than the usual challenges:

For us young French Canadians, being in England was very exciting and interesting. When I met my future wife, I had to use my hands to explain and express myself, but I learned very fast. When I arrived back in Canada, my parents did not know that I was married, so they were very surprised that I had married an English girl. And they didn't speak a word of English.

Bringing my wife to Canada was the best thing for me and my family, who love her very much. All our little nephews and nieces learned to speak English, and now they are happy about it. I love my wife very much, and there is no other woman like her. She is everything my heart desires.

Roger Robitaille was another French-Canadian serviceman who found some difficulty with the language, especially the accents, of Britain:

I could speak and understand English, although French was my native tongue, but I was not prepared for Yorkshire! I could understand Connie's aunt fairly well, but her uncle was like a foreigner to me. I used to smile and nod, and hope that I didn't look too stupid. I never really thought about the changes Connie would have to go through in Canada. I just thought that any change would be for the better; after all, it was my country.

I think the main thing that has happened to me because I married an English girl is I learned so much about the UK. If I had married a French-Canadian girl, I would never have travelled so much. I would have missed the Yorkshire dales and the lovely Lake District. How I enjoy walking through the countryside and all the moors! After many trips back to England, I have so many friends and all the people are so helpful, especially when they hear my accent and call me "the colonial." I have even learned to say *owt* and *nowt*. I've learned to enjoy the test matches and understand what the ashes are. However, I do not understand the English humour; maybe that's because I don't always know what they are saying.

Marrying a war bride has brought many contradictions into my life: lots of happiness, a wealth of information on the UK, Yorkshire pudding, bangers and mash, toad in the hole, roast pork sandwiches, jam butties, Blackpool illuminations, and so much more — three children and two beautiful grandchildren.

Gerry Poirier, a native of Montreal, went against his family's wishes, but he doesn't regret a thing:

The last thing my family said to me before I left Canada was, "Vas-pas marier une anglaise" (Don't marry an English girl). So I was a little concerned about bringing my wife to Canada, although I was sure she would be happy there. She had been corresponding with my family in French, and they had been very impressed with her command of the language and the effort she made. I returned home before she arrived, so I was able to prepare the way.

Being married to a British war bride has broadened my horizons and given me a new slant on life. All our children and our great-grandchild are fluently bilingual, as are most of our grandchildren, and they've had the advantage of living in two different cultures.

After coming up through Italy, France, and Belgium, Art Byle's unit was billeted in the town of Assen, Holland:

My good friend Sergeant Clarence Miner became friendly with a family nearby, where he would play checkers. This family had a beautiful young daughter who was helping her dad and mom with the interpreting, as they took English in their schools. One day, Clarence mentioned to them that he'd like to bring over a young fellow of Dutch descent — that's me — who would make a good husband for their daughter. They had some reservations, as their daughter was only sixteen at the time and I thought, when I saw her, that she was too young for me. But we hit if off well, and after a nine-month courtship we were married on 27 December 1945. We were driven to the town hall first, as was customary over there, and then had the church wedding. We rode in a coach pulled with horses, just like the Queen! When we entered the church, the organist played "O Canada" and the minister said, "He came, he saw, and he conquered!" We thought it quite amusing.

Despite being warned about Mary Jane's temper by her mother, Stu Brooks knew he had found the woman for him:

I met my future wife at a dance in Banstead, Surrey. She was dancing with someone and would smile at me every once in a while over his shoulder. I saw her home that evening, and we soon became close friends. From then on, we became very important to one another and decided to marry and make a life together in Canada after the war.

I always enjoyed being stationed in England — the tea rooms, the pubs, the beautiful countryside. I even became accustomed to and quite comfortable with the weather. There are times when I think back whether I should have stayed there after the war instead of returning to Canada.

I found that being married to an English girl gave us some challenges. We had to relate to one another's different cultures and problems. She learned from me and I from her, but mostly she gained a lot of knowledge about Canada and its history from books. I was a little concerned about bringing my wife to Canada because I was a bit of a stranger myself to my family, after being away for over five years. But the odd V-2 rocket was dropping in England at that time and I was worried about her and my small son's safety.

When Signalman Rufus Chudleigh arrived in England, he enjoyed the time he had off to socialize with the locals. He met Stella in East Grinstead, and they were married the day after VE Day:

Meeting and marrying Stella changed my life completely. Now there seemed to be more of a goal and purpose to my life, something I had been lacking before. I had some concerns about it when I considered our different backgrounds and cultures, but I told her all I could about life in Canada and hoped for the best! What has marriage to a war bride brought to my life? Happiness!

It was natural that in a town such as Aldershot, which played host to a large number of troops, the novelty wore thin and the hospitality was not as warm as elsewhere. George Edward Zwicker was first posted to the Aldershot Command, and he found that the local residents did not exactly take kindly to the Canadian soldiers. But then he was sent to the Oxford area and his luck changed:

The balance of our stay in England gave us the opportunity to meet and become rather good friends with some of the most gracious people one could meet anywhere. The welcome we received in general can only be appreciated by the soldiers themselves and measured by the number of war brides who braved the transition to a new and very different country. Many of the old friends have since passed away, but the memories still linger in my mind, as I am certain they do in many other Canadian soliders', and we shall never forget them.

I first met Joan at the wedding of her sister Joyce, who also married a Canadian soldier, a wartime friend of mine. I think Joan mistook me for someone else on my arrival at the church, because she started ordering me around and scolding me for being late. Now that part hasn't changed since 1945, and one of my favourite witticisms at parties is, "I'll have you know that I always have the last word in my household. . . . I always say, 'Yes, dear.'"

Our courtship in England was short, since our regiment was off to Scotland for the preparations for our move to the Mediterranean theatre of war, but we did keep in contact for about two years before the Canadians were moved to France and Belgium. During this time we were making plans for marriage, with our Wassermann tests and all other documents completed before I left Belgium, or so I thought. Unknown to me, however, my commanding officer had not signed the marriage permission, so Joan and I spent every day for a week travelling from Orpington to London trying to find an officer from the 4th PLDG, but without success.

Finally, one of the officers at Canada House said he would sign it for us. I am not sure if it was out of pity or that he just wanted to get rid of us, but we headed straight for Westminster, where we could get a licence to marry without the three-day delay. We then headed for the nearest telephone booth and told Joan's mother to ice the cake, which had already been baked.

I was born and raised on a farm in Nova Scotia, and Joan was born in London and lived the war period of her life in Orpington, Kent, and was in the ATS. It must surely have made one wonder about our compatibility as man and wife. After Joan's arrival in Mahone Bay in March 1946, it didn't take long to discover that she was not suited to farm life. I recall the first time she ventured to the stable and I managed to get her through the tail ends of two rows of milk cows, but my problem was to get her to come back out. Her next encounter was with a bucksaw, cutting firewood, with which she had minor success, but this aspect of farm life also did not conduce itself to a city girl.

It was generally agreed at this point that farming was not our life's ambition, so we moved to Peterborough, Ontario. A shortage of housing compelled us to live in a two-room trailer for a few months until the birth of our first child. Two baby girls followed, completing our family. I must give Joan full credit for the upbringing of our three children. We are now happily and comfortably retired. We still share the same bed, and most mornings Joan still gets her cup of tea in bed.

Irving Penny met a certain "lass from Lancashire" who changed his routine existence into a lifelong love affair:

Thursley Common was a dreary, damp, and dismal place to put a camp for the newly arrived Canadian troops, and the long line of squat red-brick barracks did little to relieve the monotony; the troops were restless and bored. Once-a-week films and the bimonthly visit of an ENSA party (during which the front several rows were reserved for commissioned officers, who would later entertain the artists in the officers' mess) did little to ease the tedium of daily drill and weapons training.

You can see why, when a friend arrived back off a forty-eight-hour pass with the story of having met a beautiful showgirl on the train, and that he had arranged a date with her for two weeks hence, *but* only on the condition that he bring a friend along for her friend and I was to be the friend, I jumped at the opportunity. Alas, as so often happens, the fickle-fingered fiend called Fate intervened, and I was posted guard commander for that week. Try as I might, I could talk no one into replacing me, even for money. Disappointed, I asked my friend to get her address so that I could write a note of apology, and this he did.

My disappointment was certainly lessened when, less than a week after I had written, I received a friendly note from the young lady saying that their show had come off the road for refit and they would be filling in with a show in Aldershot for two weeks. Maybe we could get together then? With Aldershot a mere two hours' walk away across the fields, you bet we could! And so it was, some weeks and several letters later, that I found myself backstage in a theatre in Aldershot, only being allowed there after showing the doorman my invitation, nervously pacing and awaiting the finish of the act to meet my pen pal.

And then my life changed. Down from the stage came a tiny dream in a wispy costume of pale green chiffon, gorgeous, barely five feet tall, and with beautiful, dark reddish-brown hair, long and curly. I fell madly in love with her at first sight and have remained so for forty-nine years. The dream drifted up to me and said, "I suppose you are it?" I just couldn't think what to say so I kissed her, which I think she did not truly appreciate at the time.

She did forgive me eventually, although she had complained to her friend that she found me a terribly dull person. Some weeks later, when I proposed to her, she said yes. Oh, happy, happy day!

Irving found that his unit was about to be moved, so he immediately married his fiancée (on a seventy-two-hour pass). He was not prepared to "take a chance on some other character cutting me out." He was eventually sent to the Mediterranean:

We had been in action for two weeks when I learned that I was the father of a son who, incidentally, I would not see for nearly eighteen months, or until I forgot to duck one day and was invalided home with the resulting wounds.

Back in England, scheduled for repatriation to Canada, and I still had not seen my wife or son. Although I was still on crutches, one understanding doctor, a woman doctor, said that if I would sincerely promise to be back on time, she would give me a seventy-two-hour pass to travel to Manchester, my wife's home town. I would have done anything for the chance to see them, and so a couple of hours later I was on a northbound train.

It was late evening when the train arrived in Central Station, and I suddenly realized that I had forgotten to telegraph my wife, but now it was too late. She now tells me that for months she had been saving small things out of her rations to make a special welcome-home cake for me and that she had used some of her precious clothing coupons to buy the material to make a special dress in which to welcome her returning husband. But, as it happened, a soldier on crutches knocked on the door to have it opened by a beautiful woman . . . who had just washed her hair and now had it wrapped in a towel and who was dressed in an old dressing gown. "Who is it?" she asked, then burst into tears when recognition dawned.

My son, now eighteen months old, would have none of this rude stranger who had come into his home. His daddy was that picture on the mantle that he kissed every night before going to bed. He even insisted on sleeping in the same bed between us. Oh, the joys of adjusting to fatherhood!

One day together, and then back on the train south, only to find that my repatriation draft was already on the move. Fortunately, one of my buddies had cleared my kit and even signed for my pay, so within an hour of my return we were on our way to Scotland to catch a ship for Canada. Five more months were to elapse before my wife and son arrived in London, Ontario, and we were able to begin what I can only describe as a wonderful married life. No man has ever had a better wife. I envy no man fame or fortune, for I would not trade one year of my life with my "lass from Lancashire" for anything you could name. God has been very, very good to me, and I know and appreciate it.

As for the sentiments of the war brides themselves towards the men they journeyed so far to be with, they are expressed in a toast given by Mary Hayward Pedersen at one of the war brides' conventions in Saskatchewan:

I've been asked to make a toast,
To the ones we love the most. . .
Our husbands — God bless 'em.
Over land and air and sea,
They came for you and me,
Our husbands — God bless 'em.
We met in different ways
In those dark and dreary days,
In air-raid shelters, dance halls,
And the pub,
Where we'd go and sing and shout,
While the bombs fell round about,
To drown out all the noise from above.
Playing in an army dance band
Is how we met.
And I tell you I'm not diddlin'
When I say it didn't take long to find
I kinda liked his fiddlin'.
But I'm sure we all agree,
We've been lucky, you and me,

To come to this great land
We now call home.
So, please rise and make a toast,
To the ones we love the most,
Our husbands — God bless 'em.

8

"Canada . . . My Home"

*I*T IS NOW *more than forty-five years since a unique army
of young women arrived on the shores of Canada. Some found
they could not cope with living so far from their loved ones back
home, and they returned. Who can blame them? The love between
a war bride and her husband rested on shifting sand, for time was
so precious during the war that lifetime decisions were often made
and sealed within a matter of weeks. Having made their commitment, however, most of these wives worked diligently, against great
odds, and created a satisfying life for themselves, their husbands,
and children.*

*When Amelia Burke remembers her long journey to Canada, she
thinks of all the other war brides who shared her experiences:*

There are times when I wonder what became of those other young
women, those war brides who travelled to Canada like I did. We
had to renew our relationships with our husbands, get to know
them again, make homes in a new land, and take the good with
the bad. Were they as homesick as I was at times? Did they watch
for the mailman, then cry over the letter from home when it did
come? Did their hopes and dreams come true? I wonder.

*The war brides had various ways of helping themselves get through
the difficult transitional period. Connie Ellen Burrill, who settled
in Yarmouth, Nova Scotia, found an approach that worked for
her:*

I came to Canada with a rather biblical attitude of "Your people shall be my people" and "Your country — my home." This has proved to be a good attitude for me. I do not forget my English heritage, but I like living in Canada as a Canadian citizen.

Slowly, the country began to assimilate these new arrivals. After settling in Chaplin, Saskatchewan, Veronica J. Moore gradually grew accustomed to the prairie way of life, and she later realized that, at heart, she had become a Canadian:

My husband passed away after only ten years in this country. The next summer I returned to England with my two children to see if I wanted to live there again. In spite of all the beautiful countryside in England, I knew that Canada was well and truly my home, and after six weeks returned here.

The life Renee Murray found in Manitoba was not easy, for she was used to city life in Edinburgh. However, she did her best, and she, too, has found that she has truly become part of her new country:

Now, many years have gone by and my young pilot is no longer by my side—he died eleven years ago—and I miss him dreadfully. I've been asked if I'd ever go back to Britain now that I'm alone and I can only answer, "Why? I'm Canadian."

Jean M. Chartrand, now a member of both the Manitoba and Saskatchewan war brides' associations, had to learn the ways of Canada on her own, without the benefit of other war brides to laugh and cry with:

At a time when we needed a war brides' association, we couldn't afford to form one because of travelling to a meeting centre, leaving little children behind, and many of us could not afford to spend the money. Today, we have many war brides' associations across this vast country of ours. They are a blessing when we can get together, meet old friends, meet new ones, sing old songs, dance the old dances of yesteryear, or just plain reminisce over old times and the terrible *faux pas* we made when we came to our new homes!

Joan Frances Schnare has no regrets about coming to Nova Scotia, although she admits she had some difficulties at first. She loves getting together with other war brides and says that the tears they shed now are from laughter:

Unfortunately, my husband died in 1983, and I thank him for the years we had together, even though he said he only married me to have a good meal! The rations were skimpy back then.

Janine Thompson recalls that those early years on a farm in Nova Scotia were hard and that "some things would make your hair stand on end." Nevertheless:

Would I do it all again? Who knows. But now I'm not sorry I did. Canada is such a wonderful country, and I like country living, and, of course, my own wonderful family is here with me. I always remembered two things that Dad told me: "Your life is what you make it" and "Every cloud has a silver lining." Eventually they do.

Nan Casey feels that moving from Holland to a remote mining camp in the British Columbia mountains was all worth it:

I have been back to Holland several times, but I have never been sorry that I married my Canadian soldier and started a new life here. Canada is a wonderful country!

Although getting used to life in Bear River, Nova Scotia, presented many challenges, Pat Miller looks back on her life in Canada with deep affection:

I love the Canadian way of living and feel proud of the Canadian label, every bit as much as I did when termed a Londoner.

Eunice Partington found a lot of happiness on her prairie farm. She tells us what being a war bride has meant to her:

214

As I look back on the past forty-six years, I thank Canada for what she has given me and I have no regrets as to the life I chose. Of course, I still glance back with fond memories of my days in England's green and pleasant land and hope that I will have the chance to return one more time in the near future, before I am laid to rest in the land I learned to love.

Getting used to life in the small town of Belmont, Nova Scotia, was not easy for Audrey Pratt. Nevertheless, she is proud to call both England and Canada home:

I must be honest and admit that life in Canada was certainly a struggle at first. My husband's family was very encouraging and did their best to make me feel welcome, and I soon learned to adapt. I have been very fortunate that I have been able to return to England on many occasions and that my family has been able to come from England to see me. I feel very fortunate that I have two such great countries to call home.

After returning to live in London, Evelyn Nicholson and her husband left England for the second time, leaving a heartbroken family behind. She seems torn between her two countries:

The introduction of the charter flights made such a difference to the war brides and their families. My heart still leaps when the plane circles over the little fields of England before landing at Gatwick. I feel sad when I leave to return to Canada, leaving my sister and brother and their families. But once on the plane, my thoughts turn towards Canada and home. There are three children, seven grandchildren, loving in-laws, and good friends waiting for me, and I still have my loving husband at my side.

Despite the years, Phyllida (Rickford) Miller has never forgotten the country she left, although her life has been "full and interesting." Today she makes her home in Regina:

I have never ceased being homesick for England. I miss the gorgeous countryside, the green trees, masses of flowers, woodlands and pasture land, and the seaside. And especially the ancient historic sites and buildings, witness to a history that I am rooted in. And, oh, for the music of English voices all around me and that wonderful, quirky sense of humour which I seldom find here! So many lovely things. . . . I still carry the British passport, and my heart has truly never left home.

Kay Garside, who came to Canada to live on a farm in Saskatchewan, returned on a visit to England nineteen years later, but she found it very different from the England she had left. She recalls what being a war bride means to her:

People often ask me how I could leave my family, friends, and homeland. I don't know what to reply. If my daughter had wanted to do the same thing, I would have been horrified. We were young; the idea of going to another country was exciting. At the time of my marriage, there seemed no end to the war and Canada was a far-off place. Most of us lived for the day and didn't look very far ahead into the future. There might not have been a future for all we knew. We didn't ask enough questions; I didn't, anyway.

The wonder is how so many of us stayed, had reasonably good lives, and are still here with no intention of returning to live in Britain. Our children are here and we are Canadians now. But there is still that strong link with our birthplace, and it will never break until we are gone.

Many of us are now widows. We support each other as best we can. There is a special bond between us, hard to explain to anyone else. When we lose a husband, I think we lose a little more than other couples. We went through so much together—the war, coming to Canada. It's a special bond.

Here is what Lilian Pearson has to say when asked if she would go through the hardship of being a war bride all over again:

Yes, I would. I believe I have the best of two worlds—to have been born in beautiful England and to have spent my young days there, and now to live on the Canadian prairies with my husband still with me to enjoy our retirement right here.

For Peggy Moir, the flowers of England still bring back fond memories:

I have grown to love and appreciate Canada but still enjoy the occasional trip to my English village home. I always have a twinge of homesickness every spring, and still miss picking bluebells and primroses.

Henriette Reid enjoyed many happy times with her husband. She has never regretted coming to Canada:

My life has been one of one adventure after another. With my husband, I've met many of the "great names" here and also lots of nice people from many lands. I've been a Canadian now for over forty-five years and love this country. At seventy-eight, without children and with the loss of my husband some years ago, I toyed with the idea of returning to my sister in England. But I've been away too long—I like ice in my drinks, air-conditioning, and the comforts we take for granted in Canada—so I will stay.

Mary Hayward and Andy Pedersen met through their music and they are still active performers today. Mary reflects on what being born in England has meant to her:

Oh yes, I still miss dear old England — the seaside, the bluebell woods, and the wild parsley in the hedgerows. I often wish for shopping in Bond Street, the pantomines at Christmas, and the London shows. Once a Limey, always a Limey — but still I am pleased and proud to be a Canadian.

Marjorie J. Crawford was met by Earl in Winnipeg on her nineteenth birthday. Her long trip from Brighton proved to be well worthwhile:

Forty-five years have gone by since I started on this journey. Five children, eleven grandchildren, and one great-grandchild. The last six years I've been alone. There have been bad times, sad times, glad and a lot of happy times, and some very, very funny times, but this I know for sure. It's not so vast and desolate anymore. Canada is my country and it is my home.

When reflecting on her experiences as a war bride, Vera Davison admits to some regrets:

I have mixed feelings about leaving my family, home, and country in 1946 to come so far away. Of course, there have been good things. Nova Scotia is a lovely province and, like England, one is never far from the sea. The people are casual and friendly, and there is not much of a class system here.

The thing I regret the most is missing so many years with my family in England. Letters and short trips do not take the place of growing older with them. Another regret is becoming an outsider in both places — in the country where I was born and in my husband's country. In Canada, no matter how kind people are, one is always outside the circle, especially in a village. It cannot be helped. One loses touch to a certain extent with England. You see everything with different eyes. It's still your home, but you have been away and experienced a different lifestyle.

I'll always wonder what it would be like to move back to England. There are probably many war brides who have no regrets. They are blessed.

After coming to Vancouver, Beryl Smallwood spent time living in a log cabin in the Cariboo, then moved to Ontario and finally back to British Columbia again:

There is nowhere in Europe that we could have lived such a wonderful full and varied life. I have never used the words "back home" to describe England. *This* is home. I have never been back—about the only war bride who hasn't.

A Jamaican war bride, Eileen M. Barkwell, came from a house with servants to live in primitive conditions in an Ontario village:

According to the way we think, the original pioneers had a dreadful time, but we had some hardships, too, compared to the way the present generation lives. I would not change with them; they don't know they are living. Our appreciation of what we achieved far outweighs theirs, because it took us a lot longer to do it and life was simpler then. Imagine no TV, no rockets to the moon and no men in space, just our own amusement with our friends and helping each other whenever needed. Satisfaction guaranteed!

Joyce Horne hopes that other war brides have been as fortunate as she has:

I have had a wonderful life here, and although I have been back to England several times, I am glad Canada is my home. I have not met many other war brides, but those I do know seem to think as I do — that our choice to marry one of those "bleedin' Canadians" was the right one.

Unfortunately, Kay Legault has some misgivings about leaving Britain for a new life in Montreal:

I cannot say that I have had a very happy life here, as there were so many differences, but Louis was a good man and we had enough to get by. I had a very hard time with my in-laws. They couldn't speak much English and also I was not a Catholic, so that didn't go down too well. Life was quite tough. If I had to do it all again, I think I would stay in my own country.

Gladys Cook's husband Les eventually became mayor of Woodstock, Ontario, and she says that opened up many new and interesting experiences for her. She recalls their forty-fifth wedding anniversary:

Our eldest son proposed a toast to his mum and dad. In his reply, my husband made this comment: "Forty-five years ago, the opening notes of a beautiful symphony were written . . . and the music is still going on." And someone said these wartime marriages wouldn't last!

Patricia Enright-Howlett reflects the positive attitude that so many war brides still carry with them today:

It takes a long time to say, "I am a Canadian." I am. I feel emotional when the Canadian flag is raised at the Olympics. Canada has been good to me, and if you asked, "Would you do it again?", you bet!

Joy Stanfield looks back on the hardships of her first years in Port Credit, Ontario, and reflects on how lucky she was:

Despite tragedies and heartbreaks along the way, we built a good life and it was worth it. Had I not been a teenaged bride, it would have been harder, but I adapted quickly and my Oxford accent soon disappeared. I made up my mind when I left that I would never go back, and I never have. Fortunately, I have never been homesick; frequent, copious letters, and now phone calls, filled the gap.

This young, sheltered war bride is now a contented OAP, being two days younger than the Queen. Our lives were intertwined when we were children, although on different levels. She came frequently to Aldershot, cradle of the British army. I envied her the beautiful coloured shoes she wore, but not her life. Mine has been so much happier and exciting.

Margaret Solomon's life with Tony continues to be a love story:

Now, as I look back, those years were some of the best of my life, spent with this guy who still shares my bed and whom I still love very much. Many envy me. He had been a hard worker, very independent, a good father to our three beautiful daughters and grandfather to six fine grandchildren, and he still calls me "Lady." He says the best thing the government ever did for him was to send him overseas to meet and marry me. It's been tough and rough at times, but marriage for the two of us has been something books are written about that have happy endings, and we would do it all again.

I'm very glad that I came to Canada with my soldier boy — to be truly Canadian with a Scottish heritage to pass on to my children and grandchildren, along with my Canadian soldier husband and his Ukrainian heritage. We call it porridge and perogies! Thank you, Canada—my new home!

Maureen McDonald looks at her wonderful family today and says, "I would not change the problems we went through to get to where we are today for anything." And despite the rough conditions that Vera G. Bonham had to live in at Macleod, Alberta, she does not regret a thing:

Looking back on it now, if I had to do it all again I wouldn't hesitate. Canada is a beautiful country and it has given me a happy and plentiful life, for which I am very grateful. I often tell my husband Dave how thankful I am to him for bringing me over here. I'm sure I have had a lot fuller and richer life here in Canada than I would have had back home.

Ivy L. Cline, who met her future husband Harry during an "excuse-me" dance in Epsom, has never looked back:

Although I am alone now, I have wonderful memories to sustain me and have never regretted my move to become a Canadian. One of Harry's favourite sayings was that he went to Epsom and came home a winner!

Even though Audrey Roberts's wartime marriage ended in divorce, she is glad she came to this country. Coincidentally, she now has a very happy marriage with a man who was also stationed in England during the war:

I have always prided myself on my self-discipline and determination (perhaps the war years stood me in good stead) and am thankful that I didn't quit when the going was really rough. Canada has been good to me—a land of opportunity for those willing to work and invest in it. May we continue to grow in love and strength, united in this wonderful land—as CANADIANS (no matter what our ethnic origins may be).

Marg Pallot says, "It was a giant leap from a small village in the Scottish Highlands to the large industrial, French-speaking city of Montreal." She believes that the commitment war brides brought to their marriages made all the difference when the going got rough:

Canada is a great country. It has been very kind to me in many ways. Would I do it all again? A tough question that is difficult for me to answer. I am glad, though, that I belonged to the generation that considered marriage a lifetime commitment. "For better or worse" had real meaning for us, and my early days as a Canadian often required its practice. I wonder if today's youth would handle it all differently.

Despite ongoing problems with her husband's health, Joyce Young considers herself blessed that he is still living with her when so many other war brides are now widows. She believes that war brides gained something from their early struggles:

It was very hard leaving our country, families, and friends, and I often think how heartbreaking it must have been for our parents. But I do believe all the troubles, sorrows, and hardships we encountered have made better people of us.

Like so many other war brides, Lilian Olson had to struggle through the lean times in order to achieve the benefits she enjoys today. She believes the priorities of the war brides stood them in good stead:

It is not what one has in assets that is important. Instead, it is the setting of goals and working towards achieving them and enjoying those things that are available, such as close friends, the great outdoors, and the reward of work well done. It seems to me young couples today have to have everything at once, such as a house, cars, TVs, VCR, video cameras, etc., before they feel able to enjoy living. They do not seem to have the stamina that we had starting out in a foreign place with nothing but a caring husband.

During the writing of this book, I was invited by the war brides to attend their First International War Brides' Convention in Regina. More than 450 war brides and their husbands attended — it was a remarkable experience. Now past their sixties, they sang and danced the night away, carried back to that time when, as young women, they first set foot in a strange land to meet a husband who, in most cases, would stand by their side through incredible hardships.

These war brides have a right to be proud. So does Canada.

Appendix

Canadian War Brides' Associations

Alberta War Brides Association
Kay Young, President
9246-154 Street
Edmonton, Alberta
T5R 1T5

Fraser Valley War Brides
Kathy Ballentyne
130-32880 Bevan Way
Abbotsford, B.C.
V2S 1T3

Greater Vancouver War Brides Association
Bea Ackerman
5104 Ruby Street
Vancouver, B.C.
V5R 4K3

Manitoba War Brides Association
Cecilia Knight, President
Box 7
Clearwater, Manitoba
R0K 0M0

New Brunswick War Brides Association
Doris Lloyd, President
Box 15
Plaster Rock, N.B.
E0J 1W0

Okanagan Valley War Brides Association
Joan Jennens, President
577-1255 Raymer Avenue
Kelowna, B.C.
V1Y 8R8

Ontario
Although there is no provincial association for war brides in Ontario, if
you want to get in touch with a club near you, contact:

Irene (Marchand) Manning
752 Kipps Lane, Suite 110
London, Ontario
N5Y 4V4

Saskatchewan War Brides Association
Peggy Gliddon, President
2808 Montague Street
Regina, Saskatchewan
S4S 1Z2

Vancouver Island War Brides Association
Audrey Waddy
2231 Rosewood Avenue
Duncan, B.C.
V9L 3E8

Index of Names

Abelson, Gertie, 50
Adams, Doris Nelly, 24–25
Ament, Pauline Elizabeth, 48, 127–28
Ames, Bridie, 61
Anderson, Lilian, 104
Arbuckle, Nellie, 15
Armott, Daphne, 110

Bannon, Margaret, 50–51, 122
⚓ Barkwell, Eileen M., 137–38,
    177–78, 218–19
Barrett, Alice, 186
Beatteay, Robin, 166–67
Beattic, Elsie, 160
Bell, Renée, 160–161
Benn, Betty, 33, 130
Biggs, Katherine, 29–30, 122, 170–71
Black, Enid, 168–70
Bleakney, Kay, 37, 70, 134–35
Bonham, Vera G., 221
Bourassa, Marie, 174–77
Brink, Wynne, 179–80
Brock, Gloria, 18, 50, 65, 134, 171
Brock, John, 196–97
Brooks, Mary Jane, 44–45
Brooks, Stu, 205–206
Bruguiere-Taylor, Eileen, 19, 133
Buan, Joan, 19, 187–88
Burke, Amelia, 212
Burrill, Connie Ellen, 87–88, 144, 212
Burris, Laura Lillian, 41–42, 69–70,
    164
Butler, Joan Bryant, 58–59
Buzzell, Evelyn, 72, 115
Byle, Ann, 28
Byle, Art, 205

Campbell, Betty, 119–20
Casey, Nan, 154, 214

Chalklin, Peggy, 132, 159–60
Chartrand, Jean M., 55–56, 67–68,
    87, 105–106, 145–46, 213–14
Chippure, Constance J., 182
Chollet, Grace, 113
Christoffersen, Doreen, 64
Chudleigh, Rufus, 2, 19, 206
Chudleigh, Stella, 19, 104, 181
Clark, Ivy E., 117
Clements, Phyllis, 25–26
Cline, Ivy L., 19, 221
Clyne, Dorothy, 154
Collins, Joan, 165
Cook, Gladys, 219
Cornish, Elly, 135
Cornish, Les, 197
Cottrell, Phil, 202–203
Crawford, Marjorie J., 48, 102,
    217–18
Crossman, Della, 100
Cutting, Joan, 99

Davison, Vera, 4, 11–12, 85, 152,
    218
Delmage, Ruth, 21, 51, 83–84, 101
Derkach, Doreen, 112
Deshane, Jean (Imrie), 3
Donaghy, Freda Muriel, 49, 50
Dumaine, Joan, 3–4
Dumaine, Paul, 203
Dykes, Phyllis, 131–32

Elliott, Doug, 195–96
Enright-Howlett, Patricia, 23, 90, 220

Farrow, Charlotte, 75, 140
Fleming, Ronnie, 26, 112
Fletcher, Joan, 48–49
Fletcher, Russ, 197–99

Index of Names